TWISTING ARMS AND FLEXING MUSCLES

The International Political Economy of New Regionalisms Series

The International Political Economy of New Regionalisms Series presents innovative analyses of a range of novel regional relations and institutions. Going beyond established,formal, interstate economic organizations, this essential series provides informed interdisciplinary and international research and debate about myriad heterogeneous intermediate level interactions.

Reflective of its cosmopolitan and creative orientation, this series is developed by an international editorial team of established and emerging scholars in both the South and North. It reinforces ongoing networks of analysts in both academia and think-tanks as well as international agencies concerned with micro-, meso- and macro-level regionalisms.

Recent Titles in the Series

Reforging the Weakest Link:
Global Political Economy and Post-Soviet Change in Russia, Ukraine and Belarus
Edited by Neil Robinson

Demilitarisation and Peace-Building in Southern Africa:
Volume I– Concepts and Processes
Edited by Peter Batchelor and Kees Kingma

Demilitarisation and Peace-Building in Southern Africa:
Volume II – National and Regional Experiences
Edited by Peter Batchelor and Kees Kingma

Demilitarisation and Peace-Building in Southern Africa:
Volume III – The Role of the Military in State Formation and Nation-Building
Edited by Peter Batchelor, Kees Kingma and Guy Lamb

Twisting Arms and Flexing Muscles

Humanitarian Intervention and Peacebuilding in Perspective

Edited by

NATALIE MYCHAJLYSZYN
Concordia University, Montreal, Canada

and

TIMOTHY M. SHAW
University of London, UK

Routledge
Taylor & Francis Group
LONDON AND NEW YORK

First published 2005 by Ashgate Publishing

Published 2018 by Routledge
2 Park Square, Milton Park, Abingdon, Oxon OX14 4RN
605 Third Avenue, New York, NY 10017

Routledge is an imprint of the Taylor & Francis Group, an informa business

A Library of Congress record exists under LC control number: 2004020207

ISBN 13: 978-0-815-39871-4 (hbk)
ISBN 13: 978-1-351-14384-4 (ebk)

Contents

List of Contributors

Robert Astroff is a Ph.D. candidate in Political Science at the University of Toronto, Toronto, Canada.

David Carment is Associate Professor at The Norman Paterson School of International Affairs, Carleton University, Ottawa, Canada.

Major (ret'd) David Last is an Associate Professor, Department of Politics and Economics at the Royal Military College in Kingston, Canada.

S. Neil MacFarlane is Lester B. Pearson Professor of International Relations, and Director, Centre for International Studies at Oxford University.

David Meren is a Ph.D. candidate in History at McGill University in Montreal, Canada.

Natalie Mychajlyszyn is Assistant Professor, Department of Political Science, Concordia University, Montreal, Canada.

Dane Rowlands is Associate Professor at The Norman Paterson School of International Affairs, Carleton University, Ottawa, Canada.

Timothy M. Shaw is Professor of Commonwealth Governance and Development, and Director, Institute of Commonwealth Studies, School of Advanced Study, University of London.

Donna Winslow is Chair of Anthropology, Vrije Universiteit in Amsterdam, The Netherlands.

List of Abbreviations

ACCORD	African Centre for the Constructive Resolution of Disputes
ADF	Anarchist Democratic Forces
ADFL	Alliance of Democratic Forces for the Liberation of Congo-Zaire
CCR	Centre for Conflict Resolution
CIDA	Canadian International Development Agency
CIMIC	Civil-Military Cooperation
CIS	Commonwealth of Independent States
CRC	Conflict Resolution Catalysts
DRC	Democratic Republic of Congo
ECHR	European Convention on Human Rights
ECOWAS	Economic Community of the West African States
EPZs	Export-Processing Zones
FAZ	*Forces Armées de Zaire*
FPR	*Front Patriotique Rwandaise*
FRY	Federal Republic of Yugoslavia
HDI	Human Development Index
ICRC	International Committee for the Red Cross
IDPs	Internally displaced persons
IEBL	Inter-entity boundary line
IFIs	International financial institutions
IFOR	Implementation Force
INTERFET	International Force in East Timor
IOs	International organizations
IPKF	Indian Peacekeeping Force
ISS	Institute for Security Studies
JVP	Jatiya Vimukthi Peramuna
KLA	Kosovo Liberation Army
LRA	Lord's Resistance Army
LTTE	Liberation Tigers of Tamil Eelam
MNCs	Multinational corporations
MPLA	Popular Movement for the Liberation of Angola
MPRI	Military Professional Resources Incorporated
MSU	Multinational Specialized Unit
NATO	North Atlantic Treaty Organization
NCO	Non-commissioned officer
NDI	National Democratic Institute
NDMC	National Diamond Mining Company
NEPAD	New Partnership for Africa's Development

NFP	Neighbourhood Facilitators Project
NGOs	Non-governmental Organizations
OAS	Organization of American States
OAU	Organization of African Unity
OECD	Organizations for Economic Cooperation and Development
ONUC	United Nations Operation in the Congo
OSCE	Organization for Security and Cooperation in Europe
PAC	Partnership Africa Canada
PKOs	Peacekeeping operations
PSCs	Private security companies
RUF	Revolutionary United Front
SAIIA	South African Institute for International Affairs
SFOR	Stabilization Force
SLST	Sierra Leone Selection Trust
UN	United Nations
UNAMIR	United Nations Assistance Mission for Rwanda
UNCIVPOL	United Nations Civilian Police
UNDP	United Nations Development Program
UNHCHR	United Nations High Commission for Human Rights
UNHCR	United Nations High Commission for Refugees
UNICEF	United Nations Children's Emergency Fund
UNITA	National Union for the Total Independence of Angola
UNPROFOR	United Nations Protection Force
UNTAES	United Nations Transitional Authority in Eastern Slavonia
UNTAG	United Nations Transition Assistance Group
USAID	United States Agency for International Development
USIP	United States Institute for Peace
WEU	Western European Union
WFP	World Food Program

Chapter 1

Introduction

Natalie Mychajlyszyn

At certain times in international politics there have developed destabilizing and threatening domestic humanitarian situations that have drawn the attention of the international community. This community, which includes independent states, the inter-governmental organizations they have created as well as a multitude of non-governmental organizations (NGOs) and aid agencies, has responded in a variety of ways ranging from complete disregard to diplomatic missions to the dispatch of humanitarian assistance to the deployment of military forces.

This volume is interested in a particular segment of these responses, specifically where 'arms are twisted and muscles are flexed.' In this respect, it is interested in those cases where a particular outcome or direction of the humanitarian crisis in question and relations among the actors and stakeholders involved are intended to be influenced by the deployment of military force. At the same time, such cases of 'humanitarian intervention' are frequently much more complex than this as they become strongly connected, if not overlap, with peacebuilding, i.e. efforts to stabilize a threatening situation in the short-term with long-term consequences for the reduced likelihood of an escalation of tensions and a return to instability.[1] Indeed, peacebuilding itself has many facets which may include some combination of a military involvement or presence and NGO or official governmental development/humanitarian assistance. Thus, the scope of interest of this volume is more precisely the 'twisting of arms and flexing of muscles' that occurs at the intersect of military force, humanitarian intervention and peacebuilding.

Of course, the subject matter is not novel. Over the last decade, the academic and policy communities have devoted increasing attention to these issues, most distressingly as the number of cases prompting such attention has also increased. As evident in the events surrounding the international community's current and past involvements not only in Iraq and Afghanistan, but also in the Balkans and Africa, there has been much to hold this attention and sustain the field of inquiry. In the process, however, the tools and approaches used to date for examining humanitarian interventions and peacebuilding have left us generally less than satisfied.

Thus, the twin purpose of this volume is to make sense of the inherent conflicts and tensions as well as opportunities that arise when the international community responds to humanitarian crises by applying new analytic approaches and tools, drawing from a range of past cases, regions, and disciplines. The greater and more rewarding insights into the use of force for humanitarian purposes for academics as well as practitioners that derive from the volume benefit from a growing appreciation of non-traditional sources of humanitarian crises, the development of new models, and a greater concern for understanding the role of military forces in non-combat situations. In this way, it presents a collection of innovative approaches that in sum directs us toward more complete answers to one of the most complex problems of our generation.

In this respect, the volume is motivated by the following questions: Under what conditions and forms are intervention and the violation of the twin international principles of sovereignty and non-intervention acceptable? What is the nature of the humanitarian crises and conflicts that precipitate interventions? Why are some cases of intervention more successful than others? How well has the international community overcome obstacles in its efforts to build peace in post-conflict situations?

In its attempt to clarify our understanding about humanitarian interventions and peacebuilding the volume gathers its answers from different disciplines, newly developed models, and emerging approaches. In so doing, it draws on the discussions and papers presented at a workshop attended by its contributors and members of the academic, policy and NGO communities in Ottawa, Canada at the end of the century and at a time marked by attempts to think innovatively and retrospectively about the record of the post-Cold War era on humanitarian interventions and peacebuilding. Reflecting the multifaceted nature of the subject matter, the papers from contributors of that workshop that have found their way into this collection *inter alia* touch on international law and international institutions, strategic interests of great powers, human rights, political economics and development as peacebuilding objectives, decision-making processes at the national and inter-governmental levels, the criteria for successful missions, cooperation and clashing cultures between military personnel and civilians of non-governmental organizations, and the impact of the gradual expansion of peacekeeping missions.

The volume addresses several inter-linking themes that emerge from the 'twisting of arms and flexing of muscles.' In one respect, the security and development fields overlap each other in ways that are more appreciated and more entrenched in post-Cold War humanitarian conflicts. This not only has precipitated new ways of thinking about sources of threat, adding in this respect a political-economic prism, but also exposes a level of comprehensiveness in these crises that does not lend well to simple policy responses or linear thinking. Their comprehensive nature extends to their geographic scope whereby more and more these crises are regionalized by way of the movement of the populations affected and the actors both implicated in the crises and involved in the response. Indeed, there is a multitude of actors and interests – ranging from those of the international community, individual states, international and regional organizations, non-governmental aid groups as well as those of the disputants on the ground both internally as well as externally – who have complicated matters and whose impact, be it positive or negative, taken unilaterally or collectively, and the division of labour among them require a better understanding. The theme of division of labour extends to the need to re-consider the confusing, undefined non-combatant roles for militaries that were quickly assigned to them as the crises became more menacing, to appreciate more greatly the unprecedented partnerships between militaries and aid groups in the field as well as to develop more effective policies that take into account the accompanying resource implications of these new roles and partnerships. Thus, in light of the current trajectory of humanitarian crises and intervention, the volume more greatly appreciates the development of a new security sector and the multilateral nature of international responses.

The volume also grapples with how the context of interventions has changed and in the process influenced the core concepts that it informs. For instance, the end of the Cold War era is often presented as the touchstone for what the international community has had to confront and make sense of with little if any experience, knowledge and tools. Thus, ethnic conflicts, peacebuilding, blood diamonds, and civil-military cooperation among many other terms and concepts have entered our vocabulary and conceptual landscape. In another theme the volume considers the application of the principle of sovereignty and its twin norm of non-intervention which are frequently implicated either as villains that prevent action from being taken when necessary in response to domestic situations and humanitarian crises or as the harbingers of international order without which the entire system would degenerate into chaos.

In offering innovative and rewarding approaches to humanitarian interventions and peacebuilding, the volume builds on the body of work developed by scholars and analysts who have probed regularly the complexities of this subject matter in an effort to not only better understand but also to improve the international community's responses to humanitarian crises. Not surprisingly, the ethical dimension of interventions in general and humanitarian interventions by military forces in particular receive a great deal of their attention. Some analysts have promoted the notion of 'consent' in their efforts to clarify the muddy ethical waters of intervention.[2] Others attempt to maintain the non-violent integrity of humanitarianism in arguing that military responses for humanitarian purposes unacceptably militarizes this work, in contrast to others who defend the necessity of using military force for humanitarian purposes.[3] Indeed, some attempt to reconcile the 'military' dimension with the 'humanitarian' one by situating such operations within the framework of the just war theory since massive violations of human rights are considered in the post-Cold War era as legitimate threats to international peace and security and which warrant a forceful response.[4] Other scholars grapple with the integrity of the label 'humanitarian' in an age when national and strategic interests dominate, not every humanitarian crisis engenders an intervention and ultimately where it is abused by those looking to legitimize the use of military force.[5]

Some scholars of the ethics of humanitarian intervention focus on the actions of NGOs involved in carrying out humanitarian assistance or relief under conditions of conflict or crisis. Indeed, NGOs have recently begun to receive their share of criticism in the post-Cold War era for prolonging the war and facilitating the efforts of the combatants by, inadvertently or not, providing sanctuary for them in their refugee camps and minimizing their responsibility by 'cleaning up' after them.[6] Thus, NGOs face their own ethical dilemma about whether to continue to provide humanitarian assistance and protection when these are thwarted by combatants if they are perceived as biased, thereby leading the NGO to be targetted by one side of the conflict or manipulated for the benefit of one of the disputing parties to perpetuate the conflict, or to withdraw from the conflict since the presence of NGOs and their humanitarian efforts can aggravate the situation for the civilian population they are trying to assist.[7] One study of this dilemma argues that NGOs will need to come to terms with their perceived lack of neutrality and develop a new humanitarian ethic that allows for withdrawal as an acceptable option.[8]

The literature on humanitarian interventions also attempts to understand the effect of such interventions on the life of the conflict itself in order to inform the policy- and decision-making communities. For instance, Michael Doyle and Nicholas Sambanis look at the use of force in peacebuilding operations.[9] For them and others, peacebuilding is a range of peace support activities ranging from simply monitoring and observing a truce to traditional peacekeeping to multidimensional peacekeeping to peace enforcement through military intervention, at the heart of which are operational dimensions that are more robust than peacekeeping and less oriented toward destroying the adversary as in warfighting.[10] In attempting to identify those conditions that encourage successful peacebuilding, not only did they discover that UN peace operations influenced the probability of success in peacebuilding, but that efforts to end violence is dependent on muscular third-party interventions.[11] Virginia Page Fortna echoes these conclusions in her examination of post-Cold War era 'complex' or 'robust' peacekeeping on internal conflicts in terms of maintaining peace.[12] Thus, "peace lasts longer when peacekeepers are present than when belligerents are left to their own devices. In other words, peacekeeping works."[13]

In similar respects, as much as military interventions are often deployed – and argued to be deployed – as a last resort, other recent studies have attempted to examine whether an early military or coercive intervention is more effective in terms of shortening the conflict than an intervention later in the conflict cycle. In one such study, Bruce Jentleson argues that the international community needs to take a more realistic approach to conflict prevention and be more willing to use force early since such forms of conflict prevention – what he calls 'coercive prevention' – serve the vital interests of states.[14]

In contrast, Patrick Regan and Rodwan Abouharb argue that interventions prolong a conflict[15], with the timing of the intervention (early or late in the conflict) an insignificant factor. They examine six hypotheses in their research on the effect of intervention on the life of a conflict and conclude among others that biased interventions will shorten a conflict and that interventions by international organizations are indistinguishable from conflicts without interventions.[16] For them, interventions overall cannot be regarded as effective tools of conflict management.

Other scholars have contributed to our knowledge about humanitarian intervention and peacebuilding by making recommendations on how to improve these tools of the international community. For instance, Michèle Griffin, in examining four trends of interventions in the post-Cold War era in terms of their geopolitical, normative, financial, and multilateral contexts, most importantly argues that the international community can no longer continue to think about distinct tools and responses to conflict situations. Instead, "[t]he myth of a clean continuum from conflict to post-conflict and from relief to development has been exploded, and actors, instruments and frequently contending principles appropriate to these various stages – and politically feasible – must be employed simultaneously and in a strategically complementary manner."[17] In another respect, Mohammed Ayoob argues that humanitarian interventions should not be considered under Chapter VII of the UN Charter as they are not fundamentally threats to international peace and security and instead calls for a new procedure and amendments to the UN Charter that provide for responses to humanitarian crises as well as amending the membership of the Security Council and prohibiting the use of the veto power on questions of humanitarian crises.[18] By removing them from the current procedure that betrays the realpolitik and hierarchical nature of the international system, he argues that the international community can respond more effectively and promptly. And if there is no political will for such reforms, he further argues for the creation of a new structure – a Humanitarian Council– in the UN to take responsibility for these matters.[19] Others echo the call for institutional reforms in order to improve the international community's response to humanitarian crises, including the creation of a UN intervention force or rapid deployment force.[20]

By far the most significant recent contribution to this body of work on humanitarian interventions and peacebuilding is that of the International Commission on Intervention and State Sovereignty (ICISS), which released its report, *The Responsibility to Protect*, in December 2001. In its attempt to respond to the UN secretary-general's challenge in September 2000 to find new ways of dealing with humanitarian crises, the report ultimately argues that states have a responsibility to protect their citizens from 'avoidable catastrophes' and, when they are unable to do so, the international community takes on that responsibility.[21] Furthermore, the community's responsibility to protect entails the responsibility to prevent conflict and other deliberate crises; the responsibility to react to situations of 'compelling human need', including by way of military force although only as a last resort; and the responsibility to rebuild after a conflict or intervention.[22] The report lays out as well the criteria that would justify military interventions for humanitarian purposes, including cases of 'serious and irreparable harm occurring to human beings,' including 'large scale loss of life' and 'large scale 'ethnic cleansing;''[23] the right intention, i.e. to avert or halt human suffering; as a last resort; the military response being proportional to the objective; there being reasonable prospects of success; and, finally, that the consequences of the military intervention are not worse than the consequences of inaction.[24] More importantly, the ICISS argues that authority for approving interventions should continue to lie primarily with the Security Council, with the permanent members agreeing not to apply their veto to such cases. In the end, the 'responsibility to protect' does not challenge sovereignty, but instead reaffirms it in its modern form whereby states and the international community have a responsibility to respect the sovereignty of other states as well as the responsibility to respect the rights of its own population.[25] In this respect, the idea of a 'responsibility to protect' is grounded in the principle of sovereignty and also in emerging principles of human rights and human security that are setting new standards of state conduct towards their populations and making them accountable to the international community for their actions and changing international practice.[26]

The current volume follows in the tradition of this literature by offering new insights, tools and material based on field research and interviews into the multi-faceted dimension of 'twisting arms and flexing muscles' of humanitarian intervention, military force and peacebuilding in different cases and contexts. Chapter 2 by S. Neil MacFarlane unpacks the theoretical dimension and inherent debates that lie at the root of the policy community's challenge of confronting humanitarian crises while respecting international principles. In this respect, he outlines the linkages and tensions among international principles, questions of intervention and local conflicts by tracing historical changes to attitudes about the principle of sovereignty, the norm of non-intervention, and protection of human rights, specifically comparing these attitudes as they were expressed during the Cold War and in the post-Cold War era. He challenges conventional approaches that the post-Cold War era trumpeted a new period where collective morality and interests have displaced the narrow self-interests of states and argues instead that the legal normative framework has been and will continue to be a reflection of the interests of the great powers whose influence on shaping international law will remain unchallenged.

If MacFarlane's chapter lays out the theoretical context of the volume, then Timothy M. Shaw in Chapter 3 provides the overview from the ground-level of what is at stake and what the international community is confronted with when considering intervention as a response to humanitarian crises. In his look at Africa, Shaw describes the sources of instability at the domestic and regional levels from the point of view of regionalism and political economics. In particular, he emphasizes the heterogeneity of the conflicts in Africa and the consequences of emerging non-traditional security issues for state and national collapse, internal conflicts and regional instability. Moreover, the choices made by states, governments and non-state actors as they protect and advance their interests in these conflicts have serious implications for the political economic development of the nations concerned in particular and regional stability in general. Ultimately, Africa remains at the crossroads of either falling backwards towards anarchy or moving forwards towards peacekeeping and peacebuilding.

Robert Astroff and David Meren in Chapter 4 also focus on Africa. In their chapter, however, they take the two cases of Rwanda and Zaire in the 1990s to develop a *Conflict Intensity Abatement (CIA) Index* and measure changes in the dynamics of a conflict and assess the impact of third-party interventions on the intensity of that conflict. Accordingly, they find that third-party intervention in the case of Rwanda was only partially successful given that military force was used to achieve limited goals and the mission was conducted as impartially as possible, allowing for the possibility of the conflict to spill-over and re-occur as it did in Zaire.

The volume's partial theme of evaluating the effectiveness of third-party interveners continues in Chapter 5 by David Carment and Dane Rowlands. In this chapter, the authors challenge conventional approaches that argue for impartiality as a condition of successful interventions. Instead, they develop a model of biased interventions and evaluate in their case studies on NATO's intervention in Kosovo and India's intervention in Sri Lanka the conditions under which bias can reduce or aggravate violent conflicts. Ultimately, where biased interventions can in fact escalate the conflict by provoking the opposing combatant, such developments should not be taken to argue for a return to impartial interventions but instead should be used to prepare biased military interventions more strategically and operationally in anticipation of such an escalation.

The two chapters by David Last and Donna Winslow each look at the Balkans in considering the post-intervention environment and unprecedented relations among the key armed/military and unarmed/civilian agents, relations that have become more and more appreciated in light of the comprehensive and multi-dimensional nature of post-Cold War peacebuilding operations and the increased demand on these actors to take on non-traditional roles and tasks as part of the overall peacebuilding effort. Last in Chapter 6 focuses on the expanded role of peacebuilding for military forces that entails security, governance, relief and development and reconciliation. In all of these areas, Last notes the contribution of military forces in peacebuilding missions, but that these contributions are not linear or unilateral. He documents the challenges faced by military actors in trying to obtain their objectives in peacebuilding operations whose planning and implementation are increasingly – and necessarily – featuring civilian actors.

For her part, Winslow in Chapter 7 details the perceptions of military and civilian actors of each other and the tensions that inevitably arise as each actor in attempting to carry out their expanded and overlapping roles come into regular contact with the other. Based on extensive field interviews, she highlights the sources of these tensions as the lack of coordination between the two types of actors as well as among them (given that each type itself entails numerous groups), but most importantly the different organizational cultures of military groups and civilian relief agencies, the different tasks and ways that each group seeks to accomplish them, and different timeframes and definitions of success, among others. The future is not inevitably tense, however, as the two groups find themselves working together more and more regularly given the complex nature of post-Cold War peacebuilding operations and develop mutual respect and value as well as a common ground for improved relations.

The volume also contributes to the literature more collectively by grouping the chapters in a way that presents interesting inter- and intra-regional comparisons – i.e. Africa and the Balkans – about how we conceptualize and approach humanitarian intervention and peacebuilding. Not only do the African chapters, for instance, provide valuable insight into the similarities and differences among cases within the same region, but also across regions when compared to the more robust response taken to the conflicts in the Balkans. In addition, the volume captures the pervasiveness of such terms as 'military force,' 'humanitarian intervention,' and 'peacebuilding' as they have crossed disciplines, including political science, international law, anthropology, and international political economy, as well as issue-areas, such as security, development and culture. Most importantly, the pervasiveness of these terms is a function of the disturbing realities of the post-Cold War era, marked by civil and ethnic strife, the use of military force, and human suffering on a large scale. As a result, the linkages between these terms have become more greatly appreciated by analysts and practitioners alike.

At the same time, however, their significance and content has fluctuated in keeping with the changing circumstances on the ground and their consequences. In this respect, the terms have become pregnant with new concerns and issues for analysts and policy-makers. Some of these issues consider the methods for assessing impact, evaluating success, and risk-assessment. Other issues pertain to the multiple definitions for 'intervention,' 'humanitarian,' and 'peacebuilding,' levels-of-analysis, the distinction between state and regional interventions, and various definitions of security for different referents. Yet others concentrate on the agents of intervention, the role of states, international organizations and the challenges to traditional, sovereignty-based approaches by non-traditional ways of thinking that emphasize transnational, human-based processes.

The conclusions stemming from this volume are of considerable importance and interest in light of the evolving dynamics surrounding military responses to humanitarian crises. For instance, great power interests will continue to direct the timing and course of humanitarian interventions and, by extension, undermine any efforts to respond to these crises in a collective, morally-infused, established manner. While the outcome of these interventions will be irregular, the tragedy of their failure or success will remain with the local population rather than with the great powers themselves. Moreover, there is a significant likelihood that the crises that precipitate humanitarian interventions will proliferate and even expand to take on greater regional dimensions, suggesting that the future will continue to feature protracted conflicts and large-scale human despair unless the great powers see an interest in the particular case or region. Finally, military-infused peacebuilding brings together new actors from different organizational/cultural backgrounds that would not have worked so closely during Cold War type peacekeeping missions; as it is unlikely that any of these groups will 'assimilate' with the other, the success or failure of the peacebuilding task depends on their ability to find new ways and understandings of each other.

Thus, conversations about humanitarian intervention, military force and peacebuilding are not new. Neither have we seen the last of interventions by individual states or multilateral organizations. As is readily apparent, the topics are complicated and exceedingly complex. Whether or not the issues they raise can ever be satisfactorily addressed remains to be seen. Meanwhile, perspectives on military force, humanitarian intervention and peacebuilding will continue to be nurtured, in the process promising vital and useful information for scholarship and policy. Ultimately, such perspectives will continue to strive to provide more enriching explanations of the most perplexing phenomena of the post-Cold War era.

Notes

1 Michael Doyle and Nicholas Sambinas define peacebuilding as "an attempt, after a peace has been negotiated or imposed, to address the sources of current hostility and build capacities for conflict resolution." Michael Doyle and Nicholas Sambanis, "International Peacebuilding: A Theoretical and Quantitative Analysis (Statistical Data Included)," *American Political Science Review* (December 2000): p. 1. This volume considers peacebuilding to be wider in scope and not confined to a post-settlement activity but to any activity on the part of an international actor whose aim is to facilitate or restore peace in a situation that has seen conflict since it can also take place before a conflict erupts as a form of conflict prevention.

2 *The Responsibility to Protect*, Report of the International Commission on Intervention and State Sovereignty, International Development Research Centre, Ottawa, Canada, December 2001, p. 8; C. A. J. Coady, "The Ethics of Armed Humanitarian Intervention," *Peaceworks* No. 45, United States Institute of Peace (July 2002): p. 5, 10.

3 *The Responsibility to Protect*, p. 9; Coady, "The Ethics of Armed Humanitarian Intervention," p. 6; Hugo Slim, "Violence and Humanitarianism: Moral Paradox and the Protection of Civilians," *Security Dialogue* 32:3 (2001).

4 Coady, "The Ethics of Armed Humanitarian Intervention," pp. 19, 20.

5 Ibid., pp. 12-13, 24; Slim, "Violence and Humanitarianism," pp. 330, 337-338.

6 Slim, "Violence and Humanitarianism," pp. 329, 330.

7 Michael Bryans, Bruce Jones and Janice Gross Stein, "Mean Times: Humanitarian Action in Complex Political Emergencies – Stark Choices, Cruel Dilemmas," *Coming to Terms* 1:3, Program on Conflict Management and Negotiation (January 1999), pp. v, 5, 10, 11, 12-20.

8 Bryans, Jones and Stein, "Mean Times," pp. vi, 30.

9 Doyle and Sambanis, "International Peacebuilding."

10 *The Responsibility to Protect*, p. 57; Doyle and Sambanis, "International Peacebuilding," pp. 3-4.

11 Doyle and Sambanis, "International Peacebuilding," p. 14.

12 Virginia Page Fortna, "Inside and Out: Peacekeeping and Duration of Peace after Civil and Interstate Wars," *International Studies Review* 5:4 (2003): pp. 97, 108.

13 Fortna, "Inside and Out," p. 111.

14 Bruce Jentleson, "Coercive Prevention: Normative, Political, and Policy Dilemmas," United States Institute of Peace, *Peaceworks* No. 35 (October 2000).

15 Patrick Regan and Rodwan Abouharb, "Interventions and Civil Conflicts: Tools of Conflict Management or Simply Another Participant?" *World Affairs* (Summer 2002).

16 Ibid.

17 Michèle Griffin, "Where Angels Fear to Tread: Trends in International Intervention," *Security Dialogue* 31:4 (2000): p. 423-424.

18 Mohammed Ayoob, "Humanitarian Intervention and International Society," *Global Governance* 7:3 (July-September 2001): p. 228.

19 Ibid., pp. 228-229.

20 Coady, "The Ethics of Armed Humanitarian Intervention," pp. 32-36.

21 *The Responsibility to Protect*, pp. viii, xi.

22 Ibid., p. xi.

23 Ibid., p. xii.

24 Ibid.

25 Ibid., pp. 7, 8.

26 Ibid., p. 12.

Chapter 2

International Politics, Local Conflicts and Intervention

S. Neil MacFarlane

States traditionally have used several means by which to achieve their political goals where other states are concerned, the most extreme undoubtedly being war, the external application of organized force either to change the policy of an adversary or to destroy it. Another tool has been to affect internal change in the other state in one of two ways. On the one hand, a foreign state can support the domestic opposition struggling to remove a threatening ruler or government. On the other, a foreign state can help protect and secure a government facing an internal threat to its power. This model of foreign politics of intervening in the domestic politics of another state is perhaps as old as war itself, having played an important part, for example, in the conflict between Athens and Sparta during the Peloponnesian War.[1] Indeed, in the nineteenth century intervention was one of the principal means by which the members of the Holy Alliance attempted to stop the revolutions in Central Europe. And outside of Europe intervention in local disputes was an important method used by England and France for their colonial expansion, by the United States during its period of imperialism,[2] and by the great powers to exert control over China.

During the nineteenth century, international standards against intervention in the internal affairs of states were weak and ambiguous. With the Congress of Vienna, a large part of the Concert (Prussia, Austria, Russia) supported intervention as a legitimate way of protecting monarchies against republicanism and liberal revolutions. States beyond Europe for the most part were not regarded as equal members of international society; thus, they were not protected by the Westphalian standards prohibiting intervention. In general, the great powers believed that interfering in other states in order to protect their citizens or property was their right. Even during the prolonged fall of the Ottoman Empire, the possibility of humanitarian intervention was forcefully discussed in order to protect Christian subjects from the Sultan. Thus, intervention and European colonialism were justified most profoundly by ideas of European and white superiority and as a mission to civilize people plunged in the darkness of ignorance.

During the Cold War, since the superpowers could not risk war against each other, intervention was one of the principal means by which they pursued their global competition, primarily, but not only, in the Third World.[3] In this way, intervention was one of the principal methods of interaction between the global (structural) and the local levels. At the same time, the Third World's resistance to this practice reinforced the legal standards supporting sovereignty and the principle of non-intervention (see below).

After the Cold War the practice of intervention changed in several significant ways. First, there have been very few unilateral and formal interventions. The majority of interventions are carried out either by multilateral organizations or groups of states acting under a mandate from these organizations, primarily the United Nations. Second, considerations of national interest and international power structures have been replaced by international norms, and especially those relating to human rights. In this way one could say that, superficially at least, the character of interaction between the global and the local has changed profoundly. Likewise, during the Cold War the periphery was an issue mostly in terms of how it reflected the global competition and structural bipolarity. Today, the periphery no longer figures as a target of competition, but of governance – the imposition of standards said to be universal by international organizations that are legitimized in international law or by representatives chosen by these organizations.

Consequently, it appears that attitudes about sovereignty and the principle of non-intervention are changing. In particular, domestic political processes of the great powers, transnational links among non-governmental organizations, and the media are playing important roles concerning these changes. In this respect, state behaviour has come to be influenced less by strategic imperatives and more by domestic considerations and their impact on the attitudes of the policy community towards foreign and military policy.

Thus, this chapter addresses three questions: 1. What were the principal reasons for intervention during the Cold War? 2. How does contemporary intervention differ from the past? 3. What explains the differences between the two periods? The analysis begins with a discussion of the definitions of the principal terms followed by a review of the role of intervention in the international relations of the Cold War will be examined. The next part examines the evolution of the theory and practice of intervention after the Cold War. The chapter concludes with a discussion of the implications of the analysis for the dissonance between the global and the local in the contemporary international system. The primary argument is that the displacement of states by multilateral organizations, of strategic considerations by domestic politics, and the national interests by international standards is more apparent than real.

As a note of clarification, given that there are several possible approaches to the study of intervention, (i.e. legal, ethical, political), this analysis considers intervention from the political point of view, whereby intervention is a coercive application of power which aims to modify the target's action. The motivations of intervention can be self-interest in the traditional sense, or the pursuit of particular or universal norms and values. While intervention occurs within a reinforcing legal framework, this framework serves only to influence the direction and frequency of intervention, as will be explored more thoroughly in the following pages. But ultimately, intervention is a political phenomenon and it is regarded here as such.

The Terms of the Debate

There are three important concepts in this analysis, the first of which is "global." Global refers to a category of factors which function on the international level. They can be associated with a particular state (for example, American military power) or they can be extraterritorial (like the financial markets or the internet). They can be concrete, structural, institutional or subjective. For example, one could say that the structure of power (bipolarity, multipolarity, hegemony), the mechanisms of international economic trade, and the principles of human rights all have an important global dimension, meaning that they function on the global level.

Comparable phenomena also exist at the regional, national, or sub-national levels with more limited geographies. When referring to the relationship between the global and the local, one is speaking about the interaction between domestic structures and processes on one side and their counterparts more generally. Although the distinction between the global and the local are clear in theory, and this distinction can have analytical value, in practice the two levels are deeply interpenetrated. For instance, regional balances of power are the base for the global balance, and the global balance can determine its local equivalents. Moreover, the character of regional and local economies is clearly influenced by the international economy at the same time that the character of the international economy reflects the structures and economic standards of Western Europe and North America. Even human rights, said to be universal and anchored in the instruments of international law, is rooted locally in Western Europe.

The choice of identifying a phenomenon as global or local has important normative and political aspects. For example, one can say that the problem of underdevelopment in Africa is local, determined by weak governments, corrupt leaders, the absence of rule of law, insecurity, low skill levels or traditional skills ineffective for a modern economy. On the other hand, the problem can be classified as a global one by referring to the unequal structure and exploitation of the international economy, the economic domination of the North and structural dependence of the South. In the first case, since underdevelopment is the result of domestic factors, the international system and the North is not guilty and is not obligated to correct the situation. In the second case, that the problem is the result of a system created in and by the North for its own advantage implies a responsibility for restitution. It should be recognized, consequently, that the categorization of "international–domestic" has significant policy constraints that can not be dismissed.

It is necessary to question as well the meaning of "the war between the global and the local." Indeed, there is a certain ambiguity in this formulation: it can indicate that war exists in the space between these two levels and binds the global to the domestic, or it can suggest that there is a struggle of, or significant tension between, one level against the other, and that the global is attempting to eliminate the domestic and the domestic is resisting this threat. The analysis carried out in this chapter follows the first interpretation, but recognizes that the second also has a certain value as discussed below.

Finally, what does "intervention" mean?[4] Intervention is a commitment in the domestic affairs of a state with the intention of changing or modifying its structure of power and authority. In an attempt to influence the domestic policy of a country, political, economic, or military instruments can be used. In general, however, the concept of intervention suggests military action. While military engagement in the affairs of a state can be coercive or consensual, the concept of intervention implies an element of coercion. In this respect, when a government invites or accepts an intervention, it is with the intention of coercing its domestic opponents.

The problems emerging from this approach to intervention are obvious. At what point does military technical assistance become intervention? Indeed, the provision of weapons can be as effective as deploying military units to a conflict. Besides, the economic and financial pressure could be as or even more effective as military action in affecting the domestic politics of a country. Propaganda can also have a significant effect on the political process of a country. And inaction can have consequences as profound or even more than action. It is for such reasons that Stanley Hoffmann noted: "The subject is practically the same as that of international politics in general from the beginning of time to the present … . Anything can constitute an intervention, indeed even non-acts can constitute intervention."[5]

A discussion about the concept of sovereignty is closely related to that of intervention. The traditional understanding of sovereignty is that a state has absolute jurisdiction on its territory and that – since states have equal standing in an international system without a supreme authority – this jurisdiction is recognized by other states. From this comes the principle of non-intervention. As Hedley Bull wrote: "Intervention … is generally believed to be legally and morally wrong: sovereign states or independent political communities are thought to have the right to have their spheres of jurisdiction respected and dictatorial interference abridges that right."[6]

In this respect there is a clear separation between politics and international law. While in political analysis, what is important is the attempt to influence the internal affairs of a state, either on behalf of the government and with the consent of the recognized authorities, or against a government and without its consent, in international law it appears that the application of intervention traditionally is limited to cases where coercion is used against a recognized government of a recognized sovereign state. Therefore, the principle of non-intervention is applied mainly to intervention against a government.

It should be noted, however, that in certain traditions of international law, this principle is diluted. In the nineteenth century there were many arguments in favour of the legality of intervention for humanitarian goals. The question presented itself within the framework of the Greek war of independence (when the decisive Franco-British intervention partly was justified by the cruelty of the Ottomans towards their Greek subjects) and later, during the 1870s concerning the way in which the Ottoman government governed its Christian subjects.[7] In essence, the issue reflects the challenge of the good of the collective to override the good of the constituent parts, whereby defending certain universal values is more significant than the sovereignty of a particular state. For those who embrace this tradition of thought, it follows that whenever these universal values are violated in a systematic way by a state in its treatment of its citizens, the other states have the right to intervene to stop the offensive behaviour. Thus, sovereignty is conditional and depends on the manner in which a state builds its relations with its population.

Intervention During the Cold War

The tension between, on one side, the collective conception of human rights and the responsibility of states and the international community and, on the other side, the individualistic design of sovereignty was obvious at the beginning of the Cold War and persisted until its end. For instance, the collective current was present in the 1945 Charter of the United Nations (UN) which, in the preamble and several articles, accepted individual and collective human rights as well as noted the obligations of member-states and the organization itself to promote these rights. Two years later, the UN General Assembly unanimously accepted the Universal Declaration of Human Rights.[8] The Declaration was followed in the 1960s by the Conventions on Civic Rights and Political, Economic and Cultural Rights. Ten years later, its conventions entered in force after ratifications by the requisite number of states. These achievements demonstrated a slow but focussed movement during this period to raise human rights from the level of domestic policy and to give it force in international relations.

Humanitarian international law developed in the same way. In 1977, the Additional Protocol to the Geneva Conventions of 12 August 1949, and Relating to the Protection of Victims in Non-International Armed Conflict (Protocol II) extended the principles of protection of civilians in international war to civil wars, which once again implied a reduction in the absolute sovereignty of a state with regard to the rights of its citizens.[9] Other international treaties and conventions, for example, the Convention on the Prevention and Punishment of the Crime of Genocide,[10] and regional ones as well, for example, the European Convention on Human Rights (ECHR),[11] pushed the debate in the same direction. The ECHR especially, even though it does not have universal application, significantly undermines the sovereignty of the signatory states, particularly for those who accept the obligatory jurisdiction of the European Court. In sum, during the Cold War the evolution of the legal instruments in this field established a significant base for intervention in defence of collectively recognised and established norms.

But, while on the one hand the legal scope of states and their organizations regarding the internal affairs of other states and especially concerning human rights expanded, the legality of intervention narrowed. For instance, Article 2, Section 1 of the UN Charter declares that the organisation is based on the principle of sovereign equality of its members; Article 2, Section 4 says that all members are obliged not to threaten the use of force against other states or to use force in their relations with other states; and Article 2, Section 7 notes that the contents of the Charter do not authorize the UN to intervene in questions of domestic jurisdiction of a state-member.

However, Article 2 includes a significant reservation: that this principle is without prejudice regarding action by the Security Council under Chapter 7 of the Charter (regarding threats to peace and international security). But, although these threats are not well defined, interpretation of the Charter during the Cold War privileged *international* threats or acts of aggression (meaning not domestic ones) in its approach to Chapter 7.[12] Even so, given that the Security Council was immobilized by the bipolar structure of the international system and the veto, it was unable to act even against clear acts of aggression. The UN and Security Council's capacity to expand the definition of threat to international security and to be able to respond to the internal crises of states or the systematic violation of human rights by a government was even more limited.

Actions by other UN institutions (especially the General Assembly) and regional organizations, such as the Organization for African Unity and the Organisation of American States, also contributed to a semblance of absolute legal sovereignty and absolute prohibition of intervention. For instance, the General Assembly's 1965 Declaration on Intervention begins by insisting that no state has the right to intervene, directly or indirectly, in the internal or external affairs of a state. It continues by declaring that armed intervention is equivalent to aggression. Five years later, in the Declaration on Friendly Relations and Co-operation, the Assembly repeated this absolute position. More specifically, the eighth preamble paragraph states that intervention (in whatever form) is a violation of the spirit and letter of the Charter.[13] Similar conclusions are reached by examining the judgements of the International Court of Justice.[14] In this respect, the decision of the Court in the 1949 Corfu Channel case can be interpreted as a complete prohibition of intervention.[15]

But there is another matter that must be examined. While the norms and principles of sovereignty seem to prohibit intervention in an absolute way, if a state is sovereign and is recognized as such by the other members of international society, and if this state seeks the assistance of others in response to an internal threat, it can be concluded that this dimension of intervention does not contradict the evolution of international law on sovereignty and intervention in such cases is legal. As Raymond Aron noted: "The sending of American forces to Lebanon and of British forces to Jordan (1958) was not regarded as contrary to international law and the United Nations Charter because it occurred upon the request of the 'legal governments.'"[16]

In sum, on the normative level, the evolving position regarding intervention during the Cold War is curious. Michael Akehurst observed in this context that: "international law has developed a body of rules on human rights, which forbid states to ill-treat individuals, including their own nationals, but at the same time it has developed a body of rules restricting the (previously almost unlimited) right of states to use force."[17] With regard to intervention, the collective/normative base justifying intervention has widened but, simultaneously, the use of the instruments of intervention in the pursuit of these principles (and against the interests of established regimes) have become illegitimate. On the other hand, intervention in support of governments appears to have remained legal. In this sense, the normative evolution is profoundly conservative, and hostile to the pursuit of a liberal agenda of human rights. Moreover, the attempt to insert these rights in consideration of intervention was severely obstructed by the ideological division of the international system.

The normative evolution of intervention during the Cold War is important for understanding intervention in the post-Cold War era. At the same time these principles had little to do with the reality facing states who were operating according to unilateral, self-centred conceptions and their national interest and in a system highly competitive over power and ideology.[18] Indeed, normative motivations and constraints did not have anything to do with the official practice of intervention, which was (and this is not surprising) deeply politicized. This becomes evident in a review of Cold War interventions by the super and great powers, who were deeply influenced by structural and global considerations; regional powers, who responded to more local political issues; and, finally, multinational organisations who have had very limited experience.

Superpowers

The history of the Cold War is sprinkled with episodes of intervention by the Soviet Union and the United States in the internal affairs of other states, sometimes directly (like the US in Vietnam or the USSR in Afghanistan), and sometimes indirectly (such as through the use of allies, like Cuba in Angola and Ethiopia on behalf of the USSR). These interventions reflected on a local level the global, bipolar competition. The conflict between the two superpowers was structural and ideological, but at its core it was prone to several constraints imposed by the nuclear balance (or Mutually Assured Destruction) and even by the extreme costs of conventional war as shown by the First and Second World Wars. Thus, direct confrontation at the core carried significant risks and the superpower conflict at the global level was diverted towards the periphery where the obstacles were weaker and the stakes and risks less significant. Indeed, even in their competing interventions in the Third World, the superpowers accepted significant constraints whereby, firstly, wanting to avoid an escalation of the local conflicts that could trigger vital interests, they avoided direct confrontations. Secondly, they avoided interventions that undermined the territorial integrity of new post-colonial states, since the support of secessionism could alienate newly independent/post-colonial states over whom they wanted to increase their influence.

It would be redundant to discuss in detail the principal cases of intervention by the superpowers and their agents during the Cold War. Suffice it to say that the most significant element of their interventions is that they were justified by clearly self-centred goals and policies. Superpower intervention was neither a question of regulating conflicts, nor of defending human rights and relieving suffering. It was a question of gaining the upper hand and obtaining credibility and prestige in a global struggle over the adversary by influencing domestic matters and internal issues of states, or of preventing them, in the periphery. There was an ideological component in several cases, but the pursuit of freedom or support of socialism or national liberation mixed with the pursuit of self-centred geopolitical gains. Indeed, the ideological agendas of the superpowers were narrow and did not reflect a normative consensus of the international community. In this respect, the weak influence of ideological motives compared to the stronger role of strategic considerations in the calculations of Washington and Moscow is evident in cases where interest-based considerations contradicted ideological ones, such as American support of dictators such as Mobutu

Sese Seko or relations between the Soviet Union and its "allies" in the Middle East such as Nasser, Sadat, or Assad, and interest and influence overshadowed a commitment to principles.

The superpowers were not the only ones to intervene in the internal affairs of states during the Cold War. The role of "proxies" like Cuba in the politics and policies of the USSR was already noted. Indeed, Cuban interventions for the most part supported progressive, socialist governments in Africa and Central America. While these had an important ideological dimension, it is important to note that Cuba depended on Soviet assistance and thus Cuba had an interest in establishing and reinforcing its usefulness in Soviet foreign policy. In another respect, the countries of the Warsaw Pact (except Romania) played a significant role in supporting the 1968 Soviet intervention of Czechoslovakia as allies of the USSR with an interest in the stability of the socialist system and within the framework of the Brezhnev Doctrine.

Great Powers

France and the United Kingdom also have a varied experience of intervention during the Cold War, an experience which had its own characteristics. In one respect, their interventions were not only part of the larger structural conflict of the Cold War, but in several cases involved close political and logistical co-operation with the US. For instance, the 1958 British intervention in Jordan formed part of a broader Anglo-American strategy which aimed at stabilizing the conservative regimes of the Middle East against Arab nationalism after the fall of the government of Nouri Said in Iraq. Likewise, the 1977-78 Franco-Belgian intervention in Shaba occurred in close cooperation with the US which wanted to contain the Soviet-Cuban sphere of influence in Southern Africa.

But it should be recognized that interventions by the European great powers cannot be explained alone in terms of the Cold War between the US and USSR. Additional factors included decolonization (sometimes not very enthusiastically), the problems of disengagement and redefining relationships with their old subjects, and continuing these relations regardless of, and sometimes in opposition to, American policy. For example, Franco-British intervention in Egypt in 1956 was in response to Nasser's threat to British influence in the Middle East, and Egyptian support for the Front de Libération National (National Liberation Front) in Algeria where France's interests lay. This incident produced one of the rare moments of concordance between the US and USSR on a significant issue of international relations, and American hostility towards their intervention forced a retreat.

Within the post-colonial framework, the two powers tried to support successor governments as in the British intervention in Tanganyika in 1964 to support the Nyerere government against a coup d'état. Nevertheless, the British eventually came to halt this policy, except in Oman where they gave significant assistance to the Sultan against a revolt in the western part of the country. In contrast, France, within the framework of bilateral defence and military technical assistance agreements, intervened in French-speaking Africa several times to support friendly governments against threats internally (viz. the many interventions in Cameroon, Congo-Brazzaville, Gabon, Niger, and Mauritania), and externally (viz. in Chad in 1978-79 against Libya) in order to maintain a French sphere of influence in the area.[19] Thus, in the British and French cases, as with the superpowers, the essence of their interventions was self-centred and reflected their perceived interests. Normative considerations had very little impact on their behaviour.

Regional Powers

The third category was intervention by regional powers, such as Egypt in Yemen in 1962, India in Bangladesh in 1971, and South Africa in the affairs of its neighbours during the 1970s and 1980s. In these cases also, intervention had an essentially political dimension. In the case of Yemen, Egypt intervened in response to an invitation by the new nationalist regime that was facing a monarchical opposition supported by Saudi Arabia and within the framework of the clash between radical Arab nationalism and traditional regimes in the region.[20] India intervened in the civil war of East Pakistan to stop the waves of refugees and also to break apart its regional rival.[21] South Africa tried to destabilize, if not to overturn, socialist regimes which supported the anti-apartheid movement and which, in South Africa's perception, allowed the influence of the USSR and Cuba in the region to expand.

It is true that several of these interventions (and in particular those of India in Bangladesh, of Tanzania in Uganda in 1979, and of Vietnam in Cambodia in 1978) had important humanitarian dimensions.[22] The Pakistani government's use of violence against the population of East Pakistan is regarded as one of the main cases of genocide in the twentieth century.[23] India's invasion ended these massacres. In the same way Vietnam's actions against the Khmer Rouge stopped the genocide of fellow Cambodians. And Tanzania's invasion of Idi Amin's Uganda drove out a regime which was responsible for at least 100,000, perhaps even half a million, murders.[24] In this sense, one could say that these interventions were of a humanitarian nature.

But it should be noted that in these three cases, the intervening governments acted after their own territories were attacked, and justified their actions by asserting their right of self-defence.[25] Moreover, in the debates of the Security Council in connection with Vietnam's intervention, several states debated whether it could be justified under humanitarian reasons. Four of the five members of NATO who took part in this debate argued that even serious violations of human rights could not justify military intervention. Expressing the pluralist conception of the international community, France's representative declared that the idea that intervention could be justified because a regime was hateful was extremely dangerous and could compromise order and international law.[26]

Multilateral Organizations

The fourth category of intervention during the Cold War was that of multilateral organizations. In general, bipolarity and the global confrontation between the two superpowers greatly limited the UN's interventionism. There is only one significant case of UN intervention in a civil conflict during the Cold War in the Republic of

Congo (Léopoldville) in July 1960 which lasted until 1964.[27] In the face of an almost complete collapse of the Congo state, a military mutiny, Belgian intervention, and the danger of a confrontational engagement by the superpowers, the UN supported the Congo government by demanding the retreat of the Belgian forces and introducing a peacekeeping force, United Nations Operation in the Congo (ONUC). The UN's involvement was consensual and the mandate did not include the use of force.

In spite of the deployment of ONUC, the situation continued to deteriorate, especially due to Katanga's secessionist attempt. In February 1961, the Security Council adopted an additional resolution which considered the use of force to prevent civil war. It followed that the UN became a participant in the war on the side of the government. Several aspects of these developments are significant. Above all, the Congo government agreed to the mandate of ONUC, whose principal goals were to restore peace and stability and to preserve the sovereignty and territorial integrity of the country by preventing the secession of Katanga and by ensuring the retreat of soldiers and foreign mercenaries. In other words, it was a matter not of questioning the state and its rights towards its people, but of restoring the state. In this respect, the experience in the Congo showed the UN's limited capacity of intervening in the domestic affairs of states, and the inherent dangers to itself in its attempts.[28]

Other multilateral interventions of the period concern regional organizations. In 1965 the Organisation of American States sent a multilateral force to replace American forces in the Dominican Republic. The debates which surrounded the operation indicated a strong disillusion with American hegemonic policy in the area and reinforced regional standards of non-intervention. In other respects, the Organization for African Unity attempted to intervene in the internal conflicts of its member states, and in particular were not very effective in deploying a "Neutral Force" in Chad in 1981.[29] This experiment demonstrated the organization's weak capacity in managing conflicts. The fact that, in spite of the many conflicts in Africa during the Cold War, this was the only significant case of multilateral intervention by the OAU shows the lack of enthusiasm by member states for such a tool of regional security.

In sum, intervention during the Cold War was mainly unilateral, state-based and self-centred, motivated by the pursuit of power and other interests of states in an anarchic and competitive system. Multilateral organizations played a minor role in the application of intervention, but more significant in the elaboration of standards was the emphasis on sovereignty and non-intervention. Although international law little by little embraced human rights, this had a limited effect on facilitating intervention. In general norms had a weak influence on the practice of intervention.

The Interlude of "New Thinking"

Towards the end of the Cold War, under the influence of Soviet "new thinking," the practice of superpower intervention changed radically. Soviet leaders concluded that conflicts in the Third World were a distraction, if not a constraint, in their efforts to improve relations with the United States and attempted to remove this obstacle as quickly as possible. For instance, the Soviets decreased and then ceased their support of governments in Ethiopia, Angola and Nicaragua and withdrew their troops from Afghanistan. Financial assistance to the Cuban military presence in Africa and Central America also dropped as did assistance to Cuba in general, thereby pushing the Cubans towards a less ambitious foreign policy. Cutbacks in assistance to Vietnam had the same effect.

At the same time, Mr. Gorbachev declared the supremacy of the idea of common humanity, his desire for the "de-ideologization" of international relations and his country's support for a more active role for the UN, all in an effort to create and maintain peace.[30] The change in Soviet position in these areas and the constructive response of the Bush administration allowed for a series of UN initiatives, supported by the USSR and the US, concerning those conflicts which undermined the Soviet-American relationship in the 1970s and 1980s. With unanimous agreement of the Security Council, the UN helped to negotiate the withdrawal of the Soviet forces from Afghanistan and the Vietnamese withdrawal from Cambodia. The UN also played a prominent role in the peaceful transition in Namibia and Cambodia, the resolution of the conflicts and the political transitions in El Salvador, Nicaragua and Guatemala, and the settlement of the civil war in Mozambique. It appeared that competitive intervention was replaced by a Soviet-American concordance to reinforce peace and security on the basis of common values.

Intervention After the Cold War

The disappearance of bipolarity decreased considerably the significance of localized wars in the strategic calculations of the great powers. One could have thought that, as a result, there would be a decrease in interventions themselves. But regional powers retained their specific interests and continued to use interventions at the same rate of frequency. And at the global level, instead of disappearing or decreasing, interventions simply changed their form and content. More specifically, while unilateral interventions by the great powers disappeared,[31] the Security Council of the UN, freed from the structural contradictions among its permanent members, became much more active and responsive to threats of peace and security with an increased number of peacekeeping or peacemaking mandates.

These changes also reflected the evolving nature of war. Inter-state wars almost disappeared, but the frequency of civil wars continued to increase. Although the strategic interest in these conflicts decreased, foreign involvement was difficult to avoid because of their character.[32] First, since the beginning of the twentieth century, there have been at least eight military deaths for every civilian, but by the end of the century the reverse was true. At the same time, the number of people displaced by war dramatically increased. While in 1975, there were about 2.4 million refugees (people who migrated through an international border) worldwide, in 1995 there was 14.5 million.[33] The number of internally displaced migrants within their countries also increased significantly. Roberta Cohen and Francis Deng notice that, "when internally displaced persons (IDPs) were first counted in 1982, 1.2 million were found in eleven countries. By 1997 the number had soared to more than 20 million in at least 35 countries."[34]

Second, the explosion of civilian deaths and displacement in contemporary wars is related to the fact that the conduct of civil war takes place widely on the territory of the country in question. And, at least in multi-ethnic societies, these wars involve not only political and military groups, but entire communities and their identities. The goals of such wars are not only the conquest of territory or control of government, but also the destruction or elimination of the adversary's population. Under these conditions, the military-civilian distinction itself tends to disappear. The result is a humanitarian crisis, if not genocide.

Finally, the globalization of communication has made it impossible to hide the images of victims. As a result, the international community is strongly pressured by civil society to help and protect victims of these catastrophes. Indeed, states, inter-governmental and non-governmental organizations now deliver this assistance and protection on site, partly because states have become less and less able and willing to accommodate refugees on their territory.[35]

Thus, intervention in the post-Cold War era has been dominated at the global level by coalitions acting under UN mandates (Somalia 1992, Haiti 1994, Bosnia 1995, Albania 1997, East Timor 1999) or by particular states (France in Rwanda 1994). In some cases, regional organizations played an essential (NATO in Bosnia) or important (Organisation of American States in Haiti) role as preferred agents of the UN. In other respects, some organizations acted independently of the UN (the Economic Community of the West African States [ECOWAS] in Liberia and Sierra Leone, the Commonwealth of Independent States [CIS] in Georgia and Tajikistan, NATO in the Serb Republic [Kosovo]). However, the majority of regional operations were authorized or recognized in advance by the Security Council (NATO in Bosnia) or retrospectively (ECOWAS in Liberia and Sierra Leone, the CIS in Georgia and in Tajikistan). The great exception is, of course, Kosovo.

From the chronological point of view, a clear pattern emerges from these operations. In response perhaps to the successful multilateral settlements of many prolonged conflicts at the end of the Cold War, success in the war against Iraq in 1990-91, and with the appearance of several wars in post-Communist Europe, there was a considerable increase in the number of interventions and peacekeeping operations at the beginning of the decade reflecting a period of tremendous enthusiasm. However, this enthusiasm was short-lived following the 1993 disaster in Somalia, the consequent modification of the American view of peace operations, frustrations by the EU, Europe generally and the UN in Bosnia, and the financial problems of the UN related to the American refusal to pay its contributions.[36] Thus, the number of peacemaking and peacekeeping operations declined dramatically during 1994-7, and the role of UN forces decreased while that of regional organizations (like NATO and ECOWAS) grew. Nonetheless, by the end of the decade, the UN returned to a more active position in its effort to solve the conflicts in Timor and Sierra Leone, if not the Congo.

In contrast with the Cold War era, interventions today are generally a multilateral operation. Exceptions are rare and likely to be found in Africa, with the exception of Russia's actions in Moldova and Georgia (South Ossetia). In Africa, especially in the case of the Democratic Republic of Congo, traditional explanations prevail of unilateral and competitive military support for one side or another in a civil war that involves the interests of neighbouring countries. Nonetheless, it should be stressed that these cases are exceptional.

Another feature of interventions in the post-Cold War era is that, for the most part, they have been justified (see below for arguments that they were not justified) based on the so-called universal values of human rights. One could even say that this "new interventionism" has taken on a liberal and collective character, whereby the liberal agenda has moved the parameters of the intervention issue to the centre and collective ideas appear to have taken on the more traditional and pluralist designs of international order. These changes are especially evident in the evolution of the quasi-legal doctrines of "humanitarian" intervention which actively disputed the domination of traditional ideas about sovereignty and the rights of states, bringing us to a discussion of the normative dimension of intervention after the Cold War.

Before beginning this discussion, however, it should be noted that the domination of states with regard to intervention has been challenged not only at the top by multilateral organizations, but also at lower levels by transnational private corporations. The examples of the latter include the role of Executive Outcomes in Angola, Sierra Leone, and Papua-Guinea[37] and Military Professional Resources Incorporated (MPRI) in Croatia and Bosnia in assisting government armed forces.[38] In considering this phenomenon, however, several of its aspects must be emphasised which question its importance for a discussion on the evolution of interventionist practice. For instance, the purchase of private military services and people is not new. Moreover, in all the cases named above, the governments in question contracted the services of these private companies; thus, they are not cases of intervention without government consent.

Whether the actions of private military corporations can be labelled "non-state" must also be considered. On the one hand, they are non-state actors. In some instances, their actions are tolerated by the interested great powers, like the role of Executive Outcomes in Angola[39] and Sierra Leone. When the great powers changed their minds, the corporations withdrew.[40] Their operations also depended on the goodwill of the countries in which the corporations were based. For example, when the South African government began to inquire about the activities of Executive Outcomes, it introduced a bill requiring government authorization for each of its operations, thereby complicating the corporation's business. Finally, these operations are vulnerable to the attitudes of international financial organizations which exert an inconsistent, but important, control on the budgets and expenditures of governments who engage these companies.

On the other hand, these private military corporations, such as MPRI, are not non-state actors. It is an enterprise comprising for the most part former American soldiers with close ties to the Defence Department and American intelligence services and which mostly is contracted by the American government to provide military assistance. In other words, it is an agent of the American government and its actions reflect American policy. In general, therefore, one could say that the interventionist actions by private companies are not an important challenge to the primacy of the state with regard to interventionism.

Turning now to a discussion of normative questions, the understanding of sovereignty evolved in the early period of the post-Cold War era. In this respect, in January 1992 the heads of states and governments of the Security Council members requested the new secretary-general of the UN, Boutros Boutros-Ghali to compile "an analysis and recommendations on ways of strengthening and making more efficient within the framework and provisions of the Charter the capacity of the United Nations for preventive diplomacy, for peace-making and for peacekeeping."[41] In his answer, Boutros-Ghali noted many major changes in the international system: the fall of ideological barriers to collective action in security matters, agreement among the permanent members on vital questions before the Security Council, the retreat of authoritarianism with the growing wave of global democratization, the peaceful emancipation of the East-Central European countries and former Soviet republics from communism, the globalization of communication and economic transactions, the increasingly central role of human rights issues in international relations and in the work of the UN, as well as, more negatively, the deterioration of regional security, serious economic problems of the South, and explosive increase in the numbers of refugees and internally displaced persons. He concluded from this evidence that there were increasingly strong reasons to abandon the idea of absolute sovereignty in the pursuit of common and universal values. As he said, "The time of absolute and exclusive sovereignty ... has passed; its theory was never matched by reality."[42] In this context, the secretary-general affirmed that there was a growing sentiment under the conditions of the post-Cold War era of an opportunity to achieve the major goals of the UN: justice, human rights, social progress, and greater freedom for all.

Boutros-Ghali's idea of relative sovereignty reflected an opinion that was spreading, at least in the North. In particular, there was a growing tendency to tie sovereignty to the behaviour and responsibility of the state in its relations with its own citizens. As his successor, Kofi Annan, said in 1998, "The Charter protects the sovereignty of peoples (*sic*). It was never meant as a license for governments to trample on human rights and human dignity. Sovereignty means responsibility, not just power."[43] Thus, the systematic violation of human rights could undermine state sovereignty and decrease the force of legal protection against intervention,[44] especially when intervention occurs under the mandate of an organization authorized to use force, such as the UN under Chapter VII of the Charter. This was an argument used in particular by France in articulating the idea of "necessary intervention" in humanitarian crises, which implies a similar right to intervene in the domestic jurisdiction of a state without the consent of that state.[45] The legal basis of such an idea is found at the end of Article 2, Section 7 in the only exception in the Charter regarding the prohibition of interventions whereby non-intervention of the UN in domestic jurisdiction did not prevent the application of Chapter VII, which establishes the rights and responsibilities of the organisation regarding threats to international peace and security. It is not surprising, therefore, that the Security Council expanded its interpretation of "threats" in its effort to respond in an effective manner to humanitarian issues related to civil war.

Thus, the logic was more or less clear and valid: a humanitarian crisis or the systematic violation of human rights in civil wars created consequences that threatened the security of neighbouring countries or the region in question. For example, waves of refugees could destabilize countries located next to or near the state undergoing the crisis. Or, retreating soldiers could find refuge themselves in a neighbouring country and, after re-grouping and resting, return to battle and provoke military attacks against the country providing refuge. Also, ethnic conflicts could draw in members of the same ethnic group from contiguous countries. The reasoning for such a position is evident in various UN resolutions passed during this period. For example, Resolution 688 identified the repression of the civilian population in Iraq – and especially of the Kurds – as threats to international peace and security. The resolution also defined as threats the Kurdish movement which transcended state boundaries and cross-border military incursions in response to Iraqi government repression, leading to the need to end that repression.[46]

In another example, Resolution 733 noted the implications of the military and humanitarian situation in Somalia in 1991-92 for regional security and the uncommitted *concern* of the Security Council that the Somali affair constituted a threat to international peace and security, required the secretary-general to take necessary measures to ensure the delivery of humanitarian assistance and invoked Chapter VII of the Charter in imposing an arms embargo.[47] With each subsequent resolution concerning the domestic situation in Somalia (Resolutions 746, 751, 775),[48] the Council repeated its concern with the situation and its implications for international peace and security. Only in the final resolution, Resolution 794, did the Council forego any references to a concern and instead clearly determined that the Somali situation constituted a threat to peace and security, noted the obstacles to and danger faced by the delivery of humanitarian assistance, declared its determination to ensure an environment in which humanitarian operations could be carried out safely in order to restore stability, security, and the rule of law, and invoked Chapter VII to authorize a military operation carried out by the United States and without the consent of the Somali government.[49] In the case of Bosnia, the UN authorized force to facilitate the protection of migrants and minority populations in protection zones and delivery of humanitarian assistance, and then, under the auspices of NATO, to end the conflict.

In these three cases, it appeared that a new standard emerged, allowing, if not demanding, intervention in the internal affairs of states where the basic rights of citizens (and in particular the right to survival) for a significant portion of the population was in question. In subsequent cases, this evolution widened further to include the protection of law and democratic institutions. For instance, in 1994 in Haiti, the Security Council authorized Operation Uphold Democracy in an effort to restore the elected government of Bertrand Aristide,[50] leading to the resignation and exile of the de facto government in Port-au-Prince. In 1997, the UN authorized (retrospectively) the intervention of ECOWAS to remove the "illegitimate" regime and restore the elected government in Sierra Leone.

It can be concluded from this series of resolutions that the international community was in the process of accepting multilateral intervention on the normative level, i.e. on behalf of the protection and promotion of human rights. On a more significant level, these developments represented a possible change in the balance between order and justice as goals of the international community in favour of the promotion of justice and the consequent amendment to the substance of sovereignty. In such extreme cases as Bosnia, Kosovo, and East Timor, the pursuit of collective principles culminated in the suspension of the state's sovereign rights and the establishment of international forms of administration. In short, it appears that the liberal and collective agenda has been victorious over the pluralist ideas of the international community.[51]

But such a conclusion would be made in haste. First, there has been a significant resistance to the erosion of sovereignty, as demonstrated in the debates of the Security Council concerning the above cases. Regarding Iraq, for instance, a notable portion of the Council (including China, Cuba, India, Yemen, and Zimbabwe) expressed reservations regarding the implications for sovereignty of Resolution 688, leading China and India to abstain from the vote for these reasons. The Security Council debates and the resolutions themselves reveal tremendous sensitivity towards this issue. In this respect, Resolution 688 simultaneously reaffirmed the sovereignty of Iraq and authorized an intervention into the country's internal affairs. After the adoption of the resolution, and in light of the opposition expressed by Iraq as well as actions by French, American and British businesses (see note 46), the Secretariat of the UN tried intensely to obtain Iraqi consent for an international presence, and succeeded in reaching an agreement with Iraqi authorities on the deployment of a small force of "UN guards." And finally, the role of this case in setting a legal precedent is obscure since Iraq was the aggressor, had been vanquished recently by an international coalition authorized by the Security Council, had sanctions against it, and in whose internal sovereign affairs the UN already played a significant role (viz. the attempt to control weapons production).

Moreover, the debates of the Security Council and their resolutions regarding the cases of Somalia, China and Zimbabwe among others underlined their unique character in an effort to avoid setting a precedent regarding humanitarian interventions and the violation of sovereignty. Regarding Somalia, of particular importance is the absence of a recognised sovereign authority and a functioning government with the power to consent to intervention and the lack of emphasis placed on this critical factor in the debate. Moreover, China is more likely to have not opposed the authorization of an armed intervention into Somalia not because it supported a softer interpretation of sovereignty but because it believed that the African group would oppose it. When the African group instead supported the authorization, China found itself in a difficult position of appearing to privilege humanitarian intervention over sovereignty.[52]

The debates and resolutions regarding Haiti also demonstrated the resistance of several members (including China and a group of now sufficiently strong Latin American states, i.e. Brazil, Mexico, Cuba, Uruguay, and Venezuela) to interfere in the domestic affairs of states in order to promote democracy. In the case of Haiti, the Security Council emphasised again the uniqueness of the situation. Indeed, any judgement about the significance of the case for expanding legitimate intervention was complicated by the fact that the government-in-exile (which was recognized as the legitimate authority) consented to the resolution and which played an essential role in the resolution's adoption. Moreover, while the de facto authorities also consented to the resolution, they had little choice in the matter.

In the cases of Croatia and Bosnia, intervention was not strictly speaking an issue as the governments consented to the presence and role of foreign forces. Nonetheless, the third incident of the former Yugoslavia – NATO intervention in Kosovo in 1999 – demonstrates the normative ambiguities surrounding the question of humanitarian intervention. In this case, NATO did not even attempt to obtain Security Council authorization because it was certain that such a resolution would be vetoed by Russia and China.[53] Without a Security Council mandate under Chapter VII, NATO's action violated the UN Charter.

On the other hand, states are thought to have obligations towards populations victimized in war or experiencing genocide. Some argue that in such situations, and when the Security Council can not make an appropriate decision, to not act is unacceptable. Within this framework, several NATO members expressed the opinion that, even if the action violated the Charter, it was legal because it conformed to general international law and the criteria of "overwhelming humanitarian necessity."[54] Moreover, as International Commission on Kosovo suggested that the action was illegal, but legitimate.[55] Thereafter, the non-aligned countries unanimously declared that, "we reject the so-called 'right of humanitarian intervention' which has no legal basis in the UN Charter or in the general principles of international law."[56] Later, in their Treaty on Friendship and Cooperation signed on July 16, 2001 and in their bilateral declaration issued at the same time, Russia and China declared:

> The heads of state of Russia and China note that the formation of a fair and rational new international order is coming up against a number of challenges. Russia and China will be making joint efforts for strengthening the leading role of the UN and its Security Council in world affairs and for countering any attempts to subvert the fundamental norms of international law with the help of such concepts as 'humanitarian intervention' and 'limited sovereignty.'[57]

In sum, the movement of the international community towards accepting liberal and collective standards of intervention is not clear. First, the consent of states remains very important in Security Council decisions, which questions the scope of the erosion of traditional sovereignty.[58] Second, the Council regularly emphasises the unique circumstances of each situation and, consequently, the exceptional character of interventionist behaviour.[59] Third, Security Council debates, general comments, and the political reactions of many significant states indicate that this normative evolution is stronger among Western states than others. Specifically, the Western agenda is resisted by a coalition of Russia, China, and the majority of countries of the South. Although the normative dimension of intervention is much more prominent after the Cold War, these standards are not universally accepted and sometimes are highly contradictory. The fact that co-operation among the permanent members of the Security Council, which was evident at the beginning of the 1990s, weakened over the course of the decade suggests that the consensus necessary to define particular situations such as "threats to international peace and security" (which is necessary to cancel Article 2, Section 7 on domestic jurisdiction) is increasingly difficult to obtain. In short, there are significant reasons to doubt the consolidation of a liberal doctrine on multilateral intervention in the post-Cold War era.[60] Moreover, if this normative evolution is seen as a reflection of Western unipolarity and hegemony in the post-Cold War world, one can anticipate that, in the long term, Russia's likely recovery and China's (perhaps India's) economic and military growth will not only dilute this hegemonic capacity but also the effects of ideological and normative Western and American hegemony.

This conclusion is reinforced upon closer examination of the behaviour of states promoting the "normativization" of intervention. If the practice of intervention were guided by universal standards, it should be universal in its application. But it is not. There is a long list of failed states where, even though the rights of the population were more or less systematically violated, the international community did not react in a manner compatible with the liberal normative position. Sudan is an eloquent example whereby, despite the current phase of its on-going civil war since 1983 during which time there have been several hundred thousand civilian deaths and a million migrants, the international community remained on the sidelines.

In the case of Rwanda, the commander of the United Nations Assistance Mission for Rwanda (UNAMIR), the UN peacekeeping force in the country, informed the Secretariat of the possibility of genocide in January 1994. The principal civil servants of the Department of Peacekeeping Operations read the telex, but showed it to neither secretary general nor the Security Council. The UN refused the request to expand the mandate of the peacekeeping force in order that it prevent the crisis. In April 1994 when the genocide started, and in the face of the murders of Belgian peacekeepers, instead of reinforcing the force, the Security Council decided to reduce it. Several members even advocated the complete withdrawal of UNAMIR. In simple terms, the Council did not have the will to expand the mandate of UNAMIR so that the force could more effectively address the crisis. For several weeks, the Secretariat and several members of the Council refused to label the situation as a genocide in order to avoid their obligations under the genocide convention.[61] It was only in July 1994 that the Security Council reacted, by authorizing Operation Turquoise where French units occupied the south-west of the country to protect a population threatened by civil war, and well after the crescendo of the atrocities of the earlier period. Close to 800,000 people perished during the genocide and approximately one million were displaced.

More recently, the contrast between the international reaction to the Kosovo crisis and the lack of any reaction towards the war in Chechnya provides a powerful example of the issue of selectivity regarding interventions on behalf of grievous humanitarian considerations whereby the humanitarian damage of the latter has exceeded considerably that of the former before NATO's intervention. In general, the selectivity of multilateral responses to humanitarian crises that are tied to war raises questions about the global legitimacy of the "new interventionism."

This explains in large part the linkages of the normative agenda with considerations of specific interest. With the exception of Somalia, intervention occurs where the interveners perceive political interests that support the action. In northern

Iraq, intervention of the three great powers was closely related to the fact that the Kurdish migrants were destined for their ally, Turkey, and that Turkey, facing an uprising by its own Kurdish population, was not willing to accommodate several hundred thousand more Kurds into the region experiencing the most insurgency. The attention received by the conflicts in Yugoslavia reflects the problem which they posed for the great European powers, especially the problem of the movement of large populations. Moreover, after a certain period of time, the credibility, if not survival, of the European and Euro-Atlantic institutions was threatened by the continuation of the conflicts and the Serb challenge. The invasion of Haiti was the result of the large Haitian migration to Florida, a critical state in the American electoral process, and the influence of the black caucus in Congress and of black votes on the electoral base of President Clinton. In the case of East Timor, the activism of Australian civil society and an interest in regional stability generated the political will for Australia to play the principal role in this multilateral intervention. In general, intervention does not occur where common interests do not exist, or when political interest militates against (viz. Chechnya). Even the case of Somalia shows the essential role of national interest, and the speed of the international withdrawal after the events of October 1993 indicates the fragility of international involvement when national interests are not in question.

The consideration of national interest helps us to understand not only the actions of those who intervene, but also the policies of those who do not oppose the intervention. For example, given the attitude of India and China regarding intervention in internal affairs, one would have expected their strong opposition to the 1991 actions in Iraq. Yet, this did not occur. This was a time when India was negotiating several bilateral economic agreements with the US, and it did not want to complicate the negotiations. In the Chinese case, two years after the events of Tienanmen, it wished to keep its critics at bay and did not want to risk any behaviour that would have led to more criticisms.

At the time of the decision on Haiti and Rwanda, Russia wanted the UN's authorization and financial assistance for its intervention in Georgia. The result was a type of trilateral agreement: the US and France did not oppose the UN resolution on Georgia, and Russia did not oppose those on Rwanda and Haiti. In the pro-democratic case of intervention in Sierra Leone, the absence of any opposition from China and Russia demonstrates this explanation, perhaps by way of African support for the intervention and the desire of these two permanent members to not alienate the African group on a matter where their own interests were not in question.

Conclusion

In sum, it would be premature to postulate that normative considerations replaced national interests in decisions to intervene even with the significant evolution of the form and content of intervention since the end of the Cold War. Interventions before were almost exclusively formal and unilateral. They were justified mainly by considerations of self-interested political gains. The normative and legal contexts were ambiguous. From one side, the collective standards were injected in international law.

On the other, the prohibition of interventions were strengthened. In any case, the normative framework had little to do with the practice of intervention.

After the end of the Cold War, and in the context of the transformed character of war, the disappearance of the competition of power and ideas, and the establishment of the hegemony of American and Western values, multilateralism dominated the reasoning for intervention. The view that sovereignty was conditional, and based on the performance of states in protecting the rights of their citizens, became more prominent. It followed that the legal prohibition of intervention weakened.

Intervention during this time had an extremely normative substance. Collective values – the management if not the settlement of conflicts, and the protection of human rights – gained force compared to definite political objectives. Intervention itself appeared to be governed by standards, such as the authorization by a multilateral institution, considerations of humanitarian international law, and the prohibition of genocide.

However, rather than conclude that state pluralism is being replaced by humanistic considerations, several reservations about the process need to be considered. Instances of unilateral and self-interested interventions persist. Not only does the consent of states for intervention retain its importance, but selectivity suggests that political interests continue to play a significant role in decisions on intervention. And the normative evolution is strongly, perhaps even more so, disputed by a coalition including Russia, China, India, and a majority of the South. The normative component of contemporary intervention can be simply a demonstration of one particular international structure, and, if one examines the history of hegemons, probably temporary.

Notes

1 See, for example, the history of competing interventions of Corcyra and Corinth in the internal affairs of the city of Epidamnus. Thucydides, *History of the Peloponnesian War* (Harmondsworth, UK: Penguin, 1986), pp. 49-53.

2 The Spanish-American war began with the Americans interfering in the anti-colonial struggle in Cuba. American control in the area of the Panama Canal was established by the organization of a secessionist movement which had had revolted and, with American assistance, broke off from Colombia. The history of American foreign policy in Mexico and the Caribbean is sprinkled with interventionist periods as part of the US's attempts to establish and maintain an exclusive zone of influence in the region. See Walter LaFeber, *The American Age: US Foreign Policy at Home and Abroad. Volume I, 1750 to 1920* (New York: Norton, 1994), pp. 197-202, 206-212, 239-250.

3 For a discussion on intervention during this period, see S. Neil MacFarlane, *Intervention and Regional Security* (London: International Institute for Strategic Studies, 1985). See also Zaki Laïdi, *Les contraintes d'une rivalité: Les superpuissances et l'Afrique (1960-1985)* (Paris: La Découverte, 1986).

4 For a useful discussion on the definition of intervention, see Hedley Bull, "Introduction," in *Intervention in World Politics,* ed. Hedley Bull (Oxford: Oxford University Press, 1984), p. 1.

5 Stanley Hoffmann, "The Problem of Intervention," in *Intervention in World Politics*, pp. 7-8. See also MacFarlane, *Intervention and Regional Security*, pp. 1-2.
6 Bull, "Introduction," p. 2.
7 Tom J. Farer and Felice Gaer, "The UN and Human Rights," in *United Nations, Divided World: The U.N.'s Roles in International Relations*, eds. Adam Roberts and Benedict Kingsbury (Oxford: Oxford University Press, 1993), p. 242.
8 GA Res. 217 (III)A, 10 December 1948.
9 For the text, see Adam Roberts and Richard Guelff, *Documents on the Laws of War,* second edition (Oxford: Oxford University Press, 1989), pp. 449-458. The Convention entered into force 7 December 1978.
10 Signed 9 December 1948, entered into force 12 January 1951. The Convention established that genocide is a crime under international law and charged the signatory states to prevent it and punish it (first article).
11 Signed 4 November 1950, entered into force September 1953. The principal goal of the Convention was to create a mechanism to strengthen the 1948 Universal Declaration. The text is available at www.echr.coe.int/Eng/BasicTexts.htm.
12 There are two significant exceptions: the sanctions against South Rhodesia concerning its unilateral declaration of independence from the British colony (1966-1979) and the arms embargo against South Africa during apartheid (1977-1994). See, among others, Margaret P. Doxey, *United Nations Sanctions: Current Policy Issues* (Halifax: Centre for Foreign Policy Studies of Dalhousie University, 1997), pp. 1-3.
13 See, for example, the absolute prohibitions of intervention in: UN General Assembly, "Declaration on Intervention" (21 December 1965) and UN General Assembly, "Declaration on Principles of International Law concerning Friendly Relations and Cooperation among States" (24 October 1970).
14 It is true that the declarations and resolutions of the General Assembly do not comprise 'hard law,' but when the General Assembly supports a vote with a large majority or unanimously, one could say that the action in question reflects the custom of state society, which is a recognized source of international law.
15 For a very useful discussion of these issues, see Michael Akehurst, "Humanitarian Intervention," in *Intervention and World Politics*, pp. 108-111.
16 Raymond Aron, *Peace and War: A Theory of International Relations* (Malabar, FL: Robert E. Krieger, 1981), p. 118.
17 Ibid., p. 95.
18 Concerning the declarations of the General Assembly, Rosalyn Higgins noted: "[C]ertainly many states regard it in practice as entirely acceptable to bring various pressures to bear, to influence the internal or external events of other states. One thus has constantly the problem of identifying the reality, and measuring it against the rhetoric." Rosalyn Higgins, "Intervention and International Law," in *Intervention and World Politics*, p. 38. Raymond Aron recognized the same difficulty in a more acute way: "since international law ... is based on the sovereignty and the equality of states, it is not a reflection but a negation of the present reality." Aron, *Peace and War*, p. 567.
19 For useful discussions on France's military policy and interventions in Africa, see Dominique Moïsi and Pierre Lellouche, "French Policy in Africa: A Lonely Battle against Destabilization," *International Security* (Spring 1979); John Chipman, *French Military Power and African Security* (London: International Institute for Strategic Studies, 1985); and John Chipman, *French Power in Africa* (Oxford: Basil Blackwell, 1989).
20 Albert Hourani, *A History of the Arab Peoples* (New York: Warner, 1992), p. 411.
21 It is important to note that the Indian military invasion was preceded by an aerial attack of Indian territory by Pakistan.

22 For a discussion of the humanitarian dimension of this case, see Nicholas Wheeler, *Saving Strangers: Humanitarian Intervention in International Society* (Oxford: Oxford University Press, 2000), pp. 55-128.

23 See Leo Kuper, *Genocide: Its Political Use in the Twentieth Century* (New Haven: Yale University Press, 1981), pp. 173-174.

24 Amnesty International, *Political Killings by Governments* (London: Amnesty International, 1983), p. 44.

25 In the Security Council debates about Bangladesh, the representatives of India at the time justified their invasion with reference to humanitarian issues. But each state having the right to correct the transcript, in the final version these references disappeared. See Akehurst, "Humanitarian Intervention," p. 97.

26 UN Document, S/PV.2109, p.4.

27 See Jane Boulden, *Peace Enforcement: The United Nations Experience in Congo, Somalia, and Bosnia* (Westport, CT: Praeger, 2001), pp. 21-50.

28 See Georges Abi-Saab, *The United Nations Operation in the Congo* (Oxford: Oxford University Press, 1978); and Conor Cruise O'Brien, *To Katanga and Back* (New York: Grosset and Dunlap, 1962).

29 See Eric Berman and Katie Sams, *Peacekeeping in Africa: Capabilities and Culpabilities* (New York: United Nations, 2000), pp. 47-56.

30 *Pravda* (7 December 1988).

31 The last stage was US action against Manuel Noriega in Panama in 1989.

32 For useful discussions of the character of contemporary wars, see Pierre Hassner, *Violence and Peace: From the Atomic Bomb to Ethnic Cleansing* (London: Central European University Press, 1997); and Mary Kaldor, *New and Old Wars: Organised Violence in a Global Era* (Cambridge: Polity, 1999).

33 Adam Roberts, *Humanitarian Action in War*, Adelphi Paper no. 305 (Oxford: Oxford University Press for the IISS, 1996), p. 12. After 1995, the number of refugees diminished but it remains higher than previous levels.

34 Roberta Cohen and Francis Deng, *The Forsaken People: Case Studies of the Internally Displaced* (Washington: Brookings, 1998), p. 1.

35 Adam Roberts, "More Refugees, Less Asylum: A Regime in Transformation," *Journal of Refugee Studies* 11:4 (1998): pp. 375-395.

36 James Mayall notes that: "by the end of 1993 there were clear signs that the governments of the major powers were more interested in limiting than in extending their international commitments." James Mayall, *The New Interventionism, 1991-1994: United Nations Experience in Cambodia, former Yugoslavia and Somalia* (Cambridge: Cambridge University Press, 1996), p. 1.

37 For a comprehensive analysis of Executive Outcomes, see David Shearer, *Private Armies and Military Intervention*, Adelphi Paper 316 (Oxford: Oxford University Press for the IISS, 1998), pp. 39-55.

38 See Ibid., pp. 56-63.

39 At one time, Angola was the source of seven per cent of the EU's imported oil, and a large number of American corporations, notably Chevron and Texaco, had important investments in countries who were threatened by the actions of UNITA.

40 When the EU decided that the presence of Executive Outcomes was an obstacle to the implementation of the Lusaka Accord in Angola, it quickly demanded their withdrawal.

41 S/23500 (Statement by the President of the Council) (31 January 1992).

42 Boutros Boutros-Ghali, *An Agenda for Peace: Preventive Diplomacy, Peacemaking and Peacekeeping* (New York: United Nations, 1992), paragraphs 1-19.

43 Kofi Annan, "Reflections on Intervention," 35th Ditchley Foundation Lecture, 26 June 1998, in *The Question of Intervention: Statements by the Secretary-General* (New York: United Nations, 1999), p.6.

44 On this point, Boutras-Ghali's predecessor, Javier Perez de Cuellar, stated in 1991 that "it is now increasingly felt that the principle of non-interference with the domestic jurisdiction of States cannot be regarded as a protective barrier behind which human rights could be massively or systematically violated." See "Report of the Secretary General on the Work of the Organization," A/46/1, 1991.

45 See Mario Bettati and Bernard Kouchner, *Le devoir d'ingérence* (Paris: Denoël, 1987); and Mario Bettati, *Le droit d'ingérence: Mutation de l'ordre international* (Paris: Odile Jacob, 1996).

46 S/Res/688 (5 April 1991). France, Great Britain, and the United States followed a simultaneous trilateral initiative outside the Security Council. In the first three weeks of April 1991, the air forces of the three powers carried out 875 flights to deliver relief to displaced Kurds. They also sent provisions by truck and helicopter, using military personnel and equipment. These interventions occurred without the consent of the Iraqi authorities and the Iraqi government strongly protested this action as a direct interference into the internal affairs of the country, what was prohibited by international law.

47 S/Res/733 (23 January 1992).

48 S/Res/746 (17 March 1992); S/Res/751 (24 April 1992); S/Res/767 (27 July 1992); S/Res/775 (28 August, 1992); and S/Res/794 (3 December 1992).

49 S/Res/794 (3 December 1992). For a comprehensive discussion of the Council debates on Somalia, see Neil Fenton, *Consent, Coercion and Sovereignty in United Nations Security Council Mandated Operations, 1991-1995*, D. Phil. Thesis, Oxford University, 2000, pp. 146-178.

50 S/Res/940 (31 July 1994). For a discussion of the Council debates and actions in the case of Haiti, see David Malone, *Decision-Making in the UN Security Council: The Case of Haiti, 1990-1997* (Oxford: Clarendon Press, 1998).

51 See Mayall, *The New Interventionism*, pp. 3-4.

52 Sir David Hannay, cited in Fenton, *Consent, Coercion and Sovereignty*, p. 170.

53 Adam Roberts notes that: "Russia and China had consistently made it clear that they would veto any proposal for military action against Yugoslavia regarding its conduct in its own territory." See "NATO's 'Humanitarian War' over Kosovo," *Survival* 41:3 (Autumn 1999): p. 104.

54 Ibid., pp. 106-107: "In this perspective it cannot be right to tolerate acts which violate widely supported legal norms just because the Charter does not explicitly provide for military action in such circumstances, or because a veto on the Security Council makes UN-authorized action impossible."

55 Independent International Commission on Kosovo, *The Kosovo Report: Conflict, International Response, Lessons Learned* (Oxford: Oxford University Press, 2000), p. 4.

56 See http://www.nam.gov.za/ungamin/com2309.htm, paragraph 171. This sentence is repeated exactly in the "Declaration of the Summit of the South," adopted at the G-77 Summit in Durban in April 2000. See www.nam.gov.za/south/77south.htm, paragraph 54.

57 "Moscow Joint Statement of the Heads of State of Russia and China" (18 July 2001 - 1347-18-07-2001), section 7.

58 It must be recognized, however, that in several cases consent was not entirely voluntary. For example, in the case of Timor, Indonesia consented to the intervention by the UN-sanctioned International Force in East Timor (INTERFET), a military coalition headed by Australia. But, Indonesia agreed to the intervention under extraordinary pressure from financial institutions and states such as the United States.

59 It must be noted, however, that more recently several UN resolutions have omitted references to the specifics and unique character of situations where the UN contemplated intervention (for example, resolution 1132 [1997] on the intervention of ECOWAS to restore the democratic government of Sierra Leone after a coup d'état).

60 This conclusion applies especially to situations where sovereignty has been suspended. In 1996 James Mayall noted that there was little support – neither in the Third World nor in the West – for the creation of protectorates or the resurrection of a regime of international trusteeships. Mayall, *The New Interventionism*, p. 23.

61 See "Report of the Independent Inquiry into the Actions of the UN during the 1994 Genocide in Rwanda," S/1999/1257 (15 December 1999).

Chapter 3

Human Insecurity and Problematic Peacekeeping in Africa: Beyond 'Blood Diamonds' and HIV/AIDS[1]

Timothy M. Shaw

> "Close to a fifth of the continent's people now live in countries disrupted by wars and civil unrest that inflict enormous costs on these economies."
>
> African Development Bank[2]

> "The continent comprises many Africas."
>
> D. G. Anglin[3]

> "In future research (on new regionalism) there is a need to ... analyze systematically the achievements as well as negative effects of regional conflict resolution, regional interventions and peace-keeping operations in concrete cases as well as within a comparative framework."
>
> Schulz, Soderbaum and Ojendal[4]

2002 may come to mark a turning point for the continent of Africa, not just because it was the year in which the New Partnership for Africa's Development (NEPAD) was launched[5] or the lackluster Organization of African Unity (OAU) metamorphosed into the African Union (AU), nor because the G-8 meeting in Canada met with African leaders over the region's developmental and democratic deficits, but rather because it was the year in which the profound threats posed for human security by a mix of blood or conflict diamonds and the HIV/AIDS virus finally came to be acknowledged. It was also the year in which South Africa cajoled several factions in the Congo to talk and agree on peace, while renewed civil conflicts and ecological challenges in turn reappeared in Southern Africa. In short, both human and national security were under threat in addition to the continued ubiquity of both conventional and non-traditional conflicts.

Yet the somewhat synthetic and sanitized NEPAD, which was a centrepiece at the Kananaskis Summit of the G-8 in mid-2002, hardly mentions inconvenient issues such as conflict. Rather, despite growing criticism from the continent's civil society,[6] it concentrates on partnership with the G-8 and the Organization for Economic Cooperation and Development (OECD), promising to deliver good governance if enhanced flows of assistance and investment flow. It dismisses issues of conflict and security in less than one page (paragraphs 72-78), asserting that peace is a core value, even if its realization is somewhat problematic and vague. Thus, NEPAD advocates capacity-building, facilitated by enhanced economic performance – which may reinforce the Ottawa Process and accelerate the 'Kimberley Process' – although the G-8 communiqué was more assertive about conflict, ecology, HIV/AIDS, information technology, etc. NEPAD itself largely overlooks the connection between impoverishment/inequality and conflict, yet if effective and sustainable steps are to be taken about blood diamonds, landmines and small arms,[7] let alone HIV/AIDS, then NEPAD II will have to confront such fundamental dilemmas.

The turn of the century in Africa was distinguished by three interrelated, yet rather divergent, sets of issues which swirled around the conflict nexus. First, although most contemporary conflicts started within one particular country, all spilled-over at least one border and in some cases, for instance, Congo, Liberia or the Sudan, over several. Second, as indicated in the next section, and most controversially, a novel genre of analysis was advanced which asserted that there were economic rather than merely ethnic or personality factors behind current wars; and these economic interests are promoted through cross-border trade in diamonds and other minerals in exchange for weapons. But third, simultaneously and somewhat in contradiction, there was also a growing awareness that not all the continent's conflicts were the same. Rather, perhaps somewhat reluctantly, there began a creeping recognition that its several long-standing struggles – all of which have pronounced 'regional' dimensions – have considerable vintage and difference. As *The Economist* noted, long-standing conflicts in West Africa "have merged, to become a single regional war."[8]

As a result, this chapter focuses on the emergence of a political economy of violence approach around the troubled cases of Angola and Sierra Leone, with their distinctive regional features, while recognizing that the continuing struggles in the Horn of Africa – most recently between Ethiopia and Eritrea – may have little if anything to do with the (political) economy. Moreover, the chapter recognizes that conflicts are rarely static, and that any investigation of such ongoing struggles must appreciate the distinctive periods in all of the continent's continuing battles, especially during and after the Cold War's bipolarity, apartheid in and around South Africa, and now, the late-twentieth versus early-twenty-first centuries. The dynamism of these conflicts pose profound dilemmas for even well-intentioned "humanitarian interventions," specifically, how to transcend them through "the responsibility to protect"?[9]

After an overview of Africa's several interrelated conflicts – and the set of analytic and policy responses to them from non-state as well as state actors, intra- as well as extra-continental sources – at the start of the new millennium, the chapter turns to a pair of distinctive regional cases, proceeding from the most to the least orthodox, formal and inter-state. The penultimate section focuses on the "discovery" of and the myriad of responses to "conflict diamonds." It concludes by abstracting a set of possible futures for this pair of regional conflict-types which entail profound policy as well as analytic implications; not just the desiderata of advancing human development/security through peacekeeping/peacebuilding, but also the possibilities of authoritarian or anarchic regimes. Such an analysis in part consists of a juxtaposition of the literatures and genres of regionalism, including integration, interaction, and competition, against security, such as the causes and responses to conflict, as well as emphasizing the prospects for non-state activity, including both non-governmental organizations (NGOs) and think-tanks which can lead to regional peacebuilding, tracks two and three negotiations, as well as policy networks and communities.[10]

Surprisingly, at least until recently, uncomfortable dimensions of inequalities or poverty with their potential for conflict were rarely treated in debates about or criticisms of "globalizations"[11] – at least until 11 September 2001 – despite the proliferation of analyses and discourses around them. As Robert Wade laments in a critique of established fields of study which are echoed in the final section below:

> The global distribution of income is becoming ever more unequal. Anybody interested in the wealth and poverty of nations must be interested in the global distribution of income … . Despite its importance, this issue has received rather little attention within the fields of development studies, international relations, and (until very recently) international economics.[12]

Overview

This section highlights the salient interrelated sets of issues around Africa's ongoing regional conflicts, to which the chapter returns at the end, specifically, analytic or theoretical approaches and policy or applied responses.[13]

Conceptual Frameworks

Just as Africa is heterogeneous, so likewise are the causes and characteristics of its ubiquitous conflicts especially if the analysis stretches over time, particularly during and after the Cold War and/or apartheid. Notwithstanding the power of the 'new' political economy of violence perspective, the apparent diversities in causes and courses, scale and spill-over of both conflicts and peacebuilding partnerships suggest the need to reconsider whether there can ever be one singular continental perspective or rather a group of regional forms. Africa has had a varied set of historical experiences, in terms of imperial connections and economic relations, let alone ecological contexts. Similar to Samir Amin's proposition in the early 1970s of distinguishing an analytic trio of Africas, at the turn of the millennium, learning from Douglas Anglin's opening assertion, we might identify three distinct regions in terms of both types of conflict and peacemaking responses by way of insights drawn from the embryonic perspectives termed "new regionalisms:"[14]

a) *orthodox inter-state/-regime* conflicts and responses (e.g. Ethiopia and Eritrea);
b) *semi-orthodox*, semi-state (economic) conflicts and responses (e.g. Angola, Congo and Sudan); and,

c) *non-orthodox*, largely non-state, conflicts and responses (e.g. Somalia and West Africa).

As is evident below, the emerging political economy of violence perspective relates more to types c) and b) than a). The apparent resilience of conflict in Africa has begun to generate this critical analysis which is novel in approach, but disturbing in terms of implications, let alone curious in terms of origins and correlates.[15] More specifically, the political economy of violence perspective[16] suggests that at least some of these resilient wars are more about economic resources and survival than, for instance, ethnicity, ideology, region, religion, etc. The next subsection as well as the final section begins to identify some of the problematic implications of such a perspective for several interrelated analytic approaches, as well as for state and non-state policy choices/directions.

In particular, the chapter raises a series of questions about a set of implications arising from this emerging political economy of conflict genre for all three established actor types in the "governance" nexus, or "triangle,"[17] i.e. not just for states but also for private sectors and civil societies,[18] suggesting that the state "corner" is shrinking while the other two are growing. Clearly, the African state is in "transition" as it downsizes and redefines itself given two decades of neo-liberal conditionalities; hence, the relative rise of NGOs and multinational corporations (MNCs).[19] But both of these are themselves beginning to confront troubling questions about their own attitudes to and practices in such ubiquitous and seemingly endless conflict situations.[20] Moreover, the triangle may be severed or dysfunctional in situations where one or all of the parties seek to destabilize rather than advance peace. As indicated in subsequent pages, this may lead to it being superseded by a quadrangle.

As William Reno argues,[21] as weak(ened) African states lose control throughout their countries of agendas, armies, identities, media, resources, territories, etc., so conflicts multiply over the shrinking national cake (c.f. Rwanda, Sierra Leone, Somalia etc). Effective authority for governance comes to reside elsewhere, leading to an inability to contain either the causes or consequences of conflict. Such a regime vacuum presents profound dilemmas for the prospects of efficacious humanitarian intervention[22] or "responsibility to protect."[23] In turn, the expectations of and pressures on not only private security companies (PSCs) but also NGOs, including think tanks, intensify as surrogates of effective national regimes.

Inequalities and insecurities, exacerbated by the escalating incidence of HIV/AIDS in almost all the continent, especially the south, have helped to spawn a new set of non-traditional security issues focusing on human security[24] such as economic, ecological, gender and social security, especially threats from gangs and guns, droughts and floods, migrations and refugees, infectious diseases and viruses, etc.[25] In turn, these have served to intensify traditional as well as new varieties of insecurity or threat, exacerbated by the proliferation of non-state (i.e. private) as well as state security formations.

Furthermore, as examined further below, the diminished African state[26] can no longer afford much of a regular military establishment, if it ever could. However, at least until 1990, the logic of the Cold War helped to keep both regimes and armies in business. But the post-bipolar era has posed challenges to the sustainability of the political economy of armies as well as mafias.[27] As military budgets decline, so statutory forces have had to begin to learn to fend for themselves, hence the apparent willingness of some African governments to "sell" statutory forces to the United Nations (UN) and other organizations involved in peacekeeping, even if some or all of the "off-budget" proceeds go into private pockets rather than national exchequers. Moreover, men in uniform take them off after hours to pursue private gain as bandits, pirates, etc. A final challenge presented is that of demobilized soldiers having few life skills other than using their weapons to secure their own basic human needs.[28]

As militaries become more autonomous, so their relationships with state and business also change. As a result, it is imperative to recognize that the "triangle" of state-civil society-economy may become quadrilateral in which the military acts in a manner increasingly independent of the state in both economic and security (and hence political) matters: soldiers in business and soldiers as mercenaries. Thus, established notions of civil-military relations are challenged, leading towards the imperative of reform of the military sector.[29]

Policy Responses

Regional conflicts in Africa – both more traditional and non-traditional – have increasingly become of global concern. This is particularly so for diasporas and for crisis or developmental NGOs, now stretching to include consumer groups sanctioning particular offending companies who induce ameliorative reactions from brand managers.[30] As a result, unlike during the Cold War period, Western involvement is no longer an echo of broader bipolar tensions. Yet, the internal causes of wars cannot be separated from their international contexts, particularly neo-liberalism as ideology and globalization as condition. In short, the characteristic mixture of economic stagnation and growing inequality is a flammable one (even if it has not always lead to overt antagonism and confrontation) because of some authoritarian reactions as well as anarchic conditions.[31]

The emergence of regional arms races as well as conflicts – rather than any anticipated "peace dividend" (which was restricted to a few cases like Mozambique) – has profound developmental implications as human and financial resources are diverted into the military away from efforts to address HIV/AIDs and other challenges. Thus, prospects for regional development recede as conflicts both escalate and proliferate and "off-budget" incomes and expenditures become priorities for regimes and leaders alike. Such negative consequences increase as the proliferation of short-term peace-keeping operations brings in more militaries and NGOs into the area. These developmental implications of civil wars are further magnified if parallel private sectors and interests are acknowledged. Moreover, the longer-term implications of protracted conflict for both civil-military relations as well as the corruption of civic culture/civil society is equally worrisome, tending to undermine any apparent progress towards formal democratic processes.[32]

A kaleidoscopic of inter-regime and regional "alliances" has come to characterize African inter-state relations since independence. In addition to continental coalitions around the founding of the OAU, a series of sub-continental networks emerged in eastern and then southern Africa in the post-colonial era over regional integration and national liberation. Definitions of regions remain fluid and problematic. Indeed, at present both the Horn and the Great Lakes regions are characterised by "inter-locking wars" based on tactical rather than continuing patterns of alliance.[33] The succession of Kabila I by Kabila II indicates how fluid these tactical arrangements are as the kaleidoscope of interrelated intra-African armies, parties, regimes and extra-African associates shifted again in 2001-2002.

Mining companies, international financial institutions (IFIs) as well as national regimes have come to sanction the hiring of private security forces in difficult times and places, such as in Angola, the Congo and Sierra Leone.[34] Given restrictive limits on the terms of any commitment of statutory forces from the North – at least prior to September 11 – and reflective of the new revisionist/realist mood, informed analysts such as Herbert Howe[35] have begun to countenance mercenary interventions when necessary if other actions and sanctions have been insufficient and ineffective. But perhaps even more surprisingly, NGOs engaged in peacebuilding have likewise come to consider the possibility, if not the necessity, of such contracts. In a report for CARE Canada and related Canadian and global NGOs, Bryans, Jones and Stein come to recommend that, "NGOs should consider the privatization of security for humanitarian purposes."[36] Such hitherto unthinkable possibilities pose profound challenges for both analysis and practice.

Moreover, nowadays both conflicts and responses to them increasingly involve a heterogeneous range of state and non-state actors from local to global levels. Thus, in addition to official actors, private companies and NGOs are now associated with peacekeeping policies and practices in Africa as elsewhere.[37] As Lloyd Axworthy reflected after his years as foreign minister in Canada, "Actualizing the concept of human security requires all actors – states, international organizations, non-governmental organizations and business – to act responsibly."[38]

Given the complexities as well as protractedness of contemporary peacebuilding, let alone constraints on governments' budgets and roles, we can expect such non-state actors to come to play increasingly central roles in peace operations in the new century. Almost all state and inter-state institutions are under pressure from and coordinate with a variety of non-state agencies in both specific and general policies and practices over peace support measures.[39] Kofi Annan in his millennium review characterized these as "complex peace operations,"[40] rather than "complex political emergencies,"[41] thereby acknowledging the responsibility to protect rather than intervene.[42] Such continuous forms of communication and coordination among the trio of actor types at all levels, as illustrated below, can be regarded as a novel variety of governance. In this respect, the notion of "tracks two and three governance" embraces these processes and policies, with implications for the pattern of long-term human development and security in different regions of the continent.

In the 1990s, a set of non-state think-tanks emerged within and around Africa as partial responses to its conflicts. Since then, they often have played regional rather than just national roles and have tended to be concentrated in Southern Africa. Moreover, the regional salience of such embryonic analytic and/or advocacy communities[43] has varied considerably, with the result that any progress towards any regional security community[44] is uneven and certainly not unilinear. These think-tanks may also be involved in direct track-two type confidence-building and peacebuilding activities in addition to engaging in informed analysis and creative policy inputs.[45] While these not-for-profit institutions have become especially well-developed in post-apartheid South Africa, e.g. African Centre for the Constructive Resolution of Disputes (ACCORD), Centre for Conflict Resolution (CCR), Institute for Security Studies (ISS), and South African Institute for International Affairs (SAIIA), they may also be found elsewhere, such as the Centre for Foreign Relations in Dar es Salaam in Tanzania and the Nigerian Institute for International Affairs in Lagos. In sum, they have come to reflect growing continental and global concerns, such as peacekeeping, small arms, landmines, etc. And, typically, they are connected with national NGO networks and have begun to engage in training in both military and NGO terms for indigenous capacity in peacebuilding.

The maturation of such institutions and their roles is apparent in two comprehensive compendiums at the turn of the century on conflict prevention and peacekeeping on the continent.[46] Yet, given state and economic declines the demand for third-party interventions by, preferably indigenous, tracks two and three far outstrips the institutions' abilities to respond given their meagre resources which are out of proportion to the pressures. Clearly, an effective continent-wide network of such indigenous as well as international human security think-tanks and NGOs would be an essential first step towards a sustainable track two and three capability.[47] But their roles are likely to be more circumscribed in inter-state than less formal conflicts, as indicated in the pair of case studies below.[48]

Angola, Congo and the Great Lakes

Middle Africa – from the Horn to Southern Africa – offers two contrasting, albeit complicated – sets of conflicts which together challenge naïve, ill-informed perspectives: Congo and the Great Lakes on the one hand, and Angola on the other. The latter is the most divisive and intense, the former the most complex and regional. Indeed, as noted by Boya, "The debilitating war in Congo is the widest international war in Africa's history and poses an unprecedented foreign policy challenge."[49] The quagmire of Congo – "one of the world's most complicated wars … one of the world's most troubling … "[50] – soon overwhelmed the embryonic grouping of new Africans. The Congo always has confounded its rulers, from Leopold II to Mobutu, both of whom ran it as a personal colony or fiefdom. Likewise, Kabila II soon succumbed to illusions of grandeur even while his idiosyncratic rule consisted of selling off whatever remained of the family jewels to fellow African presidential protectors.

Whilst there has been a series of largely African state-led efforts in regional, continental and global fora to negotiate and implement cease-fires, such as the mid-1999 Lusaka Accord, the April 2002 Sun City and July 2002 Pretoria talks, in reality Congo has been partitioned by a group of neighbouring leaders who have paid their statutory forces by allowing access to resources and loot, leading to profound long-term implications in terms of casualties, strained civil-military relations, proliferation of corruption, etc. Just as the Congo was initially the possession of the King of Belgium rather than the Belgian state, by century's end Congo continued as a possession divided among African regime and party leaders.

Across the border between Congo and Angola, Canada's then-Ambassador to the UN in New York, Robert Fowler, given Canada's two-year seat on the Security Council, served as Chair of the UN's Panel of Experts on Violations of Security Council Sanctions against União Nacional para a Independência Total de Angola [National Union for the Total Independence of Angola] (UNITA). He prepared the first critical report for the UN on causes of the conflict in Angola, which named UNITA's high-level accomplices in Africa and Europe, as examined further in the next section.[51] It raised a number of sensitive interrelated issues for policy discourses within the UN and its member-states. In particular, the impact of diamonds and oil on the duration of civil strife for both sides, at least until the assassination of Savimbi in early 2002, suggested that human security and development are lofty ideals for the majority who live under intolerable conditions. Subsequent UN reports focused on the Congo and West Africa with equally telling data.

Moreover, the bounty in Congo as elsewhere is not static: as global markets in diamonds and gold, for instance, change, so does the interest of mafias, mercenaries, miners, smugglers, soldiers, etc. For example, as the price of hard metals such as platinum escalated early in the new century, informal sector suppliers in the Congo began to concentrate on titanium rather than diamonds or gold. The complexities and dynamics of such interrelated, regionalized struggles on the continent are well-captured by Margareta Sollenberg et al.[52] with important implications for policy as well as analysis:

> Three types of external (intra-African) military involvement can be seen:
> a) external military assistance, including either arms sales of direct military support to a government, e.g. Zimbabwe's involvement in the Democratic Republic of Congo (DRC);
> b) direct military intervention of foreign troops directed against a government, e.g. Rwanda's and Uganda's intervention in the DRC; and,
> c) indirect external intervention, that is, support of various kinds to rebel groups operating against a government, e.g. Sudan's support of the Lord's Resistance Army (LRA) and the Anarchist Democratic Forces (ADF) in Uganda in the form of arms and logistic assistance.
> A fourth type of external involvement, that by countries outside Africa, has become less explicit since the end of the Cold War, although it still exists.[53]

This last type of external involvement increasingly involves private, extra-continental, economic and strategic interests than those of states. As *Africa Confidential* cautioned: "The political cost of the arms-for-oil scandal is growing fast in Luanda and Paris. It reaches right across the power elite in the two countries."[54] But if Congo/Great Lakes/Angola are complicated conflicts, their complexities pale in contrast to those in West Africa, the least formal or traditional set of wars.

Both these regional conflagrations, however, reveal the ubiquitous, corrosive character of diamonds and related high value products like oil and gas: states who control their production can import materiel (and operatives) who keep them in power.[55] Thus, UNITA transformed itself after the end of the Cold War into a regime which controlled the alluvial diamond fields instead of Western, especially US, assistance. But as its territorial reach shrank by the end of the 1990s, especially with the loss of access to the Cuango Valley, its diamond income declined. By the end of the century, while the Popular Movement for the Liberation of Angola (MPLA) secured an annual income of US$1 billion from diamonds, UNITA's income declined to US$100 million. In short, Jonas Savimbi was facing an uphill struggle even before his assassination in early 2002.

West Africa and "Blood" Diamonds

> Instead of attracting and mobilising a popular following in Sierra Leone to overthrow the country's corrupt and inept government, [Revolutionary United Front (RUF)] commanders have fought the government with guns bought with diamonds, brought from Liberia, or captured from their enemies. They do not have to rely on the goodwill of local inhabitants or the contributions of their energies and wealth, and they do not have to engage in the arduous political and organisational task of building a mass movement to fight their way to power. The RUF bases it political power on control over diamonds, much as had the corrupt Sierra Leone politicians that the RUF criticised.[56]

Other than the long-standing and destructive conflict around Angola, the most controversial and resilient contemporary struggle has been in West Africa:[57] the interrelated conflicts in Guinea, Liberia and Sierra Leone, concentrated around the confluence of their three borders. A 2000 report by Smillie, Gberie and Haleston for Partnership Africa Canada (PAC) on the economic causes of the continuing conflict in the country and region of Sierra Leone was a primary catalyst in mobilizing efforts around the production chain of blood diamonds and the possibilities of sanctioning the illegal sector and its formal associates at certain choke-points.

In short, given the rather dramatic change in state-economy-society relations in post-colonial Sierra Leone, accelerated by structural adjustment conditionalities as well as corrupt regimes, the established diamond sector became informalized and criminalized under the Siaka Stevens regime. Thus, the Sierra Leone Selection Trust (SLST) was superseded by the so-called National Diamond Mining Company (NDMC) with its Lebanese connections, with the result that the national income, infrastructure and integrity rapidly declined.

However, in contrast to the Fowler report, the PAC report helped inform and generate parallel debates in a variety of institutions, including the US Congress, the

Canadian Parliament and the UN, centred on the remarkable "Kimberley Process," inaugurated in May 2000 in the South African city where the industry began. This process brought together crucial stakeholders, such as capital, labour, environmental and women's groups as well as non-violent and local communities, in an attempt to contain the negative impacts of informal sector extraction and distribution particularly in Southern Africa and to develop a new form of governance appropriate to local to global interests.[58] Symbolically, coinciding with the Kimberley Process and the escalation of the war in Sierra Leone, De Beers and Debswana opened the extension of the Orapa mine in Botswana. The contrast between growth levels and standards of living and human development and security in two small diamond-producing African states, Botswana and Sierra Leone, could not be starker, with profound implications for analysis and praxis.[59] As Ralph Hazelton suggests:

> South Africa, Botswana and Namibia have been at the forefront of the campaign to halt conflict diamonds and to create a certification system which would assist in this. They, along with the diamond industry, have also been the most vocal champions of 'prosperity diamonds' and 'diamonds for development.' NGOs focusing on conflict diamonds have been accused of neglecting this side of the coin and of endangering the entire diamond industry.[60]

Kimberley Process: Divergent Corporate and Regional Interests

Corporate, inter-regional and other responses to the blood diamonds campaign have been illustrative of a wider process of private sector reactions to such increasingly frequent and articulate allegations of inappropriate and/or illegitimate or illegal operations that have included threats of consumer and other boycotts or sanctions.[61] Following revelations from intra- as well as extra-continental sources of diamonds as a primary cause of conflict,[62] De Beers undertook a series of interrelated defensive or pre-emptive corporate strategies. These included negotiations at multiple levels with and initiatives by the World Federation of Diamond Bourses and the International Diamond Manufacturers Association, especially their new World Diamond Council, intense discussions about corporate and (inter)national regulations to contain the threat to the industry from the approximately four per cent production of blood diamonds, advancing itself as a consumer brand,[63] rather than a diamond explorer or miner. In late 2000, De Beers created a strategic alliance with the leading luxury goods brand in the world, Moet Hennessey Louis Vuitton (LVMH). With LVMH the De Beers brand intends (if the European Union and US authorities permit) to establish a network of upmarket retail outlets to sell its own brand of diamond jewellery, which it is to source from anywhere, not just its own mines.[64]

The Kimberley Process, which continued from May 2000 to late 2002, is symptomatic of the complexities of state and non-state foreign policy in the new century for a diversity of actors in Canada, South Africa, etc. The participants from states and inter-state institutions, business and NGOs worked through a variety of channels to advance effective sanctions, including the G-8, the OAU, the World Diamond Council, the World Federation of Diamond Bourses as well as the UN,[65] even if some international NGOs continue to express skepticism or reservations.[66] Sanctions on any remaining uncertified blood diamonds are intended not only to deter conflict, but also to support legitimate enterprises and governments, a delicate balancing act if sanctions are to be effective.

Already, the contrast in the developmental impacts of the production and distribution of gems from divergent small states such as Botswana and Sierra Leone is palpable.[67] Botswana has been Africa's – indeed at 9.2 per cent the world's – fastest growing economy for three decades and now is solidly among the middle ranks of states in the United Nations Development Program (UNDP) Human Development Index (HDI). By contrast, Sierra Leone typically comes last in the HDI.[68] As Hazelton notes, the centrality of the diamond sector in Botswana, now the world's largest, is palpable despite the contrary effect of its high rates of HIV/AIDS infection, specifically generating almost US$2 billion annually and a profit of almost US$1.7 billion, thereby accounting for 33 per cent of GDP, 60 per cent of government revenue and 79 per cent of exports.[69]

As a result, there are emerging inter-regional tensions between the formal, industrial diamond sector in Southern Africa and the informal, non-industrial sectors elsewhere on the continent, notably around Angola, Congo and Sierra Leone.[70] The former have tried to dissociate themselves from any notion that all diamonds are tainted, as any negative impact of such a global campaign on their capital- and technology-intensive production would have profound developmental implications, especially for Botswana and somewhat for Namibia. Such differences exacerbate, for example, tensions around Zimbabwe's involvement in the DRC, which has accelerated the enrichment of the Mugabe elite. Just as in the other two types of regional conflict and response – i.e. more 'traditional' contexts – distinctive patterns of alliance have become quite apparent around the issue of blood diamonds in West Africa and Angola: African states such as Botswana, Namibia and South Africa along with mining capital and organized labour concentrated in Southern Africa[71] versus warlords and informal traders, certain transnational mineral entrepreneurs centred on Congo and Sierra Leone, even Antwerp, versus Tel Aviv and other emerging centres for polishing in the Gulf and Ukraine, with profound implications for policy and practice. Such distinctive patterns of production, distribution and accumulation, let alone conflict, should come as no surprise as they were precisely the focus of Samir Amin's tentative typology of the continent's several political economies over 30 years ago. "African capitalism" may differ from that on other continents, but in turn there are pronounced inter-regional differences within the continent, especially between Southern African capital, labour, technology and infrastructure and other regions.[72]

In short, the real causes of and responses to conflict on the continent remain problematic in part because of outmoded analytic and policy assumptions and approaches and because of a growing diversity of real interests, e.g. diamond exports from countries entrenched in the DRC such as Rwanda, Uganda and Zimbabwe. Moreover, until very recently there was profound reluctance to admit that the HIV/AIDS pandemic was a profound threat to human security throughout Africa.

Intra- and extra-continental, state and non-state responses to Africa's continuing crises will necessitate a mixture of diplomacy and pressure, economics and politics, positive and negative sanctions, tracks two and three, if there is to be any prospect of a genuine and sustainable African renaissance in the first decade of the new century, as the alliance of such heavyweights as Algeria, Nigeria, Senegal and South Africa continue to advocate at the World Economic Forum and elsewhere. The political economy of violence perspective tends to retard any such prospect just as tracks two and three can advance it.

Conclusions and Projections

The actualities of African state and non-state foreign policy, international relations and political economy are in great flux as both global and local contexts continue to evolve.[73] Neither analyses nor policies towards them have kept pace with the actual shifts in the relationships among states, companies and civil societies.[74] As indicated below, such trilateral relations can lead backwards towards authoritarian or anarchic regimes as well as forwards towards peacekeeping and peacebuilding let alone human security or development, as suggested by sub-regional peace initiatives.

New Regionalisms: Onto Zones of Peace?

Therefore, distinctions need to be made to indicate the importance of pragmatic and flexible varieties of peacemaking interventions from both intra- and extra-regional sources, as well as the imperative of informed and nuanced analyses, if state and non-state policy responses are to be as appropriate as possible. At the same time, they also imply the unlikelihood of a series of distinct 'security communities' on the continent, i.e. one singular African renaissance.

Hence, it has been interesting to witness the evolution and implementation of a set of corridors, concentrated to date in Southern Africa and notably that from Maputo, which constitute potential sub-regional zones of peace. Since these involve a range of heterogeneous partners in their governance or development, such as local and national governments as well as businesses, they can be compared to a diverse range of triangles, often Export-Processing Zones (EPZs), in Southeast and East Asia.

Similarly, the diplomacy around and development of trans-frontier or cross-border peace-parks offer alternatives to regional conflict, even if they all include South Africa as a partner. The first, Kgalagadi Transfrontier Park between Northern Cape and Botswana, was inaugurated in mid-May 2000.

Both of these two types of sub-regional governance architectures for human development and security, i.e. corridors and peace-parks, may have significant longer-term implications for human security and development. This possibility may result in part from them having broader and deeper roots among a diversity of actors – communities, economic, ecological, infrastructural, functional, political, etc. – than other methods such as presidential agreements. Thus, they are more likely to form the real bases of any sustainable renaissance on the continent.

Implications for Established Analyses and Policies

The profound challenges to established analyses and policies of the variety of causes of conflict on the continent make creative, revisionist perspectives imperative to minimize the possibilities of inappropriate idealistic or cynical reactions. Such an argument is increasingly recognized inside as well as beyond the continent, even if more by inter- or non-state agencies like the UN and World Bank or Global Witness and PAC, respectively, than academia. Even so, three analytic areas in particular are in need of creative revisionism.

First, for security or strategic studies, the growing focus on the political economy of violence has profound implications that leads away from national towards human security,[75] but also towards the analysis of novel issues and coalitions. Some of these are related to Africa's current concerns such as HIV/AIDS, land-mines and other small arms, migrations, track-two diplomacy, demilitarization, demobilization,[76] etc., while others are somewhat longer-term, such as ecological sustainability, viruses, even post-conflict redevelopment.[77]

Second, development studies and policies can no longer overlook awkward factors such as the political economy of conflict, peacebuilding and reconstruction. In the emerging post-neoliberal era, rather than concentrate on self-congratulatory comparisons about external competitiveness, this field needs to incorporate inconvenient critiques of established policies that have failed to address underlying internal social inequalities. These critiques would include the emulation of UNDP's 1999 not uncontroversial advocacy of a "human security" perspective[78] and would consider the real political economy of child soldiers and private armies among other issues.[79]

Finally, issues of governance among the myriad of non-state as well as state actors cannot be separated from questions of the causes, containment and resolution of conflicts in order to facilitate sustainable forms of peacebuilding governance. Such post-conflict governance must involve a mix of interested stake-holders, including a variety of think-tanks, and lead towards security communities. Nonetheless, questions remain about the sustainability and representativeness of such networks and communities given the palpable jealousies of some African leaders.[80]

In short, even before the political economy of conflict genre became so popular, the dynamics and ambiguities of the African continent's wars have challenged a variety of analytic and policy prescriptions, with implications for a range of assumptions as well as state and non-state actors alike.[81] As a result, it is imperative to generate informed but modest new analytic suggestions and directions not just for African Studies but also for Development even Global Studies. If security analysis and policy can be thereby challenged, so likewise should be development: *ex Africa semper aliquid novi!* The months and years since 2002 continue to confirm Pliny's prediction about the continent.

Notes

1 An earlier version of this chapter appeared as "Political Economy as Causes and Consequences of Conflicts in Contemporary Africa: Where? When? Why?" in *Les Conflits dans le Monde/Conflicts in the World 2000/2001*, eds. Albert Legault and Michel Fortmann (Quebec: Institute Québecois des Hautes Etudes Internationales, Université Laval, 2002), pp. 151-177.

2 African Development Bank, *African Development Report 2000* (Oxford: Oxford University Press, 2000), p. 23.

3 D. G. Anglin, "Conflict in Sub-Saharan Africa," in *Les conflits dans le monde/Conflicts in the World, 1998-1999,* eds. Albert Legault and Michel Fortmann (Quebec: IQHES, Université Laval, 1999), p. 96.

4 Michael Schulz, Fredrik Soderbaum, and Joakim Ojendal, eds., *Regionalization in a Globalizing World: A Comparative Perspective On Forms, Actors and Processes* (London: Zed Books, 2001), pp. 266 and 268.

5 A. De Waal, "What's New in the 'New Partnership for Africa's Development'?" *International Affairs* 78:3 (July 2002): pp. 463-475; K. R. Hope, "From Crisis to Renewal: Towards a Successful Implementation of the New Partnership for Africa's Development," *African Affairs* 101:404 (July 2002): pp. 387-402.

6 P. Bond, ed., *Fanon's Warning: A Civil Society Perspective on the New Partnership for Africa's Development* (Trenton, NJ: Africa World Press, 2002).

7 Graduate Institute for International Studies, *Small Arms Survey, 2001* (Oxford: Oxford University Press, 2001); Graduate Institute for International Studies, *Small Arms Survey, 2002* (Oxford: Oxford University Press, 2002).

8 "West Africa: The War that Spread," *The Economist* (19 May 2001): pp. 15-16.

9 M. Ayoob, "Humanitarian Intervention and International Society," *Global Governance* 7:3 (July-September 2001): pp. 225-230; International Commission on Intervention and State Sovereignty (ICISS), "The Responsibility to Protect," (Ottawa: International Development Research Centre, 2001); T. G. Weiss, "To Intervene or Not to Intervene? A Contemporary Snap-Shot," *Canadian Foreign Policy* 9:2 (Winter 2002): pp. 141-157.

10 ICISS, "The Responsibility to Protect;" J. Stremlau, "Ending Africa's Wars," *Foreign Affairs* 79:4 (July/August 2000): pp. 117-132; Weiss, "To Intervene or Not to Intervene?"

11 R. Luckham et al, "Conflict and Poverty in Sub-Saharan Africa: An Assessment of the Issues and Evidence," ID21 News Issue #51, (Sussex: Institute for Development Studies, 2001); Wayne E. Nafziger and Juha Auvinen, "Economic Causes: The Political Economy of War, Hunger, and Flight," in *The Origins of Humanitarian Emergencies: War and Displacement in Developing Countries*, eds. Wayne E. Nafziger, Frances Stewart, and Raimo Väyrynen (Oxford, Oxford University Press, 2000).

12 R. Wade, "Global Inequality: Winners and Losers," *The Economist* (28 April 2001): p. 93.

13 K. C. Dunn and T. M. Shaw, eds., *Africa's Challenge to International Relations Theory* (London: Palgrave, 2001); P. J. McGowan and P. Nel, eds., *Power, Wealth and Global Equity: An International Relations Textbook for Africa*, second edition (Cape Town: University of Cape Town Press, 2002); P. Vale, L. A. Swatuk, and B. Oden, eds., *Theory, Change and Southern Africa's Future* (London: Palgrave, 2001).

14 T. Shaw, "New Regionalisms in Africa in the New Millennium: Comparative Perspectives on Renaissance, Realisms and/or Regressions," *New Political Economy* 5:3 (November 2000).

15 M. Berdal and D. Malone, eds., *Greed and Grievance: Economic Agendas in Civil Wars* (Boulder: Lynne Rienner, 2000).

16 P. Collier and A. Hoeffler, *Greed and Grievance in Civil War*, (Washington, DC: World Bank, 2000) (www.worldbank.org/research/conflict); M. Duffield, *Global Governance and the New Wars: The Merging of Development and Security* (London: Zed Books, 2001); W. Reno, *Warlord Politics and African States* (Boulder: Lynne Rienner, 1998); I. Smillie, L. Gberie and R. Hazelton, *The Heart of the Matter: Sierra Leone, Diamonds and Human Security* (Ottawa: Partnership Africa Canada, 2000).

17 T. Shaw, "African Foreign Policy in the New Millennium," in *Africa's Challenge to International Relations Theory*, eds. K. C. Dunn and T. M. Shaw (London: Palgrave, 2001).

18 This was indicated in a diagram in *Citizens and Governance: Civil Society in the New Millennium,* Commonwealth Foundation, London, 1999, p. 16.

19 S. J. MacLean, F. Quadir and T. M. Shaw, eds., *Crises of Governance in Asia and Africa* (Aldershot: Ashgate, 2001).

20 M. Bryans et al, "Mean Times: Humanitarian Actors in Complex Political Emergencies – Stark Choices, Cruel Dilemmas," *Coming to Terms* 1:3 (January 1999), CARE Canada, Ottawa; C. Spearin, "A Private Security Panacea? A Specific Response to *Mean Times*," *Canadian Foreign Policy* 7:3 (Spring 2000).

21 W. Reno, *Warlord Politics and African States* (Boulder: Lynne Rienner, 1998).

22 Shaw, "African Foreign Policy in the New Millennium," and T. M. Shaw, "Peace-building Partnerships and Human Security," in *Arnold Companion to Development Studies*, V. Desai and R. Potter, eds. (London: Arnold, 2002).

23 ICISS, "The Responsibility to Protect."

24 "Human Security," Department of Foreign Affairs and International Trade, Government of Canada, Ottawa, September 2000, www.dfait-maeci.gc.ca/foreignp/humansecurity; C. Thomas, *Global Governance, Development and Human Security* (London: Pluto, 2000); *Human Development Report 1999*, United Nations Development Program, New York, 1999; *Securipax Forum,* United Nations Educational, Scientific and Cultural Organization (UNESCO), Paris, 2000.

25 L. Axworthy, "Human Security and Global Governance: Putting People First," *Global Governance* 7:1 (January-March 2001); S. J. MacLean and T. M. Shaw, "Canada and New 'Global' Strategic Alliances: Prospects for Human Security at Start of the Twenty-First Century," *Canadian Foreign Policy* 8:3 (Spring 2001).

26 Reno, *Warlord Politics and African States.*

27 H. M. Howe, *Ambiguous Order: Military Forces in African States* (Boulder: Lynne Rienner, 2001).

28 K. Kingma, ed., *The Impact of Demobilization in Sub-Saharan Africa* (London: Macmillan, 2000).

29 Howe, *Ambiguous Order.*

30 See Naomi Klein, *No Logo: Taking Aim at the Brand Bullies* (London: Flamingo, 2000) on the Nestle, Nike and Shell campaigns and corporate responses.

31 Dunn and Shaw, *Africa's Challenge to International Relations Theory.*

32 J. Brommelhorster and W. C. Paes, eds., *Soldiers in Business: The Military as Economic Actor* (London: Palgrave, 2003); Howe, *Ambiguous Order.*

33 As suggested by *Strategic Survey 2000*, International Institute for Strategic Studies, London.

34 According to Howe, *Ambiguous Order* and G. Mills and J. Stremlau, eds., *The Privatisation of Security in Africa* (Johannesburg: South African Institute for International Affairs, 2000).

35 Howe, *Ambiguous Order.*

36 M. Bryans et al, "Mean Times."

37 E. G. Berman and K. E. Sams, eds., *Peacekeeping in Africa: Capabilities and Culpabilities* (Geneva: United Nations Institute for Disarmament Research (UNIDIR), 2000); P. Mbabazi, S. J. MacLean and T. M. Shaw, "Governance for Reconstruction in Africa: Challenges for Policy Communities/Coalitions," *Global Networks* 2:1 (January 2002); M. Mekenkamp et al., eds., *Searching for Peace in Africa: An Overview of Conflict Prevention and Management Activities* (Utrecht: European Platform for Conflict Prevention and Transformation, 1999).

38 Axworthy, "Human Security and Global Governance," p. 23.

39 These are aspects of an emerging "global compact." See www.unglobalcompact.org.

40 Kofi Annan, *'We the Peoples:' The Role of the UN in the 21st Century* (New York: United Nations, 2000).

41 L. Cliffe, ed., "Special Issue: Complex Political Emergencies," *Third World Quarterly* 20:1 (March 1999).

42 ICISS, "The Responsibility to Protect."

43 Mbabazi, MacLean and Shaw, "Governance for Reconstruction in Africa."

44 E. Adler and M. Barnett, eds., *Security Communities* (Cambridge: Cambridge University Press, 1998).

45 Mbabazi, MacLean and Shaw, "Governance for Reconstruction in Africa;" MacLean and Shaw, "Canada and New 'Global' Strategic Alliances."

46 Berman and Sams, eds., *Peacekeeping in Africa*; Mekenkamp et al., eds., *Searching for Peace in Africa.*

47 Mbabazi, MacLean and Shaw, "Governance for Reconstruction in Africa;" MacLean and Shaw, "Canada and New 'Global' Strategic Alliances."

48 The Horn of Africa is not included in part because one of its central confrontations between Eritrea and Ethiopia is *sui generis* inter- rather than semi- or non-state, even as it impacts macro-regional wars, such as that in and around the Sudan.

49 O. Boya, "Contentious Politics and Social Change in Congo," *Security Dialogue* 32:1 (March 2001): p. 71.

50 T. B. Seybolt, "The War in the Democratic Republic of Congo," *SIPRI Yearbook 2000* (Oxford: Oxford University Press, 2000), p. 59.

51 *Report of the Sanctions Committee on the Violation of Security Council Sanctions against UNITA* (New York: United Nations, 2000)

52 M. Sollenberg et al, "Major Armed Conflicts," *SIPRI Yearbook 1999* (Oxford: Oxford University Press, 1999), p. 23.

53 Sollenberg et al, "Major Armed Conflicts," p. 23.

54 *Africa Confidential* (9 February 2001): p. 1.

55 G. Campbell, *Blood Diamonds: Tracing the Deadly Path of the World's Most Precious Stone* (Boulder: Perseus, 2002); J. Cilliers and D. Christian, eds., *Angola's War Economy: The Role of Oil and Diamonds* (Pretoria: Institute for Security Studies, 2000); Howe, *Ambiguous Order.*

56 Reno, *Warlord Politics and African States,* p. 222.

57 A. Cockburn, "Diamonds: The Real Story," *National Geographic* (March 2002).

58 *Other Facets* (2001-2), Partnership Africa Canada, Ottawa.

59 *Other Facets* (2001-2).

60 R. Hazelton, *Diamonds: Forever or For Good? The Economic Impact of Diamonds in Southern Africa*, Partnership Africa Canada, Occasional Paper No. 3 (March 2002), p. 1.

61 Klein, *No Logo.*

62 Campbell, *Blood Diamonds*; Cilliers and Christian, eds., *Angola's War Economy*; *A Rough Trade: The Role of Companies and Governments in the Angolan Conflict*, Global Witness, New York, 2000; *Conflict Diamonds: Possibilities for the Identification, Certification and*

Control of Diamonds, Global Witness, New York, 2000; Smillie, L. Gberie and R. Hazelton, *The Heart of the Matter*.

63 Klein, *No Logo*; N. Stein, "The De Beers Story: A New Cut on an Old Monopoly," *Fortune* (March 2001).

64 www.worlddiamondcouncil.com; www.diamond.net.

65 *Other Facets* (2001-2).

66 See "Kimberley Process Report Card on Conflict Diamonds, Valentine's Day 2002," *Other Facets* (March 2002): p. 4.

67 Cockburn, "Diamonds: The Real Story."

68 Hazelton, *Diamonds: Forever or for Good?*; *Human Development Report 1999*.

69 Hazelton, *Diamonds: Forever or for Good?*, p. 3.

70 See Cockburn, "Diamonds: The Real Story."

71 Hazelton, *Diamonds*.

72 Dunn and Shaw, *Africa's Challenge to International Relations Theory*.

73 Dunn and Shaw, *Africa's Challenge to International Relations Theory*.

74 Shaw, "African Foreign Policy in the New Millennium."

75 Axworthy, "Human Security and Global Governance."

76 K. Kingma, ed. *The Impact of Demobilization in Sub-Saharan Africa* (London: Macmillan, 2000).

77 *Human Development Report 1999*.

78 *Human Development Report 1999*.

79 Berdal and Malone, eds., *Greed and Grievance*; E. Braathen et al, eds., *Ethnicity Kills? The Politics of War, Peace and Ethnicity in Sub-Saharan Africa* (London: Macmillan, 2000); Cilliers and Christian, eds., *Angola's War Economy*.

80 Mbabazi, MacLean and Shaw, "Governance for Reconstruction in Africa;" C. Thomas, *Global Governance, Development and Human Security* (London: Pluto, 2000).

81 Shaw, "African Foreign Policy in the New Millennium."

List of useful websites

www.accord.org.za
www.africa-confidential.com
www.africa-research-bulletin.com
www.allafrica.com
www.ccrweb.ccr.uct.ac.za
www.diamonds.net
www.euconflict.org
www.globalpolicy.org
www.humansecurity.info
www.igd.org.za
www.iss.co.za
www.partnershipafricacanada.org
www.unesco.org/securipax
www.worlddiamondcouncil.com

Chapter 4

Short-Term Gain, Long-Term Pain: An Assessment of United Nations Chapter VII Activities in Central Africa

Robert Astroff and David Meren[1]

An enduring problem faced by scholars and policy makers is the absence of specific criteria for evaluating the outcome of third-party "peacebuilding" interventions in violent intergroup conflicts. This chapter seeks to address this gap in the peacebuilding literature through an assessment of United Nations (UN) Chapter VII operations in Rwanda (1994) and Zaire (1996).

Rwanda and Zaire are glaring examples of the international community's practice of intervention without responsibility. As a result, these cases raise critical questions; specifically, how could the international community have better crafted a response to the violence that plagues Central Africa? This question is particularly relevant given the UN's Chapter VII intervention in Sierra Leone. Moreover, the proliferation of UN-sanctioned peace operations in Kosovo, East Timor and the Democratic Republic of Congo (DRC) / Zaire is evidence of a trend that makes a thorough, comprehensive examination of such Chapter VII interventions imperative.[2]

This chapter investigates the following research question: what is the relationship between the strategy and outcome of third party intervention? Its primary objective is to enhance the ability of decision-makers to intervene more effectively in intergroup conflicts.[3] It adds to the study of conflict management by offering a theoretical framework for evaluating the outcome of third-party intervention.

In order to achieve this objective, the chapter advocates the use of a Conflict Intensity Abatement (CIA) Index. The model measures changes in conflict dynamics as a means of evaluating the outcome of third-party interventions. As a result, these case studies demonstrate that "peacebuilding with muscle" is a task not to be entered into lightly, since achieving the conditions necessary for any measurable, sustainable success requires a long-term political and military commitment. The political will that has motivated such coercive third-party interventions in the past, however, has proved to be of a short-term, "quick-fix" nature that has failed to sufficiently acknowledge the complexities inherent in violent inter-group conflict. This has resulted in the perpetuation, and even aggravation, of the conflict that originally motivated the interventions.

The chapter begins with a brief description of the methodology employed in the study. The second section presents an overview of the theoretical literature on third-party intervention. This is followed by the development of a theoretical model to evaluate interventions by third-parties in violent intergroup conflicts. With this accomplished, the model is then tested against two related case studies in Central Africa: Rwanda (1994) and Zaire (1996). The application of the model to real-life situations will yield a series of recommendations, relevant not only to the on-going tensions in the Great Lakes region, but also to the management of protracted intergroup conflicts in general. The study concludes that policy-makers must take heed of the lessons learned in Rwanda and Zaire and remember that once the UN makes the commitment to intervene in a violent intergroup dispute, it must stay the course of conflict resolution.

Methodology

The framework for this paper follows Alexander George's method of "structured, focused comparison" which makes it possible to draw generalizations from a small number of cases by evaluating a minimal number of variables.[4] The methodology is "structured" as it employs a set of standardized questions that guide the analysis, and "focused" as it deals selectively with only certain aspects of each case.

In order to provide the theoretical underpinning for this study, the independent and dependent variables must be identified. It is impossible to examine every potential explanation for the outcome of third-party intervention because the processes, context and actors involved are intrinsically complex. As Jacob Bercovitch notes, "[t]he number of variables which impinge on this process is immense;" accordingly, consideration can only be given to some of them.[5] Thus, the task is to choose a specific variable that will change over the course of intervention efforts, while holding others constant, and to provide justification for why this particular factor has been selected and how it best captures variation in the dependent variable.

Independent Variable: Strategy

Evaluating the relationship between the strategy employed by a third-party and the outcome of intervention is a difficult task. Although conceptualizing or measuring the behaviour of third-parties and strategies is challenging, it is arguably the most important variable affecting outcome. Accordingly, examination of this variable is critical to gaining a more complete understanding of the success or failure of third-party initiatives. The appropriateness of the strategy is determined by comparing the optimal type of intervention predicted by the theoretical model with the tactics actually employed. Strategy is linked to outcome, as the tactics employed by a third-party affect the method and manner in which intervention is carried out.

Dependent Variable: Outcome

The formulation of specific criteria to analyze the effectiveness of third-party intervention has presented difficulty to both scholars and practitioners. Touval and Zartman rightly note that "[w]hat constitutes successful … [intervention] … is of course debatable."[6] Given that the objective of third-party intervention is to achieve a "successful" outcome, logic dictates that outcome must be considered the dependent variable for this study.

Overview of Theoretical Literature

The progression of a typical conflict is graphically depicted in the Conflict Intervention Curve (Figure 4.1). As the figure illustrates, the course of a protracted intergroup conflict can be plotted in terms of two dimensions: (1) the intensity of the conflict (y-axis) – measured by the number of people killed; and (2) the evolution of the conflict over time (x-axis). The path of a conflict is represented by a bell curve. This shape was chosen as it captures the dynamic nature of conflicts which vary dramatically in terms of intensity over time.

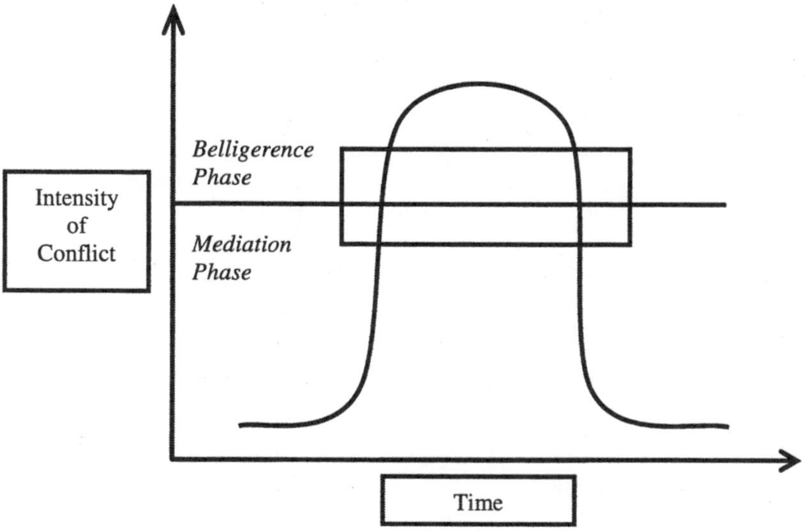

Figure 4.1 Conflict Intervention Curve

Figure 4.1 divides intervention strategies into two phases: *mediation* and *belligerence*. The *mediation phase* encompasses peaceful, i.e. nonviolent, efforts to de-escalate conflicts, while the *belligerence phase* involves forceful, i.e. potentially violent, initiatives to reduce conflict intensity.

The strategies available to third parties to promote the de-escalation of conflicts are graphically depicted in the Phases of Intervention (Figure 4.2). These tactics are grouped into three broad categories: (i) diagnostic; (ii) intercessory; and (iii) military.

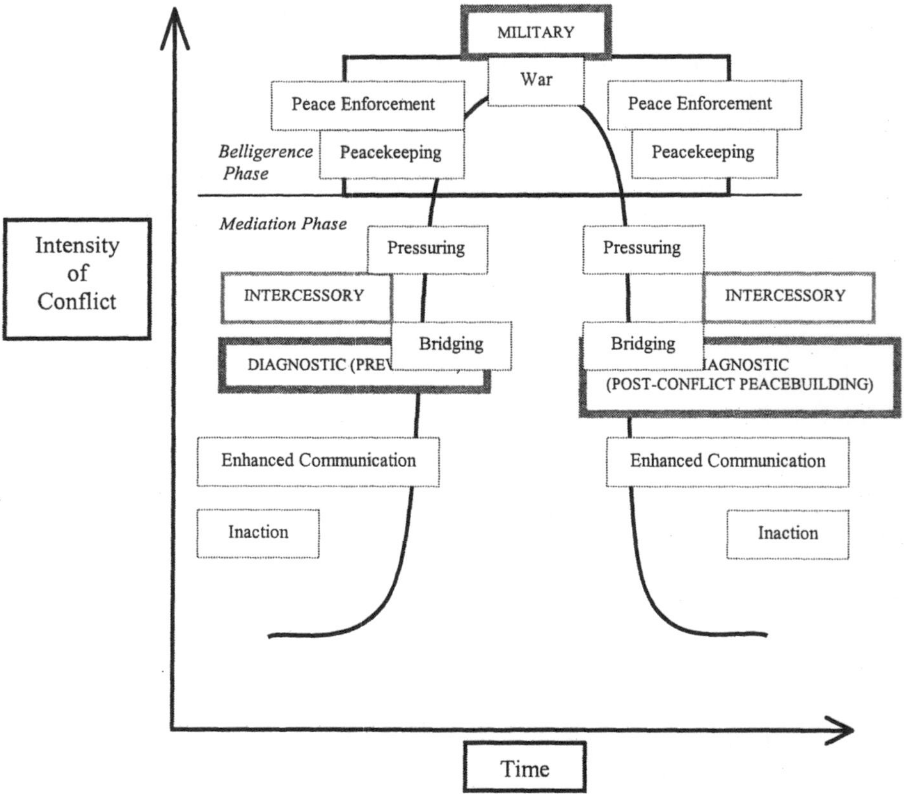

Figure 4.2 Phases of Intervention

Intervention by a third-party can take place either in the *mediation phase* (encompassing diagnostic and intercessory strategies, i.e. nonviolent tactics), or in the *belligerence phase* (encompassing military strategies, i.e. potentially violent tactics). The study hypothesizes that there is a relationship between strategy and outcome, such that the more intense the conflict, the more forceful the strategy needed to restore order.

Given that the focus of this study is on "muscular" peacekeeping and peace enforcement operations, the overview of the literature will be restricted to military strategies.[7]

While the full life-cycle of a conflict is provided, this study is confined to the boxed area in the upper portion of the diagram. The enclosed box highlights the stage where mediation and belligerence meet.

Independent Variable: Military Strategies

If diagnostic and intercessory tactics are ineffective in reducing tensions, third parties may resort to military intervention, in an attempt to move the combatants from the battlefield to the negotiating table.[8] The use of this type of strategy marks a significant change in the dynamics of a conflict, as it signifies that the disputants are engaged in combat or the possibility of violence is imminent. As a result, employing these tactics entails greater risk to third parties. Military intervention may take the following forms: peacekeeping, peace enforcement, and war.

Peacekeeping Peacekeeping is defined as:

> the deployment of military or police, and frequently civilian, personnel to assist in the implementation of agreements reached between governments or parties who have been engaged in conflict. ... [This type of intervention normally] presumes cooperation and its methods are inherently peaceful: the use of military force, other than in self-defence, is incompatible with the concept.[9]

In this context, peacekeeping is mitigative in nature; it provides a stable environment in which the de-escalation of conflict may be achieved.

Peacekeeping traditionally involves the interposition of modestly armed forces between the combatants. In some cases, peacekeepers may take on specific tasks, such as monitoring elections, the withdrawal of troops, or the decommissioning of weapons. The key, however, is the neutrality of the mission and the willingness of the disputants to accept foreign intervention.[10] Peacekeeping operations are normally associated with actions authorized under Chapter VI of the UN Charter.[11] In terms of skills, equipment, and professional orientation, peacekeeping missions require personnel trained in the maintenance of law and order.

Military police and, to a lesser extent, combat forces are best suited to this task. The use of military police is preferable due to their training in law enforcement and ingrained appreciation for the restrained use of force.[12] Moreover, deploying military police clearly distinguishes a peacekeeping mission from that of peace enforcement by providing less opportunity for the mission to "creep" towards enforcement should violence resume.[13]

Peace Enforcement Peace enforcement involves the forcible interposition of a third-party between combatants in order to facilitate the cessation of hostilities, deter renewed aggression, and create an environment conducive to the declaration of a cease-fire and the commencement of de-escalation efforts. Unlike peacekeeping, peace enforcement requires neither the consent of the disputants, nor the cessation of hostilities. Peace enforcement requires the skills, equipment, and professional orientation of combat forces; consequently, the same personnel utilized for enforcing the peace may be inappropriate or poorly suited to the tasks of peacekeeping, given that their training is likely focussed on fighting wars, not keeping peace. The political, military, and legal implications of peace enforcement are tantamount to an international declaration of war against one or more of the combatants. These operations are normally undertaken pursuant to Chapter VII of the UN Charter.[14]

The combative nature of peace enforcement often requires military forces to retain the command, control, communication, and intelligence gathering functions of a mission. Furthermore, the rules of engagement prescribed for peace enforcers are permissive – that is, commanders of peace enforcement operations are authorized to use force in carrying out their mission until all parties have acceded to the cessation of hostilities and a transition to traditional peacekeeping activities can be made. This permissive engagement policy is crucial to establishing the credibility of the enforcement effort between groups engaged in violent conflict.

Peace enforcement is not unconstrained warfare; nor is it neutral intervention. Operating without the consent of one or more of the disputants makes peace enforcers partisan from the perspective of an aggrieved and unyielding combatant. If peace enforcement occurs with the willing agreement of only one side, those who conduct the intervention may be viewed as favouring that side and as acting in a belligerent manner toward the other. This perception of unfairness may be impossible to overcome and may be reinforced if the intervening body applies its rules of engagement unevenly between the parties.

The transition from peace enforcement to peacekeeping should occur only after the implementation of a cease-fire, disengagement of the combatants and consent from the disputants for the interposition of peacekeeping forces is obtained.[15] In other words, there must be a peace to keep in order for peacekeeping to have any chance of success.

War The most violent form of intervention by a third-party is war, characterized as "sustained fighting between organized armed forces."[16] In essence, the critical distinction between peace enforcement and war is that peace enforcement is sanctioned by international law, whereas war is an act of aggression unauthorized by the international community. While traditionally not employed as a method of conflict de-escalation, this strategy was de facto used by NATO in an attempt to end the conflict between Serbs and Kosovars in Former Republic of Yugoslavia (FRY).

Dependent Variable: Outcome

An enduring problem faced by international relations theorists has been the absence of a precise definition for "effective" or "successful" intervention. For instance, Bercovitch describes a successful mediation outcome as "[a]ny mutually acceptable compromise that restores conditions and stops hostilities and violence."[17] Meanwhile, Touval and Zartman define mediation success as "the conclusion of an agreement promising the reduction of conflict."[18]

Table 4.1 Conflict Intensity Abatement (CIA) Index

Conflict Intensity	Net Change	Intervention Result
Category 1a: Unabated military hostilities; political repression; no rule of law; humanitarian disaster	-3 points	Total Failure
Category 1b: Sporadic overt violence; limited political accommodation; high levels of tension and suspicion; humanitarian emergency	-2 points	Preponderant Failure
Category 1c: some prospect of violence; no institutional capacity to deal with political conflict; wary interactions; humanitarian crisis	-1 point	Partial Failure
Category 2: no appreciable change in the military, political, social, or humanitarian dimensions of the conflict	0 points	Status Quo
Category 3a: cessation of overt violence; lack of established political communication; continuing mistrust; basic human needs met	+1 point	Partial Success
Category 3b: efforts to de-escalate military tension; institution-building toward effective political discourse; tentative consensus; vast majority of population no longer at risk	+2 points	Preponderant Success
Category 3c: no prospect of violence; established institutional capacity to deal with political conflict; consensus; humanitarian needs satisfied	+3 points	Total Success

The paucity of specific definitions reflects the difficulty in distinguishing between the different levels of intervention outcome. Bercovitch points out that "[o]f all the aspects of third party intervention, the most difficult to study is the relationship between third parties and conflict outcomes."[19] The problems include knowing what variables are attributable to the intervention effort and which variables result from the dynamics of the conflict itself. There is also the difficulty of knowing when an intervention initiative begins and when to assess the effects of the effort. Should this be done immediately following the intervention, or should one look at the long term consequences of the third party's actions? There is also the problem of perceptions – one outcome may be perceived as successful by one party and as a failure by the other.

In spite of these conceptual obstacles, it is both necessary and possible to develop a model that captures the nuances of success or failure. The Conflict Intensity Abatement (CIA) Index is designed to measure the level of inter-group conflict at three points over the course of an intervention: (1) deliberation; (2) implementation; and, (3) termination. The CIA Index is also organized into three categories representing the possible outcomes of third party intervention, as measured by a change in the level of conflict intensity. The categories describing success and failure are further subdivided in order to allow for gradations in possible results. Each potential outcome is assigned a point total in order to facilitate comparison across case studies.[20]

The categories describe the military, political, social and humanitarian conditions at different levels of conflict intensity as perceived by external observers. It is acknowledged that certain outcomes may be more desirable for specific types of disputes.

Case Study: Rwanda 1994 – *Opération Turquoise*

The suspected murder of Rwandan President Juvénal Habyarimana in April 1994 unleashed two parallel processes of violence which continued unabated for the next three months: massacres of the civilian population and a resumption of the civil war. Within hours of the assassination, militant Hutus initiated a brutal campaign of violence against Tutsis, moderate Hutus, and opposition politicians. Kigali quickly descended into disorder, as soldiers and gangs of youths wielding machetes, clubs and firearms rampaged through the streets.

The worst perpetrators of the attacks on civilians were the *Interahamwe* and *Impuzamugambi* militias. The Presidential Guard bore the main responsibility for the murder of opposition politicians in early April, while the gendarmerie, often mobilized by local government officials, took part in the killings in the countryside. The atrocities committed were shocking in their brutality.

Efforts by the UN to respond to the crisis were halting, confused and ineffective. Due to its mandate under Chapter VI of the UN Charter, the United Nations Assistance Mission for Rwanda (UNAMIR) I could not use force to protect civilians from the campaign of violence.[21]

On 15 June, France announced that it was prepared, "along with its main European and African partners," to intervene in Rwanda to protect groups threatened with "extinction."[22] France initially insisted that it would not act alone, but it soon became clear that none of its Western allies intended to join the intervention. The Western European Union (WEU) met, and while some of its members offered to provide equipment, no state offered to provide troops.[23] The US supported the idea as a means of bridging the gap before the planned arrival of the 5,500 UN peacekeepers under UNAMIR II, but also declined to contribute its own forces.[24] The Organization of African Unity (OAU) criticized the initiative, stating that unilateral action might be a hindrance to arriving at a solution.[25] Three of Rwanda's neighbours – Burundi, Tanzania, and Uganda – denied France permission to stage operations from their territory.[26]

On 22 June, the United Nations Security Council passed Resolution 929 under Chapter VII of the UN Charter, authorizing France to use "all necessary means" to protect Rwandan civilians, but called for a "strictly humanitarian ... impartial and neutral" operation that would not interfere in the fighting between the rebel and government forces. Furthermore, the resolution kept the troops under "national command and control" and stated that the duration of the intervention would last only two months.[27] The operational mandate was reportedly less than the three months sought by the secretary-general, apparently due to a need to ease French domestic concerns about being involved in a prolonged conflict.[28]

Opération Turquoise was launched that same day. However, French operations were limited to western Rwanda and were inadequate for ensuring the protection of civilians or relief operations throughout the country.

The besieged Hutu government urged France to intervene in order to prevent a Tutsi victory.[29] At the same time, French efforts to assist Rwandan civilians resulted in armed clashes with the *Front Patriotique Rwandaise* (FPR).[30] As the rebels continued to advance, France requested the Security Council to authorize the creation of a safe haven in southwestern Rwanda, but the FPR rejected this proposal, arguing that France was seeking to assist the rapidly weakening Hutu government forces.[31]

On 4 July, the FPR gained control of Kigali as well as Butare, Rwanda's second largest city. Without waiting for UN approval, France unilaterally declared a safe-zone in southwestern Rwanda to protect civilians. France's military commander in Rwanda stated that any Tutsi rebel forces entering the safe-zone would be fired upon "without any hesitation" if they threatened the population.[32] Most of the people in the safe-zone were Hutu, including some 250,000 refugees who had fled from parts of Rwanda controlled by the FPR.[33]

The French government announced its intention to begin a reduction of personnel by the end of July, with a view to complete withdrawal by the end of August. In mid-July, France began to equip a force of 500 troops drawn from various African states, to assist the French contingent and facilitate the eventual transfer of responsibility to UNAMIR II.[34]

As the withdrawal of French forces approached, fear of another crisis materialized with thousands of Hutus fleeing the safe-zone in Rwanda to Zaire.[35] Nevertheless, as planned, all French forces left Rwanda by 22 August.[36]

Measuring Appropriateness of Strategies

Phase I: Deliberation Phase I of *Opération Turquoise* extends from 15 June, the date the French government announced its intention to lead a multinational rescue mission to Rwanda, to 22 June, when the Security Council passed Resolution 929 authorizing the intervention. During this time, the intensity of the conflict escalated and the death toll from the genocide continued to rise. Given these conditions, this intervention is positioned in the belligerence phase of Figure 4.2. According to the theoretical model, a peace enforcement strategy is the optimal strategy to employ at this point.

Due to continued fighting and the opposition of the FPR to French intervention, different tactics were called for than the peacekeeping efforts of UNAMIR I and II, which ultimately failed. As a result, the French government, under the authorization of Chapter VII of the UN Charter, launched *Opération Turquoise* as a peace enforcement mission with broad rules of engagement. Since the tactics predicted in theory match the ones employed in practice, the choice of strategy is considered appropriate according to the model.

Phase II: Implementation During the implementation period of *Opération Turquoise* from 22 June until the end of July when French involvement in the mission began to diminish, the campaign of genocide continued. As a result, this phase of the intervention remains situated in the belligerence phase of Figure 4.2. According to the model, peace enforcement remained the most effective strategy to use at this time.

This strategy was employed, with the French forces in theatre taking steps to ensure the safety of all parties, in keeping with their mandate under Chapter VII of the UN Charter. This included the establishment of a safe-zone in western Rwanda and confronting and disarming members of both Hutu and Tutsi militias in that area.

Table 4.2 Measuring Appropriateness of Strategies: *Opération Turquoise*

Phase	Strategy in Theory	Strategy in Practice	Match?
Deliberation	Peace Enforcement	Peace Enforcement	Yes
Implementation	Peace Enforcement	Peace Enforcement	Yes
Termination	Peace Enforcement	Peacekeeping	No

Phase III: Termination The termination phase extends from the end of July, when French forces began preparations for their withdrawal from the region, until 22 August, when Opération Turquoise formally concluded. The intensity of conflict at this point, although not as desperate as had been prior to the intervention, still remained volatile, thus justifying its position in the belligerence phase of conflict. As such, any intervention at this stage should have mandated the continuation of peace enforcement efforts.

With the conclusion of the French intervention, however, peace enforcement actions ceased, and the succeeding UNAMIR II, a Chapter VI mission, became pre-occupied with the evolving humanitarian aspects of the conflict. As such, the strategy employed at the termination of *Opération Turquoise* is considered inappropriate, according to the model.

Outcome

Phase I: Deliberation Prior to the French announcement of 15 June, the situation in Rwanda can only be characterized as a genocide in progress. Widespread military hostilities led to a state of anarchy and the onset of a humanitarian disaster of catastrophic proportions. As such, the situation at the outset of the deliberation phase is classified under Category 1(a) [-3 points] (see Table 4.3). Although the intervention occurred simultaneously with Security Council approval on 22 June, no appreciable change in the conditions occurred on the ground until the implementation phase; as such the situation remained under Category 1(a) [-3 points].

Phase II: Implementation Following the onset of genocide, the situation in Rwanda continued under Category 1(a) [-3 points] (see Table 4.3). Due to its robust rules of engagement, *Opération Turquoise* successfully reduced the level of conflict intensity. This change is reflected in the CIA Index by a positive move to Category 1(b) [-2 points] following intervention by the UN. The net change of +1 point indicates that *Opération Turquoise* was a partial success.

Table 4.3 CIA Index of Outcomes: *Opération Turquoise*

Phase	Conflict Intensity		Net Change	Intervention Result
	Before Intervention	**After Intervention**		
Deliberation	-3 points	-3 points	0 points	Status Quo
Implementation	-3 points	-2 points	+1 point	Partial Success
Termination	-2 points	-2 points	0 points	Status Quo

Phase III: Termination At the beginning of this phase, which saw the French forces preparing for their withdrawal from Rwanda, the situation remained under Category 1(b) [-2 points] (see Table 4.3). Throughout its implementation, *Opération Turquoise* met with partial success in reducing the intensity of conflict and establishing some minimal order, as the genocide effectively ended, although sporadic violence continued.

With the withdrawal of the French forces from the region, however, the international community lost an opportunity to build on and consolidate the partial success that the intervention had achieved. As a result, no appreciable change occurred following the termination of the French-led intervention. Accordingly, the conflict remained under Category 1(b) [-2 points].

Case Study: Zaire 1996 – Zaire Rescue Mission

By late 1996, the humanitarian crisis engendered by the Rwandan genocide, coupled with the ongoing collapse of the regime of President Mobutu Sese-seko, meant Zaire[37] and Central Africa in general confronted a five-way, mutually reinforcing conflict involving: (1) an ethnic war between Zaire's Tutsi civilian population and the coalition of *Forces Armées de Zaire* (FAZ) and radical Hutu militias operating out of refugee camps in eastern Zaire; (2) Zairian Tutsis and the Alliance of Democratic Forces for the Liberation of Congo-Zaire (ADFL) versus the government in Kinshasa; (3) inter-state conflict between Zaire and Rwanda, exacerbated by the refugee crisis and the other related conflicts; (4) control of the refugee population by Hutu militias; and, (5) the UN and various non-governmental organizations (NGOs) struggling to perform their humanitarian tasks, but hampered by the political-military conflicts.[38] The result was a humanitarian emergency of catastrophic proportions.[39]

By November 1996 fighting compelled the UN and the NGO community to evacuate their personnel from eastern Zaire. With both the local and refugee populations cut-off from humanitarian assistance, it was estimated that one million lives were at risk.[40] Following the failure of a French proposal in the Security Council for an international response, Canadian Prime Minister Jean Chrétien announced Canada's willingness to lead such a mission. An American pledge of support was followed by the Security Council granting Canada authority under Chapter VII of the UN Charter to lead a multinational force (MNF).[41]

Almost immediately, however, the refugee population began moving – further westward into Zaire and back across the Rwanda-Zaire border. The ADFL attacked a series of refugee camps, which caused the Hutu militias to flee, permitting the previously intimidated refugee population to leave.[42]

Within days, the MNF was thrown into doubt. On 19 November the US withdrew the groundforce portion of its commitment to the MNF. Rwandan and ADFL officials announced the force was no longer welcome. Amid reports of continued fighting and confusion over the condition and whereabouts of refugees, the groundforce component of the mission was abandoned.[43]

On 28 November Canada announced it had achieved consensus among its partners to set up the MNF's operational headquarters and to begin airdrops, if the situation warranted. By 13 December, however, the mission was effectively terminated with a report to the Security Council by Force Commander Lieutenant-General Maurice Baril, in which he stated the MNF had fulfilled its mandate to the best of its ability. The mission came to a formal conclusion on 31 December. Except for eyewitness accounts from survivors and suspected mass graves, however, the precise number and fate of those refugees who remained in Zaire is largely unknown.[44]

Appropriateness of Strategies

Phase I: Deliberation Phase 1 extends from the first week of October 1996 to the passage of Resolution 1080 by the Security Council on 15 November, which authorized the MNF. This phase saw an intensification of ADFL offensive activity, resulting in massive refugee flows within Zaire and the absolute collapse of Kinshasa's authority over the region. As such, this period is placed in the belligerence phase of Figure 4.2. This dictates that the optimal strategy according to the model is peace enforcement.

The international community recognized this to an extent. While the French initiative envisioned a peace enforcement action, the plan failed due to the lack of US and African support. Similarly, the Chapter VII mandate given to the MNF that was established by Resolution 1080 embraced the appropriate strategy. What remained to be seen was whether the participating countries had the political will to carry out this mandate.

Phase II: Implementation This phase takes place from the point of Chapter VII authorization of the MNF to the 13 December report by Baril that the force had fulfilled its mandate to the best of its ability. Implementation of the MNF coincided with a renewed ADFL offensive on the remaining refugee camps not under its control. As such, the intervention occurred in the belligerence phase. This suggests a strategy of peace enforcement to address the humanitarian disaster.

This was, in fact, the strategy intended when the MNF was mandated. By the end of this phase on 13 December, however, it had become apparent that the multinational coalition did not have the political will to pursue the desired strategy, citing changing events on the ground for the lack of implementation of the MNF. As such, the correlation between theory and practice in this phase is qualified. As will be seen below, this had serious consequences for the outcome of the intervention.

Phase III: Termination This phase occurs between 13-31 December, the date of the official termination of the Zaire Rescue Mission. Fighting continued throughout eastern Zaire during this period; as a result, this period remains in the belligerence phase. The humanitarian disaster, although mitigated by the massive exodus of refugees back to Rwanda, remained unsolved, given the flight of a significant portion of the refugee population into the Zairian interior. Their numbers, condition and whereabouts remained unknown. Moreover, the proximate cause of the humanitarian disaster, namely the political-military conflict between the ADFL, Hutu militias and FAZ, remained unresolved.[45]

As such, any intervention should have been of a peace enforcement nature. With Baril's report to the Security Council on 13 December, however, the intervention effectively ended; accordingly, the strategy employed by the international community to respond to the crisis during this phase is deemed inappropriate.

Table 4.4 Appropriateness of Strategies: Zaire Rescue Mission

Phase	Strategy in Theory	Strategy in Practice	Match?
Deliberation	Peace Enforcement	Peace Enforcement	Yes
Implementation	Peace Enforcement	Peace Enforcement	Yes[46]
Termination	Peace Enforcement	Inaction	No

Outcome

Phase I : Deliberation Prior to the deliberations on an international intervention that culminated in Resolution 1080, the situation was anarchic. With the ADFL offensive beginning in mid-October, eastern Zaire was consumed by violence, arising from the myriad of overlapping conflicts. These conditions produced a humanitarian emergency that placed the lives of hundreds of thousands of refugees and internally displaced persons at risk. As a result, these conditions place the conflict in Category 1(a) [-3 points] prior to the UN's deliberations.

At the time of the passage of Resolution 1080, these conditions had not changed significantly. The ADFL offensive continued, with its forces in control over much of eastern Zaire and the refugee camps contained therein. The political-military conflict continued unabated, and the humanitarian emergency deepened in the absence of any international aid. As a result, the conflict remained in Category 1(a) [-3 points], indicating no net change had occurred in the conflict at the end of the deliberation phase. This is not too surprising, however, given that the international community's intervention to this point had been of an investigatory, deliberative nature.

Phase II: Implementation At the outset of the implementation phase of the Zaire Rescue Mission, conditions in eastern Zaire was situated in the Category 1(a)[-3 points], given the scale of the conflict and the accompanying humanitarian disaster.

With the passage of Resolution 1080, however, events unfolded in a manner not foreseen by the international community. The subsequent ADFL attacks on the refugee camps not under its control caused the flight of the Hutu militias, and drove the refugee population to flee to either Rwanda or deeper into Zaire. Coalition leaders claimed that the mere threat of the MNF had been enough to break the gordian knot of the humanitarian crisis, saving the lives of thousands of refugees.[47] Such claims could lead to the argument that the intervention resulted in an improvement in the conflict, and as such, should be considered a success.

Although such claims may be partly true in the sense that there was an improvement, they ignore the fate of those refugees and internally displaced persons who fled into the Zairian interior, and neglect the fact that the proximate cause of the humanitarian disaster, namely, the ongoing political-military conflict in eastern Zaire, remained unresolved.

More ominously, such claims fail to acknowledge that the international community's plan to intervene was not implemented. The MNF never set foot in eastern Zaire, except for a vanguard unit sent by Canada. The refugee flows across the Rwanda-Zaire border were used by coalition members, particularly the US and UK, as reason not to proceed. In fact, the massive refugee movement was more directly attributable to the ADFL attack on the refugee camps. With these conditions in mind, the aborted implementation of the MNF produced no net change in the conflict, which remained under Category 1(a)[-3 points].

Phase III: Termination As noted in the evaluation of Phase II, the failure of the international community to follow through effectively on the mandate of Resolution 1080 meant that conditions in eastern Zaire remained at Category 1(a) [-3 points] at the beginning of the termination phase. The consensus of the MNF coalition partners was that the massive exodus of mainly Hutu refugees back to Rwanda had solved the humanitarian emergency to an extent that the MNF was no longer required.

While the UN and NGO community now had access to these newly-repatriated refugees in western Rwanda, the international community failed to acknowledge the humanitarian disaster that continued for those refugees and internally displaced persons remaining in Zaire. Further, it did nothing to address either the political-military or humanitarian issues arising from the ongoing collapse of the Mobutu regime, or the broader, related challenges throughout the Great Lakes region of Central Africa. Here again, therefore, the international community's inaction meant no appreciable net change occurred in the conflict.

Table 4.5 CIA Index of Outcomes: Zaire Rescue Mission

Phase	**Conflict Intensity**		**Net Change**	**Intervention Result**
	Before Intervention	**After Intervention**		
Deliberation	-3 points	-3 points	0 points	Status Quo
Implementation	-3 points	-3 points	0 points	Status Quo
Termination	-3 points	-3 points	0 points	Status Quo

Evaluation and Discussion

The partial success of *Opération Turquoise* may be ascribed to the fact that military force was used to achieve *limited* goals, and the attempt to conduct the mission as impartially as possible. France did not hesitate to use force when it saw its objectives threatened; those military goals, however, were limited in geographic scope. The safe-zone established by France primarily affected the FPR's ability to advance, but France refused the Hutu government's appeal to use the French forces for military gain. Indeed, when the French forces initially intervened, the Hutu foreign minister noted:

"We would like this operation to go beyond a humanitarian intervention. We would like to see the French force the [FPR] to accept a cease-fire."[48] France did not allow itself to be drawn into the conflict in such a manner, neither did it see the pursuit of a process of national reconciliation as one of its objectives. Instead, it used military force in a limited, effective fashion to address human rights concerns. The UNAMIR forces in Rwanda had no such mandate and, consequently, their influence was far less than that of *Opération Turquoise*.[49]

At the same time, however, part of the weakness of *Opération Turquoise* arose from the desire by the intervening force to minimize its involvement both in terms of the scope of activities undertaken and the duration of the mission. By establishing a safe-zone in just the southwestern part of Rwanda and declaring that troops would be present for only two months, the impact of the intervention on the protection of civilians and the creation of conditions for national reconciliation was significantly reduced.

France left Rwanda at a time when millions of people remained displaced, when the newly recognized government had yet to establish effective mechanisms for peace and stability, and when Hutu extremists had fled to the mountains or to neighbouring countries while remaining a potent guerrilla threat. Not only was the humanitarian crisis far from over, but the French withdrawal itself fostered a greater sense of insecurity among the approximately one million Rwandans who had sought shelter in the safe-zone; it also prompted another wave of refugee flows into neighbouring countries, including Zaire. As a result, while the strategy of peace enforcement was a partial success, its short duration and restricted scope limited the success of the intervention.

This limited effectiveness had serious implications for Central Africa in general and Zaire in particular. The failure of the international community to address the latent causes of the conflict in the region meant that the potential remained for a recurrence. This is precisely what occurred in 1996 with the collapse of the regime of Mobutu Sese-seko and the unleashing of the ADFL offensive in eastern Zaire.

Here again, however, the international community appears to have misunderstood the complex demands required for effective humanitarian intervention. While the Canadian-led MNF was assembled more quickly, and had a broader membership than its 1994 predecessor in Rwanda, the international coalition focused predominantly on the humanitarian aspects of the conflict, and not the underlying conditions that had provoked the renewal of violence and human suffering. Before the MNF was ever implemented, coalition members were backpedaling on their commitments, particularly the US and UK, which cited the return of large numbers of refugees to Rwanda as evidence that the intervention was no longer necessary.[50]

The MNF apparently failed to acknowledge that the refugee flows were the latest development in an on-going, complex, regional dilemma. The short-term, "quick-fix" nature of the intervention, combined with its apparent pre-occupation with the humanitarian dimension of the conflict, resulted in the MNF losing its perspective and political will. This resulted in the abandonment of any efforts to assist the large number of refugees and internally-displaced persons that remained in Zaire. It also meant that the international community willfully refrained from undertaking any serious attempts to address the roots of the on-going humanitarian crisis.

Conclusions

Implications

The first and most important contribution of the model developed in this study is that it provides a point of departure to assess the appropriate tasks and tools of intervening over the course of violent inter-group conflicts. Accordingly, this perspective allows for meaningful evaluation of the relationship between the strategy and outcome of third-party intervention.

The second contribution of the model is that it reflects the dynamic nature of violent conflicts and attempts by third-parties to de-escalate them. It may be used to evaluate a specific phase of a dispute or the entire life cycle of a conflict. Accordingly, the model has applications at both micro- and macro-levels of analysis.

How can the model be useful for decision-making? The practical implications primarily concern ways in which policy-makers can use the ideas and logic of the model to make better strategic choices. Ideally, it may assist decision-makers to avoid costly mistakes that carry severe repercussions.

The model can also help policy-makers in two additional ways. First, it can assist them to analyze problems in a manner that may be superior to previous approaches. Second, empirical research may make policy recommendations more persuasive to leaders in the sense that it shows specific linkages between procedures and outcomes. Accordingly, the combination of theory-based models and practice is essential to making informed policies.

Revision of Model

This chapter has demonstrated the effectiveness of the CIA Index against a small number of cases. In order for the framework to have broader relevance, however, it must be applied to additional conflicts in different contexts. While this study focussed on efforts by the UN to de-escalate violent conflicts within a specific section of the Conflict Intervention Cycle, the framework is designed to evaluate a wide range of disputes varying in conflict intensity. As such, the model should be used to examine a larger number of cases involving different types of third-parties and different levels of conflict intensity. In addition, the framework must be adjusted to reflect institutional decision-making processes, rather than relying on a rational actor model.

In addition, the variable of strategy must be examined in greater detail. While there exists a causal link between strategy and outcome, it would be intellectually naïve to assume that such a link provides a sufficient explanation. Future research could focus on further subdividing the range of strategies discussed in this paper, thus increasing the number and type of tactics that may be evaluated. Moreover, the expansion of the CIA Index into further gradations will provide a more nuanced assessment of intervention by third-parties.

Where Do We Go From Here?

Despite its importance as a method of mitigating disputes, the precise formula for achieving successful intervention has not been found. International conflicts are unique events; as the proliferation of Chapter VII operations has revealed, they vary in terms of parties involved, intensity, and possible responses. These features define the nature of a dispute and affect the course of its outcome. In other words, intervention is shaped by the context and character of a conflict.

Rwanda and Zaire are tragic examples of the complicated and disjointed policy-making process that often dictates the strategy and outcome of intervention efforts by third-parties. The aftermath of these conflicts has continued to present complex problems for the region and a multitude of international actors. The international community must go beyond assuaging its guilty conscience and must instead summon and maintain the political will necessary to carry out its commitment to break the cycle of violence; otherwise, the international community is destined for further instances when it will have ensured long-term pain, for the sake of short-term gain.

Notes

1 The authors wish to express their gratitude to David Carment, Harald von Riekhoff and Natalie Mychajlyszyn for their assistance and encouragement.

2 UN Security Council Resolution 1289 (2000) invoked Chapter VII of the UN Charter to revise the mandate of the United Nations Mission in Sierra Leone (UNAMSIL) to " … take the necessary action to fulfil [its] … tasks, and affirmed that, in the discharge of its mandate, UNAMSIL may take the necessary action to ensure the security and freedom of movement of its personnel and, within its capabilities and areas of deployment, to afford protection to civilians under imminent threat of physical violence … ." The Chapter VII operation in Kosovo was authorized under Security Council Resolution 1244 (1999). The intervention in East Timor was established under Security Council Resolution 1264 (1999). Finally, Resolution 1291 (2000) revised the mandate of the United Nations Mission Organization Mission in the Democratic Republic of Congo (MONUC), making it a Chapter VII mission.

3 The study of conflict abounds with terms that seek to describe violence among state and substate actors, spanning the spectrum of intensity from minor unrest to full-scale war. Rather than attempting to classify conflict narrowly as "ethnic," "religious," "social," "economic" or otherwise, this work seeks a definition that is broadly inclusive. Most conflicts prevalent in the current international environment occur between groups Samuel P. Huntington, "The Clash of Civilizations?" *Foreign Affairs* 72:3 (Summer 1993): p. 38. Compared with inter-state conflict, inter-group conflict poses more complex problems for third-party intervenors because it requires a more sophisticated application of solutions. For example, events in Rwanda between Hutus and Tutsis were affected by cross-border activities of group members in neighbouring Zaire, Burundi, and Uganda, without the

express involvement of the political elite or state infrastructures of those sovereign entities. The international community sought to contain the conflict within the borders of Rwanda; however, it soon became apparent that violence and intra-group affinities transcended these administrative boundaries. The extra-territorial aspects of the Rwandan conflict suggest that the term "inter-group conflict" has greater analytical utility than "intra-state conflict" for the purposes of this study.

4 Alexander George, "Case Studies and Theory Development: The Method of Structured Focused Comparison" in *Diplomacy: New Approaches in History, Theory and Policy*, ed. Paul Gordon Lauren (New York, NY: Free Press, 1979), pp. 43-68.

5 Jacob Bercovitch, *Social Conflicts and Third Parties: Strategies of Conflict Resolution* (Boulder, CO: Westview Press, 1984), p. 116.

6 Saadia Touval and I. William Zartman, "Introduction: Mediation and Theory," in *International Mediation in Theory and Practice*, eds. Saadia Touval and I. William Zartman (Boulder, CO: Westview Press, 1985), p. 14.

7 The scope of this paper precludes a more detailed discussion of potential strategies available to third-party intervenors. Accordingly, the reader is referred to Robert E. Astroff, "Scuttled Diplomacy: A Study of Intervention by the United Nations in Rwanda," Master's Thesis, Carleton University, 1999, for a more thorough accounting of the range of diagnostic and intercessory strategies.

8 Third parties may also use the threat of military action as a deterrent against continued hostilities. This approach combines intercessory (pressuring) tactics and the potential use of military strategies. See Frank Harvey, "Deterrence Failure and Ethnic Conflict: The Case of Bosnia," in *Peace in the Midst of Wars: Preventing and Managing International Ethnic Conflicts*, eds. David Carment and Patrick James (Columbus, SC: University of South Carolina Press, 1998), pp. 230-264.

9 Gareth Evans, *Cooperating for Peace: The Global Agenda for the 1990s and Beyond* (London: Allen and Unwin, 1993), p. 11. This definition echoes many of the key points expressed by Boutros Boutros-Ghali in his 1992 report, *An Agenda for Peace*: "Peace-keeping is the deployment of a United Nations presence in the field, hitherto with the consent of all the parties concerned, normally involving United Nations military and/or police personnel and frequently civilians as well. Peace-keeping is a technique that expands the possibilities for both the prevention of conflict and the making of peace." UN Doc. A/47/277 [1992], p. 6.

10 Richard N. Haass, "Using Force: Lessons and Choices for U.S. Foreign Policy," in *Managing Global Chaos: Sources of and Responses to International Conflict*, eds. Chester A. Crocker and Fen Osler Hampson with Pamela Aall (Washington, DC: United States Institute of Peace Press, 1996), pp. 197-198.

11 Chapter VI missions may take the form of "muscular peacekeeping," commonly referred to as Chapter VI 1/2 operations.

12 Denis McLean, "Peace Operations and Common Sense," in *Managing Global Chaos: Sources of and Responses to International Conflict*, eds. Chester A. Crocker and Fen Osler Hampson with Pamela Aall (Washington, DC: United States Institute of Peace Press, 1996), p. 328.

13 David M. Malone, "The UN Security Council and Peace Operations," *Canadian Foreign Policy* 5:2 (Winter 1998): p. 82.

14 Haass, "Using Force," p. 198.

15 K. J. Holsti, *International Politics*, 6th ed. (Englewood Cliffs, NJ: Prentice Hall, 1992), pp. 368-369.

16 Michael Lund, *Preventing Violent Conflicts: A Strategy for Preventive Diplomacy* (Washington, DC: United States Institute of Peace Press, 1996), p. 39.
17 Bercovitch, *Social Conflicts and Third Parties*, p. 113.
18 Touval and Zartman, "Introduction: Mediation and Theory," p. 14.
19 Bercovitch, *Social Conflicts and Third Parties*, p. 112.
20 For example, if a dispute moves from non-violent to violent after the intervention of a third-party (i.e. a net negative change in the CIA Index), this would represent a failure of the initiative to de-escalate the conflict.
21 For a detailed discussion of UNAMIR I, as well as a comprehensive account of the genocide, see *Rwanda: The Preventable Genocide* (Addis Ababa: International Panel of Eminent Persons, Organization of African Unity, 2000).
22 "France May Move In to End Rwanda Killing," *New York Times*, 16 June 1994.
23 "France Presses Plan For Rwanda Mission," *Washington Post*, 20 June 1994.
24 "US Endorses French Initiative For Military Mission in Rwanda," *Washington Post*, 21 June 1994.
25 *Rwanda: Death, Despair and Defiance* (London: African Rights, 1995), p. 1141.
26 "Few Allies Help France," *New York Times*, 24 June 1994.
27 UN Doc. S/RES/929 [1994]. The Security Council vote was ten in favour, none opposed, and five abstentions (Brazil, China, New Zealand, Nigeria, and Pakistan), an unusually tepid outcome to intensive French diplomatic lobbying. Despite falling under French national command, *Opération Turquoise* is nonetheless considered intervention by the international community, in much the same way as the US-led Operation Desert Storm was considered an action by the UN. In each case, rather than being placed under UN command, the responsibility for upholding the UN Charter was essentially "contracted out" to member-states.
28 "French Offer Is First Step Toward a Multinational Force," *New York Times*, 23 June 1994; "UN Supports France on Force for Rwanda," *Washington Post*, 23 June 1994.
29 "Rwanda Asks France to Help Hold Off Rebels," *New York Times*, 3 July 1994.
30 "French Force in Skirmish in Rwanda," *New York Times*, 4 July 1994.
31 "French Troops, Rebels Clash," *Washington Post*, 4 July 1994.
32 "Rebels Take Chief Cities In Rwanda," *Washington Post*, 5 July 1994.
33 "French Establish a Base in Rwanda to Block Rebels," *New York Times*, 5 July 1994.
34 *The United Nations and Rwanda, 1993-1996* (New York, NY: United Nations Department of Public Information,1996), pp. 53-58.
35 "Rwandans' Exodus From Safe Zone Swells," *New York Times*, 20 August 1994.
36 "French Troops Withdraw From Rwanda Safe Zone," *Washington Post*, 22 August 1994. In a joint statement, French President Mitterand and Prime Minister Edouard Balladur declared: "France has fulfilled its duty. ... It is now up to the Rwandan authorities and the international community to assume, as of today, all of their responsibilities." "New Tide of Refugees Heads Out of Rwanda," *Washington Post*, 20 August 1994.
37 For the purposes of this chapter the Democratic Republic of Congo will be referred to by its former name of Zaire. The name was changed upon the coming to power of President Laurent Kabila in May 1997.
38 Howard Adelman, "Responding to State Failure," paper presented to the workshop, *Peace-Building and Democratic Development: Examining Canada's Policy Options*, Carleton University, Ottawa, Canada, 26 September 1996, pp. 22-23.
39 The dictates of space render it impossible to provide a fully detailed account of the conditions in Zaire and the events that led to the international intervention. The reader is therefore referred to the following: David Meren, *Destinies with Greatness or Delusions of*

Grandeur? Causes and Consequences of Prime Ministerial Interventions in Response to International Crises, Master's Thesis, Carleton University, 1999; John Hay, *Conditions of Influence: An Exploration Study of the Canadian Government's Effect on United States Policy in the Case of Intervention in Eastern Zaire*, Master's Thesis, Carleton University, 1998; *The Fifth Estate*, CBC-TV, 18 November 1997; Terrence McKenna, documentary, *The National Magazine*, CBC-TV, 18 November 1996; Herbert Weiss, "Zaire: Collapsed Society, Surviving State, Future Policy," in *Collapsed States: The Disintegration and Restoration of Legitimate Authority*, ed. I. William Zartman (Boulder, CO: Lynne Rienner Publishers, 1995).

40 "Tutsi Offensive Imperils Hutus," *Globe and Mail,* 1 November 1996; "Relief Workers Forced to Leave," *Globe and Mail,* 4 November 1996; "Relief Workers Study Lesson in Politics," *Globe and Mail,* 6 November 1996.

41 Hay, *Conditions of Influence*, pp. 43-44; "Canada Pushes for US Support," 13 November 1996; UN Doc. S/RES/1080 [1996]). The Security Council resolution provided for: "the establishment for humanitarian purposes of a temporary multinational force to facilitate the immediate return of humanitarian organizations and the effective delivery by civilian relief organizations of humanitarian aid to alleviate the immediate suffering of displaced persons, refugees and civilians at risk in eastern Zaire, and to facilitate the voluntary, orderly repatriation of refugees by the United Nations High Commissioner for Refugees as well as the voluntary return of displaced persons, and invites other interested States to offer to participate in these efforts ... by using all necessary means." The operation was set to terminate on 31 March 1997, unless "the Council, on the basis of a report of the Secretary-General, determines that the objectives of the operation have been fulfilled earlier."

42 "UN Mission Not Needed, Africans Say: First Wave of Canadians Leave, but Full Deployment Delayed," *Ottawa Citizen,* 17 November 1996; "Refugees Stream Back to Rwanda," *Globe and Mail,* 16 November 1996.

43 *The Fifth Estate*, CBC-TV, 18 November 1997.

44 Hay, *Conditions of Influence*, p. 4.

45 Hay, *Conditions of Influence*; *The Fifth Estate*, CBC-TV, 18 November 1997.

46 This match is qualified. Although the strategy initially envisaged was of a peace enforcement nature, the MNF was never effectively implemented as it had been foreseen by Resolution 1080.

47 "International Steering Group Agrees that Zaire Force No Longer Needed," Press Release, Prime Minister's Office, Government of Canada, 13 December 1996.

48 "French Paratroopers Disarm Rwanda Militias, Saying They Are Allies of Neither Tribe," *New York Times*, 26 June 1994.

49 As the French forces were withdrawing from Rwanda, a member of Concern (an Irish NGO) lamented the lack of respect for the authority of the UN forces: "The French were a protection force and drew the line, and everyone knew not to cross it. Everyone knows that the UN has no spine, that's the bottom line." "UN Stops Returning Rwandan Refugees," *New York Times*, 28 September 1994.

50 Hay, *Conditions of Influence*, pp. 62, 66.

Chapter 5

Twisting One Arm: The Effects of Biased Intervenors*

David Carment and Dane Rowlands[1]

There is a presumption that when coalitions of states attempt to reduce the level of conflict between other warring parties, they do so in a balanced and unbiased manner. This assumption of impartiality, however, is often inaccurate and misleading. The central characteristics of traditional peacekeeping missions – the use of force for self-defence only, the interposition of troops after a cease-fire and the maintenance of tactical and strategic impartiality – no longer define operational success. Part of the shift in intervention procedures is related to the increasing prevalence of intra-state conflicts, which have proven to be decidedly more complex and often more deadly for both belligerents and peacekeepers as well as ordinary citizens caught in the fray. In order to execute complicated functions such as guaranteeing the safe passage of humanitarian aid, assisting displaced persons, and stopping the killing of ordinary citizens, peacekeepers must now resort to forceful measures directed against a combatant.

Many observers have concluded that the key principles informing conventional, essentially peaceful, missions are problematic – if not anachronistic – in an era dominated by armed conflict within rather than between states.[2] Recent studies on UN peacekeeping efforts, such as the Brahimi Report and the findings of the International Commission on Intervention and State Sovereignty,[3] recommend the development of more meaningful criteria for distinguishing between the cases where intervention should be more forceful and when it should employ less dramatic means.[4]

Critical analyses have begun by examining the traditional principles upon which peacekeeping and more forceful measures are based in order to determine why the new breed of missions succeed or fail.[5] The single most strongest explanation for the lacklustre efforts of recent missions is the problematic nature of forceful intervention in intra-state conflict. Some findings show that increases in the use of force may exacerbate tensions because of the incipient moral hazard problem.[6] Others suggest that a lack of resolve and credibility within coalitions and security organizations create additional incentives for escalation and prolonged conflict.[7]

---

* This chapter was originally published in *International Peacekeeping* 10:3 (Autumn 2003). It is re-printed here with permission from Taylor and Francis and can be accessed at http://www.tandf.co.uk/journals.

To guide the development of peacekeeping policies, additional research is required on a wide range of operational issues. In this chapter we examine the role of bias in two episodes: NATO's intervention in Kosovo, and India's intervention in Sri Lanka. These case studies are used to examine the preliminary hypotheses that have been developed in a formal model.[8] There is, as yet, little consensus on whether impartiality is necessary for the successful management of today's conflicts. A loss of impartiality and an increase in bias are often associated with more forceful and potentially risky and costly undertakings. Therefore, it is useful to know when forceful interventions are more likely to succeed by clearly specifying the conditions under which a biased intervention is likely to either inhibit violence or act as a catalyst to it.[9]

The substance of the chapter begins with a review of the literature on bias, followed by a heuristic description of the formal model of bias that appears in Carment and Rowlands (2000).[10] We then examine the details of the two case studies and evaluate the performance of the model in predicting the effects of bias. A summary of the results and a conclusion complete the paper.

Literature Review

There is a convenient analytical division within the literature on the role of third-party bias in conflict management and resolution. One component of this literature examines bias in pacific forms of third party involvement, such as mediation. A second line of research examines the role of bias in peacekeeping and peace enforcement. Each is considered in turn.

With respect to pacific forms of third-party involvement, Boskey argues that the first principle of mediation is that any agreement that results from the process should be voluntary.[11] According to Boskey, the primary purpose of mediation is to gain agreement between the adversaries without compromising the autonomy of either party. Matz challenges this claim, emphasizing that autonomy is not the same as making a decision in the absence of any constraints.[12] It is legitimate for mediators to apply pressure, and indeed adversaries invite third-party intervention precisely because they seek the resulting pressure as a means of solving a dispute that they cannot solve themselves.

Empirical support for Matz's argument is provided by Carnevale and Arad.[13] They examine the relationship between mediator pressure and party autonomy in small group settings, and conclude that third-party bias does not significantly constrain effective mediation. A third-party is more readily accepted when the parties to a dispute are aware of the biases that may be inherent in the third-party's approach.[14] This acceptance occurs when the clear communication of third-party bias creates a cushioning effect, providing a statement of interests and intent so that both sides can adjust their positions prior to and during the negotiations.[15] Carnevale and Arad's findings also support the intuitive notion that partisan and non-partisan disputants evaluate the mediator differently. The parties to a dispute act strategically, anticipating and acting on signals of mediator intent in order to maximize their own interests.[16] Finally, Carnevale and Arad show that disputants will more readily accept a biased mediator if it brings resources and prestige to the table.

Further support for these arguments are provided by Gibson, Thompson and Bazerman.[17] They ask how and why it is the case that mediators often reach agreements that are less than ideal. They argue that inappropriate agreements are frequently a result of mixed and poorly communicated signals as well as a preoccupation with mediator impartiality.

To summarize, mediation research suggests that clearly communicated third-party bias may actually act as a beneficial catalyst in dispute resolution by allowing disputants to develop a more realistic appraisal of their situation and their optimal responses. What remains unclear, however, is whether or not this conclusion is still appropriate in cases where the third-party used more active and forceful methods of intervention, such as peacekeeping or peace enforcement.

Forceful Intervention, Peacekeeping and Bias

Traditional perspectives assume that a violation of impartiality goes against the underlying precepts of peacekeeping. For example, Alan James has consistently argued that favoritism in intra-state ethnic conflict is more likely to make peacekeepers targets rather than intermediaries.[18] Citing evidence from the Congo, Lebanon and Bosnia, James suggests that outside forces should not intervene unless the three basic conditions, (specified at the outset of this chapter) can be reasonably met.[19] Similarly Krain chronicles longstanding as well as more recent explanations for why actors engage in mass killings, and traces the evolution of preventive efforts from preventive diplomacy, to economic sanctions, to military intervention.[20] He finds evidence that interventions that increase the resources available to the faction intent upon genocide will increase the severity of genocidal acts, while intervention aimed at increasing the resources of the opposing side will decrease the severity and scope of the killings.[21]

Roberts sees the problematic nature of forceful interventions in terms of "loss of consent" rather than in terms of "loss of impartiality."[22] He characterizes the downgrading of the consent of the parties to a conflict as a requirement for UN action to be at the heart of the peacekeeping crisis. He uses the crises in Iraq (the establishment of safe areas for Kurds in northern Iraq), the former Yugoslavia (the entire operation), and Somalia (no functioning government to grant consent) as case studies.[23] Roberts cites as a major problem the incongruity between the UN's stated willingness to use force within the scope of its peacekeeping operations and a reluctance to perform this role in practice; instead contracting out the use of force to regional organizations or specific countries. Like James, Roberts believes the willingness to use force leaves lightly-armed UN peacekeepers vulnerable to attack and exposes the UN to criticism for engaging in force that may have an adverse impact upon civilian populations.

Others have argued that forceful and more biased interventions are merited under specific circumstances especially when the outcome is likely to result in significant defeat of one party.[24] For example, Betts argues that intervention cannot hope to maintain impartiality even if the form of forceful intervention is limited in scope. This is because in instances where the outside power takes complete command of the situation and imposes a peace settlement the intervention will result in stability. More limited forms of intervention undertaken with the goal of impartiality may keep either belligerent from defeating the other, but will not stop the adversaries from waging war in an attempt to do so.[25] The intervening force should have no illusions as to what the application of force will accomplish: victory for one faction over the other.[26]

Empirical support for this argument is provided by Enterline and Balch-Lindsay.[27] They conduct an empirical analysis of 74 civil conflicts between 1900 and 1992. Their results indicate that third-parties have virtually no significant impact on conflict duration in cases of a negotiated settlement; but they do play a decisive role in those conflicts that are brought to a conclusion through military victory by one of the belligerents.

Carment and Rowlands argue that forceful measures are appropriate under a pre-specified set of conditions and are most likely to succeed only when the conflict is salient to the outside party.[28] Less forceful measures are likely to prevent continued fighting only when the belligerents' expected gains are low. To support this argument they develop a game-theoretic model for evaluating peacekeeping strategies in intra-state conflicts. They base their model on four variables: the mission's intensity, the salience of the conflict to the intervenor, the capabilities of the belligerent, and the belligerent's expected gains from continued fighting.[29] The authors characterize intervention as a calculation of third-party interests and the willingness of belligerents to continue fighting.[30]

In a similar vein, Lake and Rothchild argue that forceful intervention, has two primary effects.[31] First, like Krain and Betts, they believe it alters the internal balance of power. This can be useful in equalizing forces and in creating a hurting stalemate in which neither side can be victorious, thereby encouraging a negotiated settlement. Second, it can also lead to situations wherein the intervention emboldens the weaker party to the conflict, encouraging it to increase its demands and thus prolong the conflict. Accordingly, Lake and Rothchild argue that pressure must be exerted on both sides to moderate their demands.

Finally, Luttwak weighs in against intervention in any form.[32] He makes an argument counter to Krain and Lake and Rothchild that intervention, and especially peacekeeping, disallows for the possibility of a decisive conclusion, or the true exhaustion of the parties to the dispute, which would allow them to seek a long-lasting and potentially final resolution.[33]

The general conclusion that can be taken from these analyses is twofold. On the one hand, both the mediation and peacekeeping literature question the assumption that intervenors must be perceived and act impartially. Under certain circumstances, such as genocide, failed peace accords or prolonged conflict, the intervenor should make an effort to ensure the conflict reaches a specific outcome. This finding is reinforced by Zartman and Touval and Watkins and Winter who argue that an intervenor may be more effective in achieving a stable short-term outcome when the third-party has a vested interest in a specific outcome that may favour one side over another.[34]

On the other hand, while it may be accurate to assume that third-parties have the ability to impose costs through more biased interventions, it remains unclear whether they will want to or have to impose high costs in all instances and whether these efforts will succeed. Our review indicates that there may be instances where biased interventions lead to escalation and there may be instances where de-escalation is the result. Further, the literature is ambivalent on specifying the conditions in which forceful interventions will lead to increased stability. This is a significant weakness in our view because intervention is a costly process and imposes long- and short-term costs on both the intervenor and the belligerents. Failed interventions also have implications for future interventions. Biased efforts that result in failure may result in future challenges at a later stage of the conflict.

Finally, none of the studies reviewed here compare the effects of a biased intervention against those instances where no intervention took place (as suggested by Luttwak). The non-intervention benchmark is a preliminary but important step in drawing valid conclusions regarding the likelihood of escalation and the presumed impact of a biased intervention. Indeed, most analyses that are critical of a biased intervention fail to specify what the outcome would have been if the combatants engaged one another unfettered by third-party influence.

To summarize, the literature does not appear to identify a compelling, overarching framework for analyzing and understanding intervenor bias. The mediation literature suggests that under certain circumstances of clear communication, bias can be useful and effective. The corresponding literature on more forceful intervention is divided between those that emphasize the traditional requirement of impartiality, and those that believe that action in support of one side of a dispute is necessary. In the absence of consensus, we now turn to a deductive approach to understanding intervenor bias.

The Role of Bias in a Model of Intervention

There are few formal models of intervenor bias from which to derive testable propositions. Carment and Rowlands develop a model to investigate the effects of bias in intervention,[35] basing their analysis in part on an earlier model in Rowlands and Car-ment.[36] In general these approaches belong to a class of models that include the work of Becker, Wolfson and especially Hirshleifer, that have traditionally examined the be-haviour of combatants in isolation from any outside interference.[37] To these models we add the effects of third-party intervention.

The formal model presented elsewhere[38] examines the behaviour of two combatants who fight over the distribution of resources or benefits. Each group chooses to allocate its resources towards fighting or productive activities, making the best of a trade-off between fighting – by which they acquire additional resources – and acquiescing – which transforms fighting resources into goods and services that enhance the welfare of the group. As one group increases the effort it puts into fighting, its opponent will tend to do the same in order to maintain the prior resource distribution. When there is no intervention, the two groups will end up at an equilibrium where they settle on a constrained optimum in terms of the division of their effort between fighting and producing.

When a third-party intervenes and skews the resource distribution in favour of one group, the reaction of the combatant is determined by the intervention's effect on the relative marginal contributions made to the group's welfare from its different activities. In equilibrium, the group should be indifferent between putting more effort into fighting (which may yield more resources) or into working (which transforms available resources into desired products). By linking assumptions to empirically-observable conditions, the model can generate predictions for the consequences of biased intervention and other conflict-related phenomena. Rowlands and Carment provide an example of how a general model such as the one described here can be solved for specific cases that are in turn linked to independent, empirically-based characteristics.[39]

For a wide class of assumptions the model does generate some fairly robust predictions about how intervenor bias affects the behaviour of disputants. Intuitively, the intervention can be thought of as augmenting the effort of the intervenor's favoured side, and detracting from the efforts of the opposing combatant. The consequence is that the combatant favoured by the intervenor will tend to reduce their fighting effort while the opposing side will tend to increase theirs.

However even these reactions are complicated by the presence of indirect reactions. On the one hand, as the favoured combatant begins to reduce its fighting effort in direct reaction to the intervenor's support, the indirect response of the opponent is to do likewise. On the other hand, the increased fighting effort of an unfavoured combatant in direct response to the opposition of the intervenor will tend to induce indirectly more fighting effort by its opponent. The resulting equilibrium can have three characteristics, depending on the relative size of the direct reactions of the two combatants:

1. The larger the response to the intervenor and consequent increase in the fighting effort of the unfavoured combatant, and the smaller the de-escalating reaction to the intervention by the favoured combatant, the more likely that the combatants will both escalate their levels of fighting effort in equilibrium.

2. Smaller reactions by the unfavoured combatant and larger responses by the favoured combatant can result in a de-escalation of the conflict.

3. When the reactions of both combatants are more comparable in scale, the more likely there will be an unbalanced response to the intervention, with the unfavoured combatant increasing its fighting effort while the favoured combatant reduces its fighting effort.

According to the logic of the model, there are no circumstances that should generate the opposite outcome, with the favoured combatant escalating while the unfavoured combatant de-escalates. The observation of this latter situation would constitute one clear way of disproving the validity of the intuitive result derived from the model.

The absence of a single solution to the formal model corresponds to some degree with the ambiguity of the literature on bias. However, the model can be solved using specific assumptions, and thereby can generate some reasonably robust results and intuition. To investigate the plausibility of the model's predictive capabilities and the potential empirical power of the model, two cases are examined to see whether they fit the basic predictions of the model. The cases, Sri Lanka 1987 and Kosovo 1999, are used to examine whether the response of the combatants corresponds to the model's predicted behaviour. These case studies may also be useful in identifying conflict characteristics that can be used to generate empirically plausible assumptions that can be used in solving the formal models of intervention.

Case Studies

Sri Lanka 1987

Sri Lanka has experienced varying levels of inter-communal violence for several decades. The conflict between the Tamil minority that dominates in the north and east of Sri Lanka and the country's majority Sinhalese began to intensify after independence from Britain. The early 1980s saw a particularly pronounced acceleration of violence, however, and attracted the increased attention of Sri Lanka's much larger neighbour, and the regional power, India.

India's ties to Sri Lanka went beyond geography and a common historical link through the British Empire. The ethnic ties between the Tamils of Sri Lanka and their brethren in Southern India meant that the Indian government often lent moral support to the Tamil cause, though the Tamils received material support from groups within India as well. The conflict in Sri Lanka, however, was a source of some distress for the Indian government for a variety of reasons. Despite the ethnic ties to the Tamils of Sri Lanka, India had its own secessionist movements to worry about, including occasional agitation by its own Tamil minority.[40] Furthermore, Sri Lanka was becoming an increasingly unstable state in an area of economic and strategic interest to the Indians. In order to assert its power and stabilize the region, India agreed to send troops into Sri Lanka to supervise a cease-fire between the main Tamil forces, particularly the Liberation Tigers of Tamil Eelam (LTTE), and the Sri Lankan government.[41]

The Indian intervention was meant to be an unbiased one in support of a cease-fire that had already been negotiated. The Tamils in Sri Lanka initially viewed the Indian Peacekeeping Force (IPKF) as an ally who would protect them from the Sri Lankan government's troops. In turn the IPKF was initially favourably disposed towards the Tamils, and in the beginning "tried to play its role as carefully and impartially as possible."[42] The Sri Lankan government also viewed favourably the presence of the IPKF as a means of ending Tamil violence and enhancing an Indo-Sri Lankan alliance.[43]

To extremists in the two ethnic camps, however, the IPKF was clearly undesirable. Tamil extremists understood, or would come to understand, that the IPKF would not permit Tamil agitation to continue, and that the Indian government did not support the formation of an independent Tamil state. Radical Sinhalese groups, such as the Jatiya Vimukthi Peramuna (JVP), viewed the IPKF as an impediment to their campaign of violence against the Tamils.

Austin asserts that the 1987 Accord between India and Sri Lanka "was based on the assumption that Indian troops would restrain the LTTE while the Sri Lankan government dealt with the resurgence of the JVP."[44] Therefore, it is not surprising that in terms of the

Tamil-Sri Lankan conflict, the IPKF eventually came to be seen as biased against the Tamils whom they were expected to disarm and contain. Muni argues that although the success of an intervention requires that "a peacekeeper should be neutral or impartial ... the very provision of the IPKF in the agreement was biased against the Tamil militants as it was meant to help the Sri Lankan government in disarming the militants."[45] The attempt to disarm the LTTE placed the IPKF in clear opposition to the main Tamil force, and in alliance with the Sri Lankan government.[46]

The intuition of the model suggests that, in such a situation, the reaction of the Tamil forces would be to escalate their activities in reaction to the IPKF's presence. The manifestation of the IPKF's bias, in the form of attempting to disarm the Tamils, did indeed prompt the LTTE to abandon the cease-fire and renew their attacks. Smith argues that the IPKF's presence "probably created the political conditions for the LTTE leadership to strengthen the resolve of the Tamil population."[47] Hennayake suggests that the IPKF faced the same opposition as the Sri Lankan forces had dealt with prior to 1987, "possibly in even greater magnitude."[48] Though undoubtedly exaggerated, at one point the IPKF had claimed to have killed 3000 LTTE guerrillas since the commencement of its operations, "more than the estimated number of LTTE members at the war's outset."[49] Therefore, there is strong evidence that, in reaction to the intervention, the Tamils increased their fighting effort relative to both the cease-fire and pre-cease-fire periods.

At the same time the Sri Lankan government clearly reduced its operations in the fight against Tamil separatism. This outcome clearly accords with the prediction of the model. Aside from relatively minor skirmishes in the Sinhalese-dominated areas of Sri Lanka, there appears to be little evidence of Sri-Lankan troops taking on major operations against the LTTE or other Tamil groups. Instead, the Sri Lankan government let the IPKF conduct most of the operations, and bear the brunt of the Tamil rebellion.

In the wider context of Sri Lanka, however, some complications emerge. The arrival of the IPKF released much of the Sri Lankan government troops for operations elsewhere. They were needed because the agreement that brought the IPKF into Sri Lanka also provoked some reaction from the Sinhalese JVP. The Sri Lankan-JVP conflict thus erupted at the same time as the intervention. Therefore, while Sri Lankan government effort in the Tamil war fell significantly, it escalated in the war against Sinhalese extremists. Overall, however, their efforts seemed to decline in reaction to the IPKF's presence. Data from SIPRI indicate that military expenditures by the Sri Lankan government actually peaked in 1987, though this may have been related to the Sri Lankan government offensive that had taken place earlier in that year, and which had been a key catalyst of both the ceasefire and the agreement with India.[50] Government military expenditures fell in the following years. Furthermore, it would appear that the JVP was largely responsible for provoking the Sri Lankan government's military response against them, suggesting that increased activity against the JVP was not directly linked to India's intervention elsewhere. In any case, the JVP-Sri Lankan government conflict was not the direct target of the Indian intervention.

Therefore the intuition of the model seems to be confirmed by the case of Sri Lanka. The insertion of an intervention force that was perceived as biased led to an escalation on the part of the group opposed by the intervenor. The favoured combatant, however, reduced its fighting effort in direct reaction to the intervention, and was able to maintain a reduced presence even in the face of its opponent's escalation due to the concomitant increase in the intervention force.

Kosovo 1998

The conflict in Kosovo pitted the ethnic Albanians of the Kosovo Liberation Army (KLA) against the army of the Serb-dominated government of the Federal Republic of Yugoslavia (FRY). The former had been agitating for greater autonomy for Kosovo, where ethnic Albanians constituted a majority of the population. Political repression by the Milosevic government had generated increasing support amongst the Albanian Kosovars for more radical solutions, including independence.

The governments of NATO, which would eventually intervene in the dispute, were not initially supportive of the Kosovars. In early 1998, US Special Envoy to the Balkans, Robert Gelbard, stated that "the KLA is without any question a terrorist group," and denounced terrorist activity in Kosovo. The FRY government took this as a signal of the West's indifference to the Kosovo question, and as tacit acquiescence to any military action that they might direct at the rebellious province.[51] The government's campaign against the KLA and its supporters intensified and civilian casualties ensued. As a consequence, support for the KLA grew both within Kosovo and amongst NATO governments.[52]

The aggressive campaign of the FRY government was met with increasing condemnation by the West. By late 1998, the US government was warning FRY President Milosevic that, if necessary, NATO would use force to bring about a settlement in Kosovo that would include significant autonomy for the province and its Albanian majority.[53] As a consequence, by mid-October 1998 KLA statements were identifying NATO as an ally, and suggested that this alliance was perceived mutually. In interviews with the KLA, Judah concluded that "[the KLA] aims to make sure that NATO troops are brought in to enforce any deal, because their presence will mean that the Serbs will no longer be able to fight – and defeat them."[54] Although there was a brief period in which NATO governments attempted to maintain a degree of impartiality, by early 1999 it was clear that the FRY government of Milosevic was being singled out as the main obstacle to peace.[55] The bias in favour of the Kosovars becomes even more apparent from this point forward. When NATO forces finally took action, it was directed entirely against the FRY government.

While establishing the direction of the intervenor's bias is fairly easy, it is far more difficult to judge the fighting efforts of the two sides in the Kosovo conflict. In the months preceding the actual NATO intervention, FRY troops were already engaged in an aggressive campaign to crush the KLA and maintain authority over Kosovo. As the disputant targeted by the intervenor, the model's preliminary intuition is that the FRY government would be expected to increase military efforts in the dispute from this already considerable level. This intensification of the war effort was indeed the stated plan of the FRY government. Just prior to the NATO offensive, Milosevic's top general, General Nebojsa Pavkovic, publicly declared that if NATO were to bomb Yugoslavia, he would move quickly and forcefully against the KLA in order to eliminate Yugoslavia's internal enemies and prepare for external attack.[56] NATO officials later noted that the Serb campaign inside Kosovo was done with precision and speed.[57] Posen describes the interaction amongst the combatants in language that is consistent with the model's prediction: "While NATO attacked Serbia, Serbia would attack the Kosovo Liberation Army."[58] The intensification of the FRY government's campaign in Kosovo is even more apparent in Freedman, who argues that the evidence is "reasonably conclusive. It is not the case that NATO air strikes prompted the campaign against the Kosovar Albanians. There is, however, no doubt that on 24 March [1999] it moved immediately to a new and unprecedented scale of ferocity."[59] The increase in FRY capacity and operations occurred despite the material damage that NATO air strikes inflicted. Byman and Waxman note that "the air campaign had not halted Serbia's infantry and artillery attacks nor prevented Milosevic from increasing the size of his forces in Kosovo."[60]

The response of the KLA to NATO's intervention is even more difficult to identify clearly due to the irregular nature of the KLA forces and tactics. The KLA forces were initially fairly small, though the 1998 campaign by Milosevic's troops in Kosovo had led to an increase in KLA support and strength. Its fighting capacity was also bolstered by the influx of weapons from Albania. The KLA's operations were primarily limited to the southern parts of Kosovo.[61]

At first glance it would appear as if the KLA stepped up its own efforts following the initial NATO air strikes. Freedman claims that the KLA met with growing success "in re-establishing themselves in Kosovo, with numbers put at up to 10,000 by the war's close."[62] Posen, and Byman and Waxman indicate that the KLA began a successful military offensive in May, after the NATO air strikes had started.[63]

An increase in the KLA's activities agrees with the model's preliminary predictions only under limited circumstances. First, the KLA's escalation would be consistent with the model if it was in reaction to the FRY offensive. Second, the information on the actual timing of activity is insufficient to be able to make a clear judgement about the relationship between the KLA's activities and NATO's air strikes. Most of the KLA activity appears to be during the last part of the war, just weeks before the agreement between Milosevic and NATO to end the conflict, and during the time when new life had been breathed into the FRY-NATO negotiations. Thus, part of the KLA tactics may have been linked to an anticipation of the agreement and the end of NATO's campaign against FRY forces.

Lessons From the Case Studies

The cases offer qualified support for the theoretical approach described here and developed more formally in Carment and Rowlands (2000). The cases also identify some important issues that future iterations of the model will have to take into account.

The Indian intervention into Sri Lanka provides perhaps the best support for the model of the two cases considered here. There is evidence that the targeted side of the intervention intensified its activity, while the side favoured by the intervenor reduced its combat efforts. The presence of a cease-fire arrangement suggests that there was a stable equilibrium immediately prior to the intervention, and that other dynamic factors in the conflict, thus, may have played a less critical role in determining subsequent behaviour.

However, the Sri Lankan case also offers a few challenges that are outside the scope of the model. On the Tamil side, the cease-fire and intervention also altered the conflict within Tamil groups themselves, with the LTTE using the cease-fire period to neutralize less radical Tamil groups. Second, the Sri Lankan army was forced to step up its campaign against Sinhalese extremists. Therefore the model's assumptions may need to incorporate or accommodate more complex relationships within the combatant groups, and to acknowledge that there may well be more than two combatants within a conflict.

The Kosovo case offers clear challenges for the model. While its results are consistent with the model, the finding is premised on indirect evidence of the effect of de-escalation by the intervention on the favoured group, in this case the KLA. The apparent increase in its activity may have been a reaction to FRY offensives, or may have been provoked at the end of the NATO intervention in anticipation of an agreement. There was a clear tactical interaction that began to emerge between the KLA and NATO. As Byman and Waxman note: "NATO air strikes and KLA attacks had synergistic effects. KLA ground offensives drew Serbian forces out of hiding, greatly increasing the lethality of air strikes. ... As one US Army general claimed, 'What you had, in effect, was the KLA acting as a surrogate ground force.'"[64] In a case such as Kosovo, therefore, where a small, lightly armed irregular force finds itself fighting against a much larger well-trained and well-equipped regular army, this kind of "synergistic" effect might be expected.

In the absence of support from an intervenor, the insurgents may simply be incapable of mounting a credible and sustained offensive, and such actions may simply be a dangerous exercise in futility. In conjunction with a substantial and sophisticated favourable intervention, however, escalation becomes a viable option. It should be noted that such an interaction represents the kind of empirically-based observation that can be used to generate more plausible and more complex propositions from the model.

To be sure, the KLA was in the process of absorbing increased financial and material support from outside Kosovo, suggesting that the KLA was already on a trajectory to escalate and that its past levels of military action were likely to have been severely constrained by the absence of weapons and other military material. The KLA was unlikely to have reached an equilibrium level of fighting effort prior to the intervention.

In both the Sri Lankan and Kosovo cases, there also appeared to be an important "rally around the flag" effect that animated the targeted combatants. Byman and Waxman claim that: "Initially the air strikes bolstered the Yugoslav president's stature. Belgrade hosted large rallies in support of Milosevic after the NATO air strikes began."[65] Later, they suggest that NATO "attacks also inflamed nationalist passions among other segments (especially in the short term), and Milosevic proved skilled at exploiting these passions with his propaganda machinery."[66] Smith notes a similar effect amongst the Tamils, with the LTTE leadership exploiting the IPKF's presence as a means of increasing its local support.[67] While these effects are consistent with the model, and may in effect be part of the political process implicit in the decision-making of the model's combatants, it may be necessary to consider their role more explicitly. In addition, a similar psychological effect may also act for weak combatants who are assisted by an intervention that may provide both a sense of legitimacy and hope.

Other challenges for this type of formal analysis are also apparent. A key extension lies in incorporating the intervention decision itself into the model, and relating it to the behaviour of the combatants. Astute leaders, aware that increased tensions may lead to outside involvement and subsequent escalation, might prefer a low intensity campaign effective enough to accomplish specific objectives without attracting outside attention. Fox notes that the Serbian-dominated government seemed to have calculated that as long as it kept its efforts below the level of ethnic cleansing, the world would focus on ending violence in Bosnia and tolerate repression in Kosovo.[68] This point is similarly argued by Shalom, who suggests that as long as Milosevic could oppress the Albanian minority without creating large refugee flows that might destabilize the region, Washington was uninterested in the Kosovo issue.[69] As one Western observer noted, "the new Serbian tactic was 'a village a day keeps NATO away.'"[70] Similarly, India's intervention was connected to prior escalation in the conflict.

Conclusions

This chapter began by questioning the popular perception that conflict intervention must be impartial. As the literature review suggested, however, there is no real consensus about the role or effect of bias in conflict management. In many instances an impartial intervention is simply out of the question: the decision to intervene in a conflict is highly political, and is often provoked by a perceived need to correct an apparently unjust situation. Intervenors may even need to demonize one side in a conflict (and glorify the other side) in order to create and maintain support for an intervention. Avoiding bias in these circumstances will be difficult.

Research on the role and effect of bias remains limited. In this chapter we provided a heuristic description to explore issues of intervention from a theoretical perspective. The simple and preliminary hypotheses associated with the model were then examined in the context of two case studies, Sri Lanka and Kosovo. The simple hypotheses were that biased intervention will induce a reduction in fighting effort by the favoured side, and an escalation on the part of the opposing combatant. However, the results are made more complex by the opposing indirect effects, wherein the escalation or de-escalation by one side induces a similar response from the opponent.

We conclude with this policy-relevant insight. If biased intervention can lead to escalation, that does not mean that modern peace enforcement operations should aim to preserve impartiality. To properly inform and prepare intervention forces it will be necessary to have a reasonable basis for predicting combatant responses. If escalation is likely, intervenors will need to be prepared politically, and will need to plan their military operations accordingly. The credibility of conflict management efforts may be severely damaged if intervention forces are withdrawn from a combat zone in the face of unanticipated opposition, as was the case in Somalia.

This chapter constitutes but one preliminary investigation into the value of developing a predictive capacity for explaining intervention outcomes. Such an approach could become a useful tool for the international community, and for understanding a central, but poorly understood, element of modern conflict management.

Notes

1 The authors would like to thank the Social Sciences and Humanities Research Council and the Norman Paterson School of International Affair's Security and Defence Forum program in providing financial assistance for this research. David Carment also acknowledges the assistance of the Program on Conflict Prevention and Intrastate Conflict at the Belfer Center, Harvard University. We are very grateful to Carmen Buchmann, Kevin Hamilton, and Shannon Leah Smith for research assistance.

2 Peter Wallensteen and Margareta Sollenberg, "Armed Conflict, Conflict Termination and Peace Agreements," *Journal of Peace Research* 34:4 (1997): pp. 339-358.; Dan Smith, "Trends and Causes of Armed Conflict," in *Berghof Handbook for Conflict Transformation*, ed. D. Smith (2000), www.b.shuttle.de/berghof/BHandbook/articles/Core/Smith/CF.htm.

3 "A Report of the Panel on United Nations Peace Operations," *The Brahimi Report,* United Nations (July 2000), www.un.org; *The International Commission on Intervention and State Sovereignty* (2000), www.iciss-ciise.gc.ca/background-e.asp.

4 Rotberg and Albaugh, among others, argue that the collective management of complex intrastate conflicts unfolds selectively, when those who have the capability to respond also have the motivation to respond. Robert Rotberg and Ericka A. Albaugh, "Preventing Conflict in Africa: Possibilities of Peace Enforcement," *World Peace Foundation Reports*, no. 24 (1999). For example, selective responses to the humanitarian crisis in Somalia resulted in a UN humanitarian mission there in 1992 and the creation of UNISOM II and UNITAF (the predecessor mission under US command) in 1993. Both missions used forceful measures, including the disarmament of militia in the absence of local consent. In 1995, air strikes and artillery were used to compel Serb belligerents to remove heavy weapons directed at safe havens in war-torn Bosnia, bringing to an end the four-year war there. Lake and Rothchild see evidence of a movement towards a norm of collective intervention in a wide range of situations, including genocide, interference with the delivery of relief, violation of ceasefire agreements, collapse of civil order, and irregular interruption of democratic governance. David A. Lake and Donald Rothchild, eds., *The International Spread of Ethnic Conflict: Fear Diffusion, and Escalation* (Princeton, NJ: Princeton University Press, 1998).

5 David Carment and Frank Harvey, *Using Force to Prevent Ethnic Violence* (Westport, CT: Praeger Press, 2000); Jacob Bercovitch, ed., *Resolving International Conflicts: Theory and Practice of Mediation* (Boulder: Lynne Rienner, 1996); Paul F. Diehl, J. Reifschneider and Paul R. Hensel, "United Nations Intervention and Recurring Conflict," *International Organization* 50 (1996); Patrick Regan, *Civil Wars and Foreign Powers: Outside Intervention in Intrastate Conflict* (Ann Arbour, MI: University of Michigan Press, 2000); Barbara Walter, "The Critical Barrier to Civil War Settlement," *International Organization* 51 (1997).

6 Dane Rowlands and David Carment, "Moral Hazard and Conflict Intervention," in *The Political Economy of War and Peace*, ed. Murray Wolfson (London: Kluwer Academic Publishers, 1998); Alan Kuperman, "The Other Lesson of Rwanda: Mediators Sometimes Do More Damage Than Good," *SAIS Review* 16 (Winter-Spring 1996); Alan Kuperman, "Transnational

Causes of Genocide: Or How the West Inadvertently Exacerbates Ethic Con-flict in the Post Cold War Era," paper resented at the Annual Meeting of the American Political Science Association, 2-5 September 1999, Atlanta, Georgia.

7 Patrick Regan, "Conditions for Successful Third-Party Intervention in Intra-state Conflicts," *Journal of Conflict Resolution* 40 (1996); Frank Harvey, "Deterrence Failure and Ethnic Conflict: The Case of Bosnia," in *Peace in the Midst of Wars: Preventing and Managing International Ethnic Conflicts*, eds. David Carment and Patrick James (Columbus: University of South Carolina Press, 1998).

8 David Carment and Dane Rowlands, "The Role of Bias in Third-Party Intervention: Theory and Evidence," unpublished mimeo, Carleton University, 2000.

9 This approach is consistent with that espoused by Marieke Kleiboer, "Understanding Success and Failure in International Mediation," *Journal of Conflict Resolution* 40 (1996), where she argues that modelling produces an incentive for more theory-driven empirical research, which, by her assessment, is more informative for the researcher and the policy maker.

10 Carment and Rowlands, "The Role of Bias in Third-Party Intervention."

11 James Boskey, "The Proper Role of the Mediator: Rational Assessment, Not Pressure," *Negotiation Journal* 10 (1994).

12 David E. Matz, "Mediator Pressure and Third-Party Autonomy: Are They Consistent with Each Other?" *Negotiation Journal* 10 (1994).

13 Peter J. Carnevale and Sharon Arad, "Bias and Impartiality in International Mediation," in *Resolving International Conflicts: Theory and Practice of Mediation,* ed. Jacob Bercovitch (Boulder: Lynne Rienner, 1996).

14 Apart from the idea of content and source bias, the term is used by many mediators to refer to the position and framing a mediator has on a particular issue. Bias is also informed by the prior relationship between the mediator, the substance of their proposals, and by the pressure the mediator applies to persuade the parties to accept an outcome.

15 Carnevale and Arad (1996) attempted to measure two factors against one another: the extent of mediator bias and the potential for future mediation, using university students as subjects assigned to represent hypothetical countries – two disputants and one as mediator. Their results indicate that mediators are able to alter their behavior in an effort to preserve their acceptability as mediator to the disputants, suggesting there may be two basis forms of bias in mediation: (1) bias of content, which pertains to the mediator's behavior and substance of their proposals, and (2) bias of source characteristics, which pertains to expectations that stem from a mediator's closer ties to one party over the other party. The authors are unable to say conclusively whether either form of bias has significant effects on judgment of the mediator and on the nature of the settlement proposals put forward.

16 For example, pro-Israeli participants in the Carnevale and Arad experiment tended to evaluate the proposal of the mediator based on whether it was favorable to their position, while neutral participants evaluated the same proposal based on its evenhandedness.

17 Kevin Gibson, Leigh Thompson and Max H. Bazerman, "Shortcomings of Neutrality in Mediation: Solutions Based on Rationality," *Negotiation Journal* 12 (1996).

18 Alan James, "Peacekeeping and Ethnic Conflict: Theory and Evidence," in *Peace in the Midst of Wars*, eds. David Carment and Patrick James (Columbia: University of South Carolina Press, 1998).

19 According to Ruggie, peacekeeping is an attempt to overcome a coordination problem between belligerents by enhancing transparency and establishing clearly defined rules of the game. Highly intense operations are compared to a game of chicken; an escalatory ladder of means up to and including war is used to "force an aggressor off its track." John Ruggie, "The

New US Peacekeeping Doctrine," *The Washington Quarterly* 17:4 (1994): p. 29. Lake and Rothchild argue that non-coercive interventions can be helpful in raising the costs of purely ethnic appeals and in structuring the incentives of group leaders prepared to accept international norms; but that, where conflicts are intense, exhortations and international warnings may not deter or end violence. Lake and Rothchild, eds., *The International Spread of Ethnic Conflict*.

20 Matthew Krain, "International Intervention and the Severity of Genocides and Politicides," paper presented at the Annual Meeting of the American Political Science Association, 2-5 September 1999, Atlanta, Georgia.

21 Krain also presents a threat model hypothesizing that threat perceptions on the part of the genocidal faction will mean that any outside intervention aimed at re-distributing resources will not impact upon the decision to undertake a program of mass killing. Krain, "International Intervention and the Severity of Genocides and Politicides."

22 Adam Roberts, "The Crisis in UN Peacekeeping," in *Managing Global Chaos: Sources of and Responses to International Conflict*, eds. Chester A. Crocker and Fen Osler Hampson (Washington, DC: United States Institute of Peace Press, 1996).

23 Evidence supporting this argument is provided by David Roberts who chronicles the experiences of the UN operation in Cambodia from 1991 to 1993, United Nations Transitional Authority in Cambodia (UNTAC). David Roberts, "More Honoured in the Breech: Consent and Impartiality in the Cambodian Peacekeeping Operation," *International Peacekeeping* 4 (1997). He shows that UN impartiality promoted conflict there. He argues that it is misleading to assess the mission on the basis of its relative success in implementing an electoral process. He claims that some analyses of the UN's Cambodian experience over-emphasize the significance of the technical aspects of the operation (logistics, communication, training, materiel deployment). David Roberts further argues that UNTAC fundamentally failed to maintain consent from the two core actors: the government in Phnom Penh and the Khmer Rouge. This loss of consent, he argues, severely hampered UNTAC's ability to implement its broad and sophisticated mandate, which was the largest and most expensive peacekeeping operation at the time.

24 Lake and Rothchild, eds., *The International Spread of Ethnic Conflict*; Andrew J. Enterline and Dylan Balch-Lindsay, "Talking in Time: A Competing Risks Analysis of Civil War Duration, Outcome and the Role of Third Parties, 1900-92," paper presented at the Annual Meeting of the American Political Science Association, 2-5 September 1999, Atlanta, Georgia; Richard K. Betts, "The Delusion of Impartial Intervention," in *Managing Global Chaos: Sources of and Responses to International Conflict*, eds. Chester Crocker and Fen Osler Hampson (Washington, DC: United States Institute of Peace Press, 1996); David Carment and Dane Rowlands, "Three's Company: Evaluating Third-Party Intervention in Intra-state Conflict," *Journal of Conflict Resolution* 42 (1998).

25 Betts uses the examples of UN intervention in Bosnia, US intervention in Somalia, and US and UN intervention in Haiti to underscore his argument. He argues that impartial intervention can work in more limited instances – such as the cease-fire mediation between Iran and Iraq and the political receivership of UNTAC – but that these instances prove only that impartiality works best where intervention is needed least, where wars have 'burned out' and the fighting factions need only the good offices of mediators to end the fighting formally. Betts, "The Delusion of Impartial Intervention."

26 In contrast, Luttwak argues that intervention, and especially peacekeeping, disallows for the possibility of a decisive conclusion, or the true exhaustion of the parties to the dispute, which would allow them to seek a sincere agreement for a denouement. Edward N. Luttwak, "Give War a Chance," *Foreign Affairs* 78:4 (1999).

27 Enterline and Balch-Lindsay, "Talking in Time."

28 Carment and Rowlands, "Three's Company."

29 It is possible for the third-party to begin an intervention in one of three ways. The first is to remain aloof from the conflict without any military involvement. The tasks here include mediation, fact finding, preventive diplomacy and sanctions. The second strategy commits troops to a low intensity conventional peacekeeping mission. The final strategy is to engage in forceful intervention requiring substantial and favorable military capabilities.

30 Carment and Rowlands conclude that intensive initial interventions are more likely to result in cooperative outcomes. They also claim that their model identifies certain low-intensity interventions can generate desirable solutions – namely in the case of highly salient conflicts with weak combatants and high gains. The Carment and Rowlands model also shows that intensive interventions will not always work, especially when third-party credibility is low; and the model demonstrates scenarios in which it is better to let the conflict run its course rather than intervening. Carment and Rowlands, "Three's Company."

31 Lake and Rothchild, eds., *The International Spread of Ethnic Conflict.*

32 Luttwak, "Give War a Chance."

33 This is supported by an assessment by International Crisis Group: "The sad lesson from Bosnia is that reconciliation between former foes cannot be expected for years. The war produced no clear result, unlike in 1945, to allow for some form of de-Nazification and a completely fresh start." "Let's Learn from Bosnia," International Crisis Group (May 17 1999), www.crisisweb.org.

34 I. William Zartman and Saadia Touval, "International Mediation in the Post-Cold War Era," in *Managing Global Chaos: Sources of and Responses to International Conflict*, eds. Chester A. Cocker and Fen Osler Hampson (Washington, DC: United States Institute of Peace Press, 1996); Michael Watkins and Kim Winters, "Intervenors with Interests and Power," *Negotiation Journal* 13 (1997). Others who have argued in favour of a biased approach include Ruggie who suggests that outside forces should gradually escalate in order to dissuade, deny and deter an ascendant force, citing evidence from Bosnia he argues that the conflict would have ended more quickly had force been used decisively earlier on (Ruggie, "The New US Peacekeeping Doctrine"); Saideman who focuses on spoilers to peace process (Stephen Saideman, "Explaining the International Relations of Secessionist Conflicts: Vulnerability Versus Ethnic Ties," *International Organization* 51:4 (1997); Harvey who suggests that the use of force is appropriate when coupled with basic tenets of deterrence when signals to use force are credible and the third-party shows resolve and commitment (Harvey, "Deterrence Failure and Ethnic Conflict"); and Regan who uses game theoretic insights in which incen-tives/ disincentives are used to alter the belligerents expected utility namely the benefits accrued form using force (Regan, "Conditions for Successful Third-Party Intervention in Intra-state Conflicts"). For Zartman and Touval, power is the basis for this process. Power translates into leverage in the form of persuasion, extraction (producing a favourable outcome for each party); termination (the ability to withdraw from a negotiation); deprivation (the ability to affect a hurting stalemate by withholding resources from one side or shift them to another); and gratification (the ability to add resources to the outcome). They emphasize that inter-venors make as much of a calculation based on interest in deciding to mediate as is the case for adversarial parties when deciding to engage in war.

35 Carment and Rowlands, "The Role of Bias in Third-Party Intervention."

36 Rowlands and Carment, "Moral Hazard and Conflict Intervention." For models evaluating the specific effects of mediator bias and informational problems, see Andrew Kydd, "Whose

Side Are You On? Mediation as Cheap Talk," unpublished manuscript, Harvard University, November 2000.

37 Gary Becker, "A Theory of Competition Among Pressure Groups for Political Influence," *Quarterly Journal of Economics* 98:3 (1983); Murray Wolfson, "A Three-Party Model of World Conflict," in *Essays on the Cold War*, ed. Murray Wolfson (London: MacMillan, 1992); and especially Jack Hirshleifer, "The Analytics of Continuing Conflict," *Synthese* 76:2 (1988) and "Anarchy and its Breakdown," *Journal of Political Economy* 103:1 (1995).

38 Carment and Rowlands, "The Role of Bias in Third-Party Intervention."

39 Rowlands and Carment, "Moral Hazard and Conflict Intervention."

40 Shatha Hennayake, "The Peace Accord and the Tamils in Sri Lanka," *Asian Survey* 29:4 (1989): p. 407.

41 Dennis Austin, *Democracy and Violence in India and Sri Lanka* (London: Royal Institute of International Affairs, 1995): p. 73; David Carment and Patrick James, "Two-level Games and Third-Party Intervention: Evidence from Ethnic Conflict in the Balkans and South Asia," *Canadian Journal of Political Science* 29:3 (1996).

42 S. D. Muni, *Pangs of Proximity: India and Sri Lanka's Ethnic Crisis* (New Delhi: Sage Publications and International Peace Research Institute, 1993), p. 127; Carment and James, "Two-level Games and Third-Party Intervention."

43 Hennayake, "The Peace Accord and the Tamils in Sri Lanka."

44 Austin, *Democracy and Violence in India and Sri Lanka*, p. 74.

45 Muni, *Pangs of Proximity*, p. 126.

46 Carment and James, "Two-level Games and Third-Party Intervention."

47 Chris Smith, "South Asia's Enduring War," in *Creating Peace in Sri Lanka: Civil War and Reconciliation*, ed. Robert Rotberg (Washington D.C.: Brookings Institution Press, 1999), p. 19.

48 Hennayake, "The Peace Accord and the Tamils in Sri Lanka," p. 413.

49 Bryan Johnson, "Tamils Warned Against Relying on Presence of India Army," *The Globe and Mail*, 22 September 1988, p. A18.

50 *SIPRI Yearbook of World Armaments and Disarmament* (Stockholm: Stockholm International Peace Research Institute, 1999).

51 Quoted in Chris Hedges, "Kosovo's Next Masters?" *Foreign Affairs* 78:3 (1999), p. 36.

52 While FRY forces claimed to have "destroyed the core" of the KLA at this time, more independent reports noted that the actions appeared to have "swelled their ranks beyond belief." Nened Sebak, "The KLA: Terrorists or Freedom Fighters?" BBC World News, 28 June 1998. A reporter who spent time with the KLA, Judah noted that "following violent events in the Drenica region [in late winter/early spring 1998] the KLA suddenly found itself in command of an uprising." Tim Judah, "The KLA: Out From the Shadows," BBC World News, 24 March 1999. Others concurred: "no one disputes the fact that since the first Serbian operation against them in March, the KLA's influence has grown." Oana Lungescu, "The KLA: A Dilemma for the West," BBC World News, 30 June 1998. British Foreign Secretary Robin Cook was quoted as saying that Milosevic's tactics had backfired, leaving the KLA in control of more territory, with greater strength and more money. Lungescu, "The KLA: A Dilemma for the West." These observations are clearly consistent with the model's prediction of how combatants react to the behaviour of their opponents.

53 United States Information Agency, 9 October 1998, www.usia.gov/kosovo/texts/archive.htm.

54 Judah, "The KLA: Out From the Shadows."

55 United States Information Agency, 20 February 1999, www.usia.gov/kosovo/texts/archive.htm. Upon successfully bringing the KLA on board in agreement to sign, it was thought that

perhaps the Serbs would be less intransigent, and more willing to negotiate. Perhaps in this belief, it was claimed by Chris Hill, one of the Rambouillet mediators, that the negotiators would have accepted a force under "any suitable disguise" by this point. Tim Judah, "Inside the KLA," *New York Review of Books* 46:10 (1999): p. 20. If this is true, at this time, in early March, NATO was sending (private) signals that were somewhat more flexible/conciliatory than they had been seen January. Milosevic, though, would not engage the issue. In any case, by 18 March 1999, and with the futile second talks of Rambouillet behind them, diplomatic efforts aimed at securing FRY acceptance of the deal were replaced by warnings to the FRY that NATO action was likely if it did not change its stance. *Kosovo Historical Background*, Department of National Defence, Government of Canada, 1999, www.dnd.ca/eng/archive/apr99/Kosovo1_b_e.htm.

56 Jeffrey R. Smith and William Drozdiak, "Serbs' Offensive Was Meticulously Planned," *Washington Post*, 11 April 1999, p. A01.

57 Ibid.

58 Barry Posen, "The War for Kosovo: Serbia's Political-Military Strategy," *International Security* 24:4 (2000): p. 53.

59 Lawrence Freedman, "Victims and Victors: Reflections on the Kosovo War," *Review of International Studies* 26:3 (2000): p. 352.

60 Daniel Byman and Matthew Waxman, "Kosovo and the Great Air Power Debate," *International Security* 24:4 (2000): p. 24.

61 Freedman, "Victims and Victors," p. 351.

62 Ibid., p. 355.

63 Posen, "The War for Kosovo," p. 64 and Byman and Waxman, "Kosovo and the Great Air Power Debate," p. 24.

64 Byman and Waxman, "Kosovo and the Great Air Power Debate," p. 29.

65 Ibid., p. 19.

66 Ibid., p. 22.

67 Smith, "South Asia's Enduring War," p. 19.

68 Jonathan Fox, "Albanians in the Region of Kosovo," *Minorities at Risk,* 1995, www.bsos.umd.edu/cidcm.

69 Stephen R. Shalom, "Reflections on NATO and Kosovo," *New Politics* 7:3 (1999), www.wilpaterson.edu/~newpol/issue27/shalom27.htm.sto

70 *SIPRI Yearbook of World Armaments and Disarmament* (Stockholm: Stockholm International Peace Research Institute, 1999), p. 57.

Chapter 6

Twisting Arms or Shaking Hands? How to Put Peacekeepers Out of Business[1]

David Last

"What I say is that 'just' or 'right' means nothing but what is in the interest of the stronger party."

Thracymachus[2]

"The strongest is never strong enough always to be master, unless he transforms force into right and obedience into duty."

Jean-Jacques Rousseau[3]

There is a great deal of talk in military circles about end-states and exit-strategies, campaign plans and civil-military cooperation. But the implications of these big ideas may be lost on some of the generals who disingenuously call themselves "simple soldiers" while walking with presidents. If lasting peace is the fruit of victory, it comes not from war fighting, but from peacebuilding. Peacebuilding is about human development in secure communities. But the secret of peacebuilding is that it cannot be forced: twisting arms alone does not work and flexing muscles can be counterproductive. Soldiers may plan military campaigns and participate in peacekeeping, but they cannot lead in peacebuilding. Instead, lasting peace depends on balancing external pressures and building peace gradually from the bottom up. Without peacebuilding, peacekeepers become guardians of stagnant conflicts that periodically erupt. Effective peacebuilding puts peacekeepers out of business and sends them home.

This chapter argues that top-down processes in establishing lasting peace emphasize regional stability, balances of power, the positioning of key allies, and the interests of external parties. While these may be necessary, they are not sufficient conditions for lasting peace. If communities are not rebuilt from the bottom-up, intervention efforts are largely wasted. Drawing on examples from Bosnia this chapter illustrates some of the practical implications of bottom-up peacebuilding for the military players in modern peacekeeping. To put themselves out of business, military peacekeepers must become adept at fulfilling appropriate, and necessarily subordinate, roles in four distinct requirements for national reconstruction: security, governance, development and reconciliation.

What is "Peacebuilding"?

To begin, "peacebuilding" itself is defined as the long process of returning a society to conditions of just and stable peace. The Canadian Peacebuilding Coordinating Committee defines it as:

> … the effort to promote human security in societies marked by conflict. The overarching goal of peacebuilding is to strengthen the capacity of societies to manage conflict without violence, as means to achieve sustainable human security.[4]

Recent work by US Air Force Colonel Michael Dziedzic puts this in context for Balkan reconstruction. He describes a three-track process defined by social relations, institutional capacity and rule of law. Peacebuilding helps a state to move from conditions of social violence, disorder and institutional incapacity, to an orderly state under the rule of law. In this orderly state, disputes are resolved peacefully, government institutions are accountable to the public, and public and private institutions have the capacity to meet individual and social needs.[5] Dziedzic's work is a practical application to institutions of earlier concepts of peacebuilding that emphasized relationships. As Betts Fetherston, a British peace researcher, argues, peacebuilding offers a theoretical framework that helps us understand the objectives of peacekeeping and conflict resolution interventions.[6] Her analysis puts Colonel Dziedzic's pragmatic prescription into perspective. Social violence is structural as well as physical.[7] Reforming social relations and rebuilding institutional capacity and rule of law is not a simple question of replicating institutions that work in peaceful societies. Building a courthouse, appointing a judge, putting uniforms on policemen, and developing civil law codes, for example, does not add up to a working legal system. These institutions will succeed or fail depending on how individuals and groups handle conflicts. In this respect, Fetherston revives John Burton's concept of "provention," whereby the conflict must be explained precisely and in all of its human complexity in order that it lead to cooperation.[8] Thus, Dziedzic's concept of building orderly societies must be accompanied by a serious consideration of the social and structural relations that led to the violence in the first place.

Peacebuilding is the reverse of the "funnel" that drags societies into protracted conflict, as described by sociologist Louis Kriesberg. In this respect, an underlying conflict situation emerges out of inter-party relations when the parties begin to perceive themselves as adversaries who desire opposing goals. As the parties communicate with one another and pursue their conflicting goals, social conflict becomes manifested and contention occurs, escalating into coercion and, ultimately, destructive conflict.[9] Thus, peacebuilding attempts to reverse this process, an exceedingly difficult exercise and which accounts for the difficulties faced by many recent peacekeeping missions.

It follows that peacebuilding efforts must meet several requirements. First, people must feel safe before the means of violence will be relinquished. Second, good governance and civil society must be instituted to allow the peaceful resolution of disputes and to provide an alternate means of influencing decisions that affect people's lives. Third, there must be relief and development to remove some of the economic causes of conflict and the pressures of inter-group competition that exacerbate conflict. Finally, there must be reconciliation to make it possible for neighbours to live together again. This last component may be at the heart of peacebuilding, though it can be the most difficult to initiate. The peacebuilding requirements suggested above – security, governance, relief and development, and reconciliation – constitute a framework of inter-related objectives that support national reconstruction. Interestingly, joint military doctrine in general and NATO in particular identify four instruments of influence, political, military, economic, and social-psychological, that may lend themselves to supporting each of the four requirements of reconstruction.[10] For instance, the military instrument corresponds to the requirement for security, the economic instrument to relief and development, and so on. However, it would be misleading to draw such conclusions. More specifically, and as this chapter emphasizes, the military instrument is only a small, and certainly not the most important, part of the problem of re-establishing post-war communal security. Instead, all four instruments, whether found indigenously or internationally, *inter alia* permeate the four requirements for peacebuilding and national reconstruction.

Security

When the international community first intervenes in a protracted social conflict, it must do so with sufficient force to guarantee all the parties to the conflict that, first, they cannot achieve their objectives by force and second, they will not be subject to attack. It follows that the size and capability of the force needed to provide this guarantee will be balanced against the extent to which the parties co-operate. Much of the literature over the last decade on selective intervention, coercive diplomacy, and wider peacekeeping strategy addresses this balance between the military dimensions of intervention and political cooperation.[11] For instance, Steven Ratner's excellent account of "new peacekeeping" deals largely with the relationship between international legal and in-country military aspects of peacekeeping missions.[12]

At the same time, in many of these works there is a growing recognition of the importance of a civilian police force in national reconstruction, indicating the beginning of a more sophisticated understanding of the nature of communal security and its role as a foundation for durable peace. In this respect, while military forces are effective guarantors of military security against organized military opposition, they are far less so against riots and civilian disturbances such as the ones experienced in Bosnia when the refugees tried to go home. Military forces are impotent in the face of bricks through windows or threatening telephone calls in the night. Thus, a functioning civilian police force is needed as early as possible in a peacebuilding and peacekeeping mission.[13]

However, international civilian police missions generally do not have the power to arrest or detain – known as "original jurisdiction." Their mandate usually is to monitor and assist the local police, providing training on human rights and community policing.

When the local police obstruct the process or violate the agreements, as the Serb Republic police did in Banja Luka in 1998, the international police monitors may call upon the military to shut down a police station, seize illegal weapons, or take action to ensure public safety. In such instances, the international military force serves as a backup to decrease violence to levels where effective civilian police can be effective.

Moreover, there is a gap in the security capabilities of the police and military forces. For instance, police officers work in small numbers, usually alone or with a partner, directly with the community. They rely on the cooperation of the community and the salutary impact of presence and example to encourage socially appropriate behaviour in individuals.[14] In their normal pattern of employment, they are not well placed to deal with large-scale organized violence or protest. In contrast, military forces are usually organized in large formations from similarly structured and equipped forces specifically for organized violence. As a point of illustration, early in the planning phases for its intervention in Bosnia, NATO identified the existence of a "security gap" because of the potential for organized violence by and amongst civilians.

Thus, when third parties expect to assume responsibility for security, they must be prepared to engage the full spectrum of security organizations – military, paramilitary, and police. This is a lesson that has not been lost on commanders and force planners in the Balkans. The United Nations Transitional Authority in Eastern Slavonia (UNTAES) included a company of riot police to manage the security gap.[15] NATO's Stabilization Force (SFOR) eventually established the Multinational Specialized Unit (MSU) to handle political riots and civil disturbances that threatened to derail the implementation of the Dayton accords.[16]

Governance

However, police do not operate in a vacuum. Their responsibilities and duties must be supported by honest courts, uncorrupted judges, and fair laws, which in turn require a functioning government. As a result, in countries where societies and human security have utterly broken down such as Bosnia, Somalia, Sierra Leone, and other places, soldiers and gendarmes are faced with a challenge that goes far beyond the physical security they can help provide. If third parties are to support security, they must also support effective governance, which involves both a government and a civil society to balance it.[17] Beyond government and civil society, good governance requires a safe social space in which issues are debated. It may also be necessary to repair or replace the social infrastructure of democratic governance, such as a free media, freedom to associate, and community leaders free of fear.

In this respect, while military security formations are useful against direct physical violence, they are less so for promoting sustainable good governance that would allow effective community policing and the slow process of national reconstruction. While Galtung's "negative peace," or the absence of physical violence, might be achieved coercively by imposing peacekeeping forces, this can only be a temporary measure and is never very satisfactory. Moreover, while mature military forces with flexible and innovative commanders sometimes have worked effectively with civilian police, civil administrators, medical and humanitarian organizations to build the "positive peace" of a stable and equitable social order, the role of soldiers, however, is largely marginal. Indeed, a heavy foreign military presence can impede even, rather than support, democratic governance.

Relief and Development

The process of restoring security and developing governance and civil society takes years. In Guatemala, both are still at issue several years after the 1994 peace settlement. In Bosnia, while security has improved, governance and civil society are dubious since the 1995 Dayton Accord. In this case, the international community is still providing emergency relief to uprooted populations, while trying to help reconstruct essential infrastructure and develop an equitable market economy.[18]

Extremism and violence thrive on poverty and human suffering. Although the specifics vary across cultures and conflicts, refugee camps and uprooted populations provide recruiting grounds for extremists, and desperate circumstances can lead to violent solutions. While poverty by itself may not engender violence, the frustration and inequity that are generated as a result are significant influences. Thus, to repair such inequities calls have been made for "humanitarian" intervention for its own sake or as part of a larger peacebuilding strategy. However, the debacles of humanitarian strategies in Somalia, Bosnia, and Rwanda demand caution in this regard. In Somalia, the control of aid became a strategic asset fought over by rival clans. In Bosnia, food and material aid fuelled the war effort and may have prolonged the conflict. In Rwanda, extremist control of humanitarian assistance camps supported the *génocidaires* and spilled the conflict over to affect neighbouring Zaire.[19] Nonetheless, although humanitarian assistance might have a benign effect on conflict, it is still a vital part of a broader peacebuilding strategy.

Likewise, the effectiveness of initial relief and longer-term development will influence whether demobilized soldiers peacefully reintegrate into post-war society or turn to banditry and renewed fighting. In other words, development shapes the long-term prospects for peace. In this respect, warfare and social violence based on economic classes and ethnicity will recur if development replicates and extends the structural violence that generated it in the first place.

Reconciliation

When communities have experienced severe mistreatment by those against whom they were fighting, as in Bosnia, El Salvador, Guatemala, South Africa, and other places, third party assistance is needed to help them become reconciled to living and working together again. Mennonite peace researcher and practitioner, John Paul Lederach, describes reconciliation as the juncture of peace, mercy, justice and truth.[20] In general, however, reconciliation is difficult to apply. For instance, "truth" and "justice" are addressed by war crimes trials. And indeed, the cruelty of civil war implicates large parts of the population and perhaps most of the political leadership of each faction in acts that might be construed as criminal. However, the threat of war crimes trials can keep extremists fighting or in hiding, thereby dragging out the process of reconciliation.[21] In contrast, whereas "truth" and "mercy" are found in the Central American and South African truth commissions, they depend heavily on a shared Christian culture of forgiveness and reconciliation, which may not work as well in situations where cultural and religious differences are part of the structure of the conflict.[22] Moreover, the preservation of "peace" in the form of an absence of physical violence can become an over-riding objective that ultimately undermines both truth and justice. In this respect, the reluctance of international forces to arrest war criminals in Bosnia speaks volumes.

Reconciliation, whether secular or religious, is ultimately a matter for *individual* consciences and psyches. Like peacebuilding itself, reconciliation cannot be forced or imposed. No external power can coerce people or communities to be reconciled to crimes or injustices of the past. It follows from this that inter-communal reconciliation must begin with individuals and work up to encompass society. However, in order to encourage and nurture this process, some structures such as war crimes trials and truth commissions, restitution committees, and avenues for inter-communal dialogue must be set up. And these structures to one extent or another need the support of external intervention.[23]

Directing Reconstruction From the Top

These four components of post-conflict reconstruction or peacebuilding, i.e. security, good governance, relief and development, reconciliation, are not separate, but rather intricately interconnected. More specifically, the genuine security of individuals in communities requires effective governance, an accepted body of laws and civilian control over police, paramilitary and military forces. Good governance and civil society require equitable social and economic development, which may be impossible until urgent relief needs have been met. While such dangers exist in the form of relief eclipsing or distorting development and inequitable patterns of development impeding reconciliation, thereby undermining security, and preventing effective governance, ultimately, the reconciliation of socio-economic groups and geographic regions is a prerequisite for development. Therefore, all four components must be supported.

However, this is a challenge for third parties already divided over basic objectives, regional strategies, and questions of national interest. Moreover, they may attempt to impose military stability, even though lasting peace ultimately depends on the belligerent parties. Adding to the complexity is the abundance of international organizations and non-governmental organizations (NGOs) in these situations, such as in Bosnia. Thus, peacebuilding requires more than a military plan in support of political objectives. In this respect, Professor Gene Dewey of the National Defence University advocates "comprehensive campaign planning" which includes multiple annexes that attempt to reconcile (or at least describe) the plans of other interested agencies involved in a theatre of operations. Among these he lists the United Nations

High Commission for Refugees (UNHCR), the United Nations Children's Emergency Fund (UNICEF), the United Nations High Commission for Human Rights (UNHCHR), the World Food Program (WFP), the World Bank's reconstruction plan, and the United Nations Civilian Police (UNCIVPOL).[24]

However, most people involved in peacebuilding never see a comprehensive campaign plan, or any of its annexes. For most peacekeeping missions, such planning with a multi-year horizon is a vague concept. Moreover, soldiers attending coordination conferences are outnumbered by civilians. Participants might see some of the actual documents authorizing the specific mission, such as United Nations (UN) Security Council resolutions or peace agreements such as the Dayton Accord, but these focus on civilian activities. As a result, day-to-day military planning at the tactical level is guided by other documents, such as the SFOR commander's guidance for civil-military implementation. Such guides may include a list of broad priorities that reflect the stage of the mission at that time. For instance, the guide issued by Commander SFOR in 1998 included such military priorities as physical security, restarting the economy, de-mining, restoration of effective policing, return of displaced people and refugees, support to elections, and regional arms control.[25]

At the tactical level, many different influential factors operate, including the political-military plan for the given country. For instance, funds from the Department of International Development may be dispensed by a British military commander supporting demobilization. Likewise, the privatization policies of the World Bank and conditions imposed by the International Monetary Fund (IMF) shape the environment in which he must obtain his objectives.[26] In this respect, the potential impact of the US must be acknowledged since, with 17 per cent of the votes, it controls the largest single block of voting shares and drawing rights in the World Bank and the power to appoint its president who is one of 24 executive directors.[27] Nevertheless, while US government decision-making is complex, and it is difficult to predict US policy decisions, or reconcile those decisions with a military commander's understanding of the world, the US is only one of many actors engaged in a mission. Other actors include international organizations whose large memberships turn its decision-making processes into cumbersome compromises. And the multiple internal agencies of these organizations confuse matters further. For instance, the activities of the Organization for Security and Cooperation in Europe (OSCE) democratization branch and UNHCR human rights monitors reflect the different perspectives of their organizations. Moreover, the view of the world in general and of a distant mission in particular is as different in Brussels, Washington and Tokyo as is the political-diplomatic from the military within these capitals. Thus, top-down formulations of post-war reconstruction plans reflect these divergent views.

As a result, a strategic balance between military and civilian and between the competing interests of the contributing states and organizations must be struck. In theatre various fora are established to accomplish this. For example, in Bosnia the weekly meeting of the "Group Principals" in Sarajevo, chaired by the Office of the High Representative, not only attempts to coordinate the variety of activities in Bosnia, but does so while considering the pressures of the organizations operating there. The

UN, the OSCE, NATO, the European Union (EU) and the IMF all cast a long shadow. Moreover, the parties to the conflict try to influence these organizations to achieve their own ends.[28] Thus, the top-down management of peacebuilding entails not only the coordination of many in-theatre organizations, but also monitoring international and domestic forces that could support or derail the peace. It follows that the success of a political-military plan devised out of theatre depends on the ability of players in theatre to balance the pressures from many different organizations who are influencing events.

However, the international mission itself is unlikely to be a monolithic entity either. Even comparatively uncontroversial missions, such as the United Nations Transition Assistance Group (UNTAG) in Namibia (1989), with a coherent command structure and a single forum in theatre headquarters to reconcile political and military objectives, have to contend with autonomous UN agencies and self-mandated NGOs. More complex missions have no such coherent structure. In Bosnia, the Group Principals representing seven separate organizations meet weekly. The "Principals" then issue separate directives to their respective organization. Moreover, since each organization is hierarchical, not all the directives reach all the way down to the local level. The result is a situation such as that at the headquarters in Sarajevo featuring pronounced differences in perspective as each organization pursues its objectives locally but in response to external pressures. In this respect, Brussels or New York may be closer to Sarajevo than Banja Luka or Tuzla in Bosnia's provinces.

At the tactical level an officer may be assigned tasks he/she is ill-prepared to understand, let alone undertake. Vague mission mandates requiring particular skills, such as "encourage refugee return," "create a secure environment," "support the development of local businesses," do not encourage or involve easily achievable projects. In many cases soldiers lack such important skills as knowledge of the local language, an understanding of cause and effect when violence erupts, knowledge of the players, and other vital information that civilians may possess. Thus, while working in towns and communities to consolidate peace, both soldiers and civilians enter into complex, inter-organizational alliances and coalitions to make their missions more achievable. For instance, military forces might offer civilian groups protection, patrols, logistical support, or perhaps even management of aid money from the Canadian International Development Agency (CIDA), United States Agency for International Development (USAID) or another national equivalent.

In contrast to the divergent objectives evident in principal centres such as Sarajevo, the problems faced by people working at lower levels (in provincial towns, villages or rural areas) are more common. Concepts such as "security," "return" and "economic recovery" have very specific and local meanings, facilitating an overlap of organizational objectives at this level as was demonstrated most dramatically in the Bosnian Refugee Return Task Forces established at the regional level under the OSCE in March 1998. In this instance, while agreement could be reached among the individual task forces about what needed to be done, higher-level officials in Sarajevo could not be convinced. Thus, a carefully worked out plan for the return of Serbs to Drvar, which involved the provision of security by SFOR, support from the United Nations Development Program (UNDP) and UNHCR was upset when UNHCR

Sarajevo issued conflicting instructions. Similar problems are known to occur elsewhere such as in Guatemala.

Building Peace from the Bottom Up

The actual process of building peace from the bottom up is not without evident challenges at the micro-level. Among the most critical is the lack of *local* partners to share, if not carry, the burden of peacebuilding. Ultimately, none of the four requirements of peacebuilding can be achieved by outsiders, whether in or out of uniform. Community building is an intensely local affair, and only locals can accomplish it. If the process falls short of its objective, all of the top-down political-military planning serves to entrench the third-party interveners as an occupying force. Military forces have severe limitations, even when it comes to providing security, as evident in the individual criminality and mob violence that continue to impede reconstruction in Kosovo and in the border areas that have become havens for armed guerrillas threatening neighbouring Macedonia.[29]

What is needed at the local level to implement a complex peacebuilding mission? Many of the skills and tasks are fairly common in large organizations, including armies. Running meetings, developing leaders, assessing needs, and integrating services are tasks frequently performed by civil affairs officers in many armies, by UN Civil Affairs, or NGOs like CARE International or World Vision. But in an environment of fear and hatred, simple tasks such as running a meeting can become insurmountable obstacles. Rebuilding relationships across boundaries and divides, encouraging and supporting locals to take action, and overcoming mistrust require "therapeutic" skills that are rather specialized. These skills not only take a long time to develop, but also they take time to apply. For instance, NGOs may work in a region for years or decades before they can begin to accomplish their full potential.

Although some soldiers may have a natural or acquired flare for the skills involved in community level peacebuilding, they operate at an impossible disadvantage. Few, if any, will have the language and cultural knowledge necessary to work effectively with the local population. None will stay long enough to build up the relationships that make sustained peacebuilding work. Much of their daily activities is incidental to the central business of rebuilding communities.

Figure 6.1 shows how various personal problems labeled "other" comprised the largest single category during a fifteen day period of visits by the local population to the SFOR Civil-Military Cooperation house in Banja Luka. These are problems for which soldiers are not prepared. As a result, most cases are referred to another actor or denied assistance, leading to frustration on the part of the soldiers because they do not have reliable and moderate local partners to deal with these intractable cases.[30] In this respect, during the escalation of the conflict moderates were deliberate targets, often by their own side.[31] Thus, although present, moderates are reluctant to cooperate with third parties to support peace because of the serious risks they face. However, without moderates in every local community committed to peace, the entire process of post-conflict reconstruction grinds to a halt.

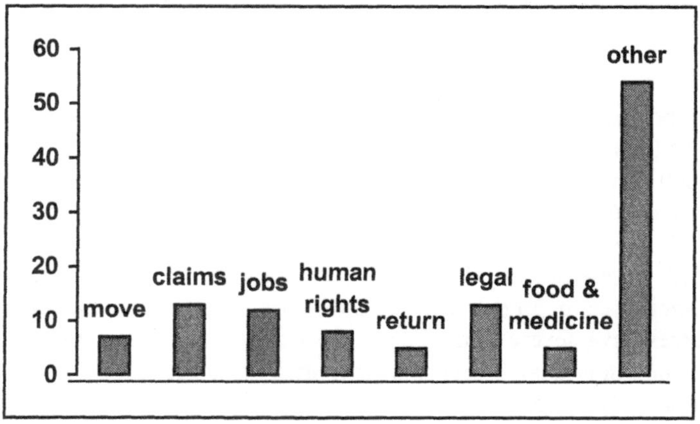

Source: SFOR House logs, Banja Luka, excluding projects and information campaign material, over 15 days

Figure 6.1 Appeals to SFOR, January 1998

In one attempt to correct this problem and promote the role of the local communities in peacebuilding efforts, from November 1997 to June 1998 the Pearson Peacekeeping Centre in Canada collaborated with Conflict Resolution Catalysts (CRC), a small US-based NGO, to experiment with local peacebuilding initiatives in a project called the Neighbourhood Facilitators Project (NFP). Directed by Gary Shapiro, an experienced international peace activist, the project's objective was to identify ways in which barriers to peace could be overcome at the community level. Its central premise was the importance of developing a range of interpersonal skills for facilitation, consensus-building, and enhancing communication. The CRC in 1997 with funding from USAID and US Institute for Peace (USIP), CRC trained twenty Bosnians of Serbian, Croatian, Muslim, and mixed ethnic backgrounds, ranging from twenty year old university students to sixty year old refugees. Most of this training was in interpersonal skills, i.e. listening, consensus building, group-facilitation, and overcoming mistrust. In December 1997 the Pearson Peacekeeping Centre worked with CRC to train nineteen international facilitators, and selected five for deployment to Bosnia. The most innovative and potentially valuable aspect of the project was the combination of mixed-ethnicity local and international facilitators in small problem-solving teams, who would work to build communications across ethnic and communal lines, and empower individuals to solve their own problems. The NFP had a project director in North America, responsible to a board and to donors, as well as to local "ownership" through a Bosnian project coordinator who worked with his international counterpart. However, the local board of directors could not function effectively and there were persistent problems with funding, eventually causing the project to close down in June 1998.[32]

In another aspect of NFP's contribution, in February 1998 Bosnian and international facilitators were brought together to establish in Northwest Bosnia a community centre with mobile teams working out of Banja Luka. The significance of this initiative is noted whereby this was a region in which some of the worst ethnic cleansing had occurred in 1992. During the course of the war and following the Dayton accord, the region was flooded with successive waves of Serb refugees from Western Slavonia, the Krajina, Western Bosnia, Sarajevo, and Eastern Slavonia. Following Dayton there was increasing international pressure to permit the return of Catholic and Muslim refugees and displaced people. Despite the extremism during the war, the region retained a multi-ethnic make up, and some acceptance of a multi-ethnic future amongst the younger generation.

Careful records and individual facilitator journals document the number and types of cases managed by the NFP community centre project (see Figure 6.2). In particular, economic appeals related to employment and micro-credit – especially in the months

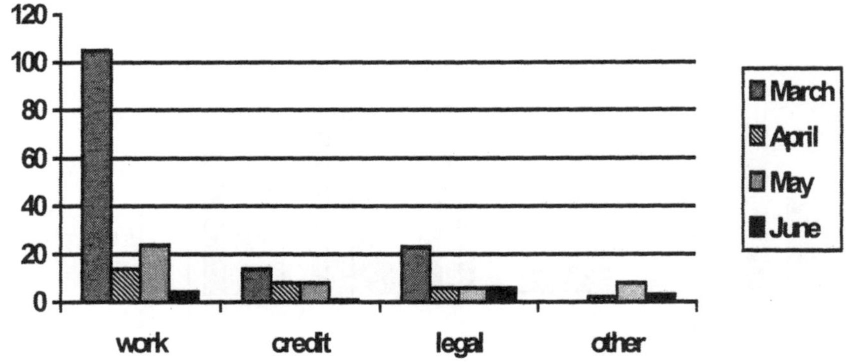

Figure 6.2 NFP Community Centre Project, Number and Types of Cases 1998

immediately after the centre opened – were dominant. One of the centre's early successes was to help a group of displaced people and ex-soldiers establish a business cooperative and apply for micro-credit to the UNDP, providing an excellent example of the social component necessary for economic reconstruction.

The economic character of many of the visits does not reveal NFP's full contribution to peacebuilding. Based on the narrative reports submitted by facilitators, each case can be characterized according to the four requirements of peacebuilding: security, governance, relief and development, and reconciliation. Reconciliation can be represented physically by the return to former communities of refugees and internally displaced persons (IDPs) from which they were expelled and who reside with others in the community. However, reconciliation must be understood to differ significantly from other more hostile situations where the returning formerly expelled population themselves expel their ethnic cleansers who claimed their properties. Regarding the other requirements of peacebuilding, in 1998 many of the economic cases handled by the NFP fundamentally enabled the return of the refugees and IDPs; in other words, people are more likely to return when there is employment opportunities. Likewise, the NFP project also supported return and security by helping people obtain necessary personal documents. Governance was promoted by forming local associations to advocate interests, for example, the elderly displaced community in Banja Luka.

Figure 6.3 below charts the number of cases managed by NFP based on the peacebuilding requirements identified in this chapter. The large "other" category reflects a wide variety of tasks including psychosocial support, accompaniment, advice, assistance with documents, and referrals to other agencies. In contrast, the larger international agencies such as UNHCR and NGOs such as the Spanish *Movimiento por la Paz, el desarme y la Libertad* (MPDL) run specific programs targeting widespread needs, but often leave more narrow needs such as those in the "other" category unmet.

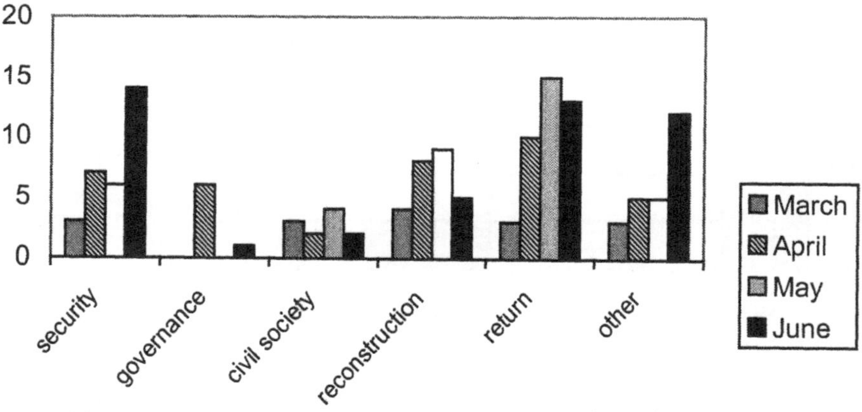

Figure 6.3 NFP Community Centre Project, Peacebuilding Contribution of Cases, 1998

NFP was a qualified success, intervening in more than 300 individual and collective cases over its short span of operation. Nevertheless, it had serious problems that narrowed its scope. For instance, low funding and bureaucratic delays limited its mobility beyond the city where many of its cases were based. The NFP was unable to register its car, and could rent a car on only a few occasions. While international facilitators participating in its project increased the mobility of teams across the inter-entity boundary line (IEBL), they were not without danger in doing so. During the troubles in Drvar in April 1998, the facilitators were targeted along with locals with spitting and insults, culminating in one seriously threatening incident.

A second problem that limited the impact of the NFP was the absence of local representation in relevant communities. The schematic below (Figure 6.4) illustrates the main towns and axes of refugee return in northwest Bosnia in 1998. Because their return involved crossing community boundaries, displaced people returning to Drvar, for example, needed a reliable point of contact to receive information and support in order to facilitate the process. Although there was a UNCIVPOL office and a CIMIC centre in Drvar, they did not provide the sort of local focus for problem-solving that the NFP provided. However, without a branch office in Drvar, the NFP's mobile teams had to re-establish contacts each visit, thereby impairing any efforts at assistance with the returns. Thus, the NFP could have been more effective as part of a coherent network of community facilitators than an isolated project.

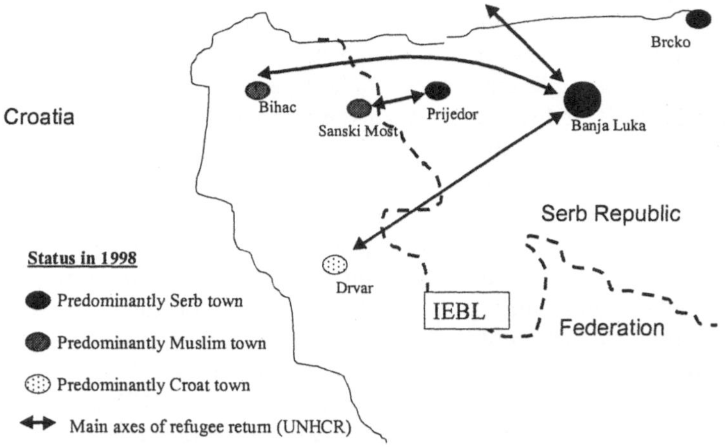

Figure 6.4 Schematic of Northwest Bosnia

Perhaps the most crippling problem faced by NFP was inconsistent and unreliable funding for paying salaries and rent. To ensure the full-time commitment of facilitators, who worked long hours and were frequently uncomfortable or at risk, the rent for the community centre and a minimum salary had to be guaranteed. However, the United Kingdom's Department for International Development, the UNHCR and other major sources of funds wanted to pay for programs, not salaries and rent. Its inability to overcome this funding problem significantly contributed to the program's closure in June 1998. By that time, most of the facilitators had been living on their own resources for six weeks or more. Moreover, after the withdrawal of the international facilitators neither the program nor its concept nor support for the local facilitators could be sustained. As a result, full local ownership, one of the program's strongest assets, was considerably undermined.

The NFP also faced other more ambivalent problems, such as its focus and expertise. More specifically, the NFP focused on process rather than programs or outcome, making it more difficult to identify in advance precisely what contribution they could make to an environment in which numerous NGOs were already working. At the same time, its lack of focus meant that it had the potential to act as the community-level "glue," bringing together other available resources and enabling the local population to solve its own problems. In this respect, the lack of focus becomes a strength. The question of expertise is related to this whereby, for instance, a total of approximately twenty days of training aimed mostly at building on existing interpersonal skills resulted in a very limited skill set on the part of its facilitators. Meanwhile, the process of selecting facilitators was very extensive and sought people who embodied a variety of backgrounds and skills. These were, in effect, "bare-foot mediators" similar to the "bare-foot doctors" sponsored by the World Health Organization in developing countries. Like the bare-foot doctors, these neighbourhood facilitators bring conflict resolution and communication skills to the level where they are most needed, i.e. the community, in order to help neighbours share the same streets and buildings again in the wake of inter-communal violence.

At this point it becomes clearer that soldiers cannot undertake the same activities attempted by the NFP facilitators for reasons of language, culture and local knowledge already enumerated in previous pages. Soldiers can help, however, to establish conditions that will allow civilians, both local and international, to do what is needed. Soldiers are well suited for this task because they are in essence a package, complete with vehicles, communication technology, guaranteed security, and they provide wide coverage of an area. At the same time, while military deployment opens the door to community-level human security, this cannot be achieved without civilian leadership.

From a careful evaluation of NFP and other peacebuilding initiatives, a model for community-based civilian peacebuilding teams can be developed that could be deployed at the same time as a military peacekeeping force. NFP was a small-scale field experiment that demonstrated the importance of interpersonal skills for local conflict resolution initiatives. It answered the question, "what does a peacebuilding 'platoon' look like?" In this respect, the "sections" in the "platoon" comprise three-person teams of mixed ethnicity, including at least one international facilitator to act as a witness and window for international resources. Four or five of these "sections" with some administrative support make up a "platoon" operating inside and outside of a community centre. The "platoons" are located in communities on either side of a communal boundary to provide mutual support in conflict reduction and population return. It is striking that by describing the model with military language it becomes more easily comprehensible to soldiers engaged in this sort of task. However, as none of the neighbourhood facilitators was military, the language of "teams," "centres" and "regions" is more appropriate.

The work actually carried out by the facilitators and the skills applied to manage the case-load over the five months that NFP operated provides a good indication of the sorts of specializations required in the peacebuilding teams. By way of an analogy, "barefoot doctors" who lack the depth of five years in medical school might specialize in infectious diseases, public hygiene, childbirth, first aid or other areas of common need. Similar areas of common need can be identified in peacebuilding operations.

While the specific requirements will vary by geographic area and the phase or timeline of an intervention, the four components of peacebuilding identified above are a good place to start. For instance, beyond the security provided by occupying international military forces and international police monitors, witness and accompaniment programs undertaken by civilian-based organizations can help provide personal security. Peace Brigades International and Balkan Peace Teams have offered training and expertise for this sort of service in the recent past. An American NGO, Impact Team International, was engaged in witness and protection work in Northwest Bosnia in 1998, assisting with the return of Serb families to the Drvar area.[33]

In addition, physical reconstruction projects in the early stages of an intervention increase special demands for construction skills. As a result, facilitators who can advise on roofing, framing, and mixing cement will be particularly valuable "problem solvers." Indeed, small-business acumen and knowledge of micro-credit procedures was very much in demand in Bosnia by 1998, as the reconstruction focus shifted to rebuilding the economy and providing employment opportunities.

Rebuilding the foundations for social and political activities require a range of organizational as well as therapeutic skills. Facilitators run meetings, but also need to recognize emotional flash points and barriers to understanding. This was particularly important in NFP when the facilitators attempted to assist tenant committees faced with competing claims for apartments among displaced people and ethnic tensions escalated. Elderly displaced people and pensioners also needed help organizing themselves to press local authorities to respect and protect their rights. The need for such skills amplifies the problems with top-down approaches where such skills are less prominently featured.

The National Democratic Institute (NDI), an American NGO that promotes civil society by helping organizations such as student associations, trade unions and clubs develop constitutions and rules of order, also confronted problems at the local level in Bosnia. Indeed, combining their organizational skills with a network of local facilitators in the relevant communities might have solved a particular problem that arose in 1998. Specifically, the development of civil society organizations on one side of the IEBL was progressing in isolation of those on the other side, reflecting the political reality of persisting barriers to inter-communal communication.[34] In this respect, facilitating the operation of civil organizations was difficult enough without eliciting further challenges in crossing inter-ethnic boundaries as part of the exercise. Even so, some groups such as pensioners' associations spoke to issues that appealed to communities on both sides of the line and, in transcending the line, could have benefited from opportunities of mutual support.

Reconciliation between communities remains one of the fundamental barriers to post-conflict national reconstruction. As the rate of refugee and displaced person returns increased in spring 2000, the risk of confrontations over housing and land increased simultaneously. Indeed, increased funding for water, electricity and sewage is only part of the solution: "continued attacks on minority returnees have underlined SFOR's uneven record in providing security for returnees."[35] Genuine security will only be achieved when the population in place accepts the returning families. To achieve this, each village, town and region must find its own balance of truth, mercy and justice, against the ongoing background of war-crimes indictments, collection of evidence and search for the missing. Neighbourhood facilitators who are displaced and local residents with a variety of ethnic backgrounds are well placed to help communities towards workable solutions for the dilemmas of return. In this respect, military chaplains, local religious leaders and a variety of NGOs are in a position to assist with inter-communal reconciliation.[36]

Conclusion

When the political objective is rebuilding a war-torn society, top-down political-military plans will always be inadequate, whether produced by one country or by a coalition. Their inadequacy becomes apparent when greater value is assigned to the need to balance external forces, rather than cater singularly to the human needs of the people affected by the conflict on whose efforts peacebuilding ultimately depends. Even a comprehensive campaign plan that links the objectives of many organizations can do little better than reflect the competing pressures that are likely to be felt at the tactical level. Taken together, these conflicting top-down pressures are unlikely to produce a winnable peace, leaving soldiers on interminable garrison duties and local populations equally frustrated.

In order to balance these external pressures, civilian peacebuilding "platoons" of local and international facilitators working in communities are required. In this respect the NFP experiment provides a model for these civilian-led, community-based units with local and international involvement, which shifts to local ownership over time. To paraphrase Dag Hammerskjold, peacebuilding is a difficult task for civilians, but only civilians can do it. Ultimately, the local parties to a conflict must provide their own solution. All we can do is offer a helping hand; twisting arms is not enough.

Notes

1 A version of this paper was presented to the 52nd Annual World Wide Civil Affairs Conference held in San Francisco, 30 June-1 July 2000. Additional research is reported in David Last, "From Peacekeeping to Peacebuilding: Theory, Cases, Experiment and Solution," Royal Military College Working Paper 01/1999.

2 Plato, *The Republic*, Book 1, trans. F. M. Cornford (Oxford: Oxford University Press, 1958), p. 338.

3 Jean-Jacques Rousseau, *The Social Contract*, in *The World's Great Thinkers, Man and the State: The Political Philosophers*, eds. Saxe Commins and Robert N. Linnscott (New York: Random House, 1947), p. 279.

4 Canadian Peacebuilding Co-ordinating Committee (CPCC), "Peacebuilding Activities Chart." CPCC is an umbrella group of non-governmental organizations involved in peacebuilding. It is sponsored in part by the Peacebuilding Branch of the Canadian Department of Foreign Affairs and International Trade.

5 Colonel Michael Dziedzic, National Defence University, discussions at the Center for Hemispheric Defense Studies, Miami, Florida, 13 March 2000.

6 A. B. Fetherston, "Peacekeeping, Conflict Resolution, and Peacebuilding: A Reconsideration of Theoretical Frameworks," in *Peacekeeping and Conflict Resolution*, eds. Tom Woodhouse and Oliver Ramsbotham (London: Frank Cass, 2000), pp. 201-203.

7 This can be found in Galtung's early work in the *Journal of Peace Research*, or in Johan Galtung, *The True Worlds: A Transnational Perspective* (New York: Free Press, 1980), pp. 67-68. Fetherston also cites W. Eckhardt, "Civilizations, Empires and Wars," *Journal of Peace Research* 27:1 (Winter 1990): pp. 9-24 as arguing that structural violence is responsible for more deaths than direct physical violence.

8 "... deducing from an adequate explanation of the ... conflict ... the structural changes required to remove it, but more importantly, the promotion of conditions that create cooperative relationships." J. W. Burton, *Conflict: Resolution and Provention* (London: Macmillan, 1990), p. 3, cited in Fetherston, "Peacekeeping, Conflict Resolution, and Peacebuilding," p. 203.

9 Louis Kriesberg, *Constructive Conflicts: From Escalation to Resolution* (Lanham, MD: Rowman and Littlefield, 1998), p. 24.

10 US Department of Defense, *Joint Doctrine Encyclopedia*, (Washington, DC: Department of Defense, 1997, www.dtic.mil/doctrine/jrm/encyi_l.pdf), p. 337.

11 See for example, *UN Peacekeeping in Trouble: Lessons Learned from the Former Yugoslavia*, eds. Wolfgang Biermann and Martin Vadset (Aldershot: Ashgate, 1998); John Hillen, *Blue Helmets: The Strategy of UN Military Operations* (Washington, DC: Brassey's, 1998); Richard N. Haass, *Intervention: The Use of American Military Force in the Post-Cold War World* (New York: Carnegie Endowment, 1994).

12 Steven R. Ratner, *The New UN Peacekeeping: Building Peace in Lands of Conflict After the Cold War* (New York: St. Martin's, 1996).

13 Robert B. Oakley, Michael J. Dziedzic, and Eliot M. Goldberg, eds., *Policing the New World Disorder: Peace Operations and Public Security* (Washington, DC: National Defense University Press, 1998), pp. 3-17.

14 M. Bard and J. Zacker, *The Police and Interpersonal Conflict: Third Party Intervention Approaches* (Washington, DC: Police Foundation, 1976).

15 UN Confidence Restoration Operation (UNCRO) Headquarters, "Planning Paper on Provision of Security for Sector East," 30 October 1995. The requirement was originally

stated as a "reinforced military police company," p. 7.

16 The MSU includes the Italian Carabinieri (a paramilitary force), and draws on the Military Police, US Psychological Operations teams (loudspeaker units), civilian police from the International Police Task Force (IPTF, a component of the UN mission) and liaison officers. Interviews by author with SFOR staff, Sarajevo, February 1998.

17 Jamie Swift, *Civil Society in Question* (Toronto: Between the Lines, 1999), pp. 4-5.

18 UNHCR, Refworld, Country Reports, www.unhcr.ch/world/euro/seo/bosnia.htm.

19 Jan Nederveen Pierterse, "Sociology of Humanitarian Intervention: Bosnia, Rwanda and Somalia Compared," *International Political Science Review* 18:1 (January 1997): pp. 71-94.

20 John Paul Lederach, *Building Peace: Sustainable Reconciliation in Divided Societies*, (Washington: United States Institute for Peace, 1997), p. 30.

21 See International Crisis Group, "War Criminals in Bosnia's Republika Srpska: Who are the People in Your Neighbourhood?" *Report: Balkans* (2 November 2000), www.intl-crisis-group.org

22 Suggested by Joseph Montville, Ph.D., Director of Preventive Diplomacy, Center for Strategic and International Studies, Annual Convention of the International Studies Association, Washington, DC, 18 March 1999. Dr. Montville is editor of *Conflict and Peacemaking in Multiethnic Societies* (Lexington, MA: Lexington Books, 1990) and co-editor with Vamik Volkan and Demetrios Julius of *The Psychodynamics of International Relationships*, Volume 1 (Lexington, MA: Lexington Books, 1990) and Volume 2 (1991).

23 Lederach, *Building Peace,* pp. 87-97.

24 Professor Gene Dewey, National Defense University, Presentation at ABCA Focus 2000 conference, Sandhurst, UK, 24 April 2000.

25 George A. Joulwan and Christopher C. Shoemaker, *Civilian-Military Cooperation in the Prevention of Deadly Conflict: Implementing Agreements in Bosnia and Beyond*, A Report to the Carnegie Commission on Preventing Deadly Conflict (New York: Carnegie Corporation, December 1998), pp. 13-14.

26 Alcira Kreimer, John Eriksson, Robert Muscat, Margaret Arnold, Colin Scott, *The World Bank's Experience with Post-Conflict Reconstruction*, Operations Evaluation Studies (Washington, DC: World Bank, 1998).

27 www.worldbank.org/html/extdr/about/content.htm.

28 Interviews by author in Sarajevo, February 1998.

29 For example, Ian Black, Rory Carroll, and Nicholas Wood, "Macedonia blames West for breeding Albanian rebels after Kosovo takeover," *Guardian Weekly*, (22 March 2001), p. 1

30 Having worked in such a centre myself, I can relate to the frustration expressed by British and American Civil Affairs teams.

31 Sociologist Anthony Oberschall has described this process in Croatia in "Polarization Dynamics in Ethno-National Conflict: Croatia and Bosnia,". paper presented to the International Sociological Association conference, Research Committee on Social Movements, Collective Action and Social Change, March 1998.

32 The project and project evaluations are reported in detail in David Last, "From Peacekeeping to Peacebuilding," and "Organizing for Effective Peacebuilding," *International Peacekeeping* 7:1 (Spring 2000): pp. 80-96.

33 Interviews by author in Bosnia, March 1998.

34 Interview by author with David Sip, NDI Community Development Officer, Banja Luka, 8 February 1998. More information on NDI's Bosnia programs is available on their web site at www.ndi.org/ndi/worldwide/ce_europe/bosnia/bosnia.htm.

35 International Crisis Group, "Bosnia's Refugee Logjam Breaks: Is the International

Community Ready?" May 2000, www.intl-crisis-group.org/projects/showreport.cfm?reportid=88.

36 David Last and Emma Kay, "The Spiritual Dimension of Peacekeeping: A Dual Role for the Chaplaincy?" *Peace Research: The Canadian Journal of Peace Studies* 31:1 (February 1999): pp. 66-75.

Chapter 7

Strange Bedfellows in Humanitarian Crises: NGOs and the Military[1]

Donna Winslow

A qualitative change has taken place in the post-Cold-War period concerning peace operations and the actors that participate in them. On the one hand are the military personnel[2] who are no longer simply protecting the sovereignty of a state. Instead militaries are intervening more and more frequently in intra-state conflicts as they often are being tasked with facilitating humanitarian relief, social reconstruction and protecting civilians in areas where there is no peace. They are also asked to broker deals, shelter the displaced, protect human rights, supervise the return of refugees, and organize and monitor elections.[3] Thus, military mandates have become wider and more ambiguous and the tasks more multi-dimensional and multi-functional. According to Williams, "the military have taken on new and significant political roles."[4] On the other hand, peace operations also are featuring larger numbers of civilian non-governmental organizations (NGOs) who perform a wide variety of relief tasks such as food delivery, monitoring elections and human rights, managing refugee camps, distributing medical supplies and services, etc. They can belong to any number of organizations with varying budgets, tasks, goals, competence, types of personnel, etc., which can make liaisons between them and the military at times difficult.[5]

Until recently, when civilian relief workers and military personnel were both involved in "traditional" peace operations, they performed their tasks separately. There was, thus, little functional need for co-operation between these groups. As former Canadian chief of defence staff, General Maurice Baril, remarked: "Humanitarian agencies and non-governmental organizations seemed to be in every area of conflict but remained independent and reluctant to modify their approach and agree to coordinate their efforts with the military force."[6]

Thus, the problem that arises is that under the new forms of peace operations, the military is expected to work not only alongside, but also in cooperation with, such NGOs and relief organizations. In the process, however, tensions inevitably arise as each actor attempts to carry out their primary objectives under such difficult and new circumstances. Given that an effective interface for civil-military cooperation is essential to the overall operation, these tensions thus can complicate, if not undermine, civil-military cooperation and can have a negative impact overall on the operation's effectiveness. In this respect, it is important to understand some of the difficulties that can arise in peace operations between members of these two communities and, at the same time, promote civil-military cooperation.

This chapter intends to examine some of the tensions which can arise between civilian relief workers and military personnel in these new forms of peace operations. The specific points of tension that will be explored relate to organizational differences in terms of: 1) organizational culture; 2) tasks and ways of accomplishing them; 3) definitions of success and time frames; 4) abilities to exert influence and control information; and 5) control of resources.

NGOs and the Military: The Context

Traditionally, interactions between the military and humanitarian workers have been characterized by avoidance or antagonism. Each group held (and sometimes continues to hold) stereotypes of the other. According to some US analysts American military personnel are described by some NGOs as "boys with toys;" rigid; authoritarian; conservative; impatient; arrogant; civilian phobic, homophobic; excessively security conscious, etc.[7] In contrast one of the battalion commanders interviewed referred to NGOs as "non-guided organizations" and other authors note the following comments: "children of the '60s"; flaky do-gooders; permissive; unpunctual; obstructionist; anarchic; undisciplined; self-righteous; anti-military; etc.[8]

One of the sources of frustration for the military is the large variety, size and apparent lack of coordination between relief organizations. In the first instance, in peace operations[9] of the post-Cold War era one can find the large international organizations (IOs) such as the United Nations High Commissioner for Refugees (UNHCR) and United Nations Children's Emergency Fund (UNICEF) as well as the well-known international non-governmental organizations (NGOs) such as CARE, OXFAM, Médecins sans Frontières (Doctors without Borders) and the International Committee for the Red Cross (ICRC). Smaller NGOs are also present in large numbers in areas of conflict. Secondly, the sheer number of non-military actors in conflict management activities has increased. For example, in 1989, 48 international NGOs were registered with the United Nations (UN). By 1998 there were 1500.[10] These NGOs may be religious or secular, may include personnel from one nation or several, may be truly non-governmental or may in fact receive large sums from government grants. Finally, a peace operation may also feature numerous small groups, each with a humanitarian interest and carrying out any variety of activities, from distributing old prescription glasses to trying to set up dental clinics. According to one Canadian Civil Military Cooperation (CIMIC) officer interviewed, "Smaller NGOs have [a] more narrow focus. They want the most bang for their money. It's an ad hoc situation."

According to Williams, humanitarian organizations form the nucleus of an international civil society whose *ésprit de corps* distrusts national military structures.[11] Miller tells us that aid workers' anti-military attitude stems from their organizations' origins.[12] In this respect, many were created to alleviate suffering caused by war (e.g. the ICRC) or to provide an alternative to military service (e.g. The American Friends

Service Committee). Pamela Aall has made the following comment on the NGO – military relationship:

> Traditionally, NGOs and the military have perceived their roles to be distinctly different and separate. NGOs have felt uneasy with military forces, either from their own countries or from the country receiving assistance, particularly when the latter are employed in the service of dictators with unsavory human rights records. Military leaders, on the other hand, tend to regard NGOs as undisciplined and their operations as uncoordinated and disjointed.[13]

In the 1990s the nature of international conflict meant that relief workers increasingly found their lives and their work at risk. A Canadian defence ministry official noted that some NGO workers had more battlefield experience than most Canadian Forces personnel.[14] Relief workers in Rwanda and Chechnya were deliberately killed in 1997. In Burundi and Sudan NGOs were expelled and workers killed because they were witness to local atrocities. In other countries workers have been victims of landmines, armed hijacking of vehicles, banditry, kidnapping, bombings, etc. As a result of these events and the deterioration of field situations, aid workers began to conclude that they needed weapons on their side in order to fulfill their mandates. For example, in Somalia:

> The ICRC suspended its normally irrevocable principle of avoiding cooperation with military forces in its relief operation in order to protect its relief convoys. The chaos in Somalia became so bad and the negotiating position of humanitarian agencies so tenuous that military force became the only viable alternative.[15]

But even security arrangements for NGOs, which ostensibly would be provided by the military, has become a contentious issue in the civil-military relationship. David Owen found the military in Bosnia "bitter in their denunciation of some of the NGOs who to them were a pestilential nuisance, resisting all attempts at coordination and then complaining that they were not properly protected."[16] A Canadian officer interviewed in Bosnia was equally cynical concerning NGOs, saying that relief groups would want nothing to do with the military, until there was a perceived security threat and only then would they establish contact to make sure that they could be evacuated or protected by the military.

Organizational Culture

At a speech on civil-military partnerships in humanitarian intervention given in Toronto, Canada in autumn 1999, Lieutenant-Colonel D. D. McAlea described obstacles to fostering civil-military cooperation:

> Number one: NGOs just don't trust the military, they're suspicious of military. Number two: they jealously guard their independence. NGOs have to be careful not to compromise their objectivity because they could loose their funding. ... There are suspicions on both sides because they have different cultures.[17]

In this paper, tension in organizational culture refers to differences in organizational goals (including values and basic assumptions), organizational composition (gender, age, ethnicity), and organizational structure. Organizational culture also refers to the way an organization carries out its business. NGOs and the military are often seen as being at odds with each other concerning their basic goals (alleviate human suffering vs. preparation for war), approaches to violence (non violence vs. controlled use of violence), approaches to nationalism (internationalist vs. strongly nationalistic) and decision-making styles (decentralized vs. hierarchical).

The military's primary mission remains fighting and winning wars, and in a theatre of operations military personnel continue to work on these skills. For example, even while carrying out its peacekeeping mandate in Bosnia, the Canadian contingent regularly carried out training exercises, including live-fire exercises. Thus, for some NGO members it is difficult to work with the military because it is difficult to forget their fundamental purpose. As one NGO member who had worked with the Canadian military on a peacekeeping-training exercise remarked, "They *seem* like nice people, both the civilian and military people mixed, but I think of military people training in acts of war ... ."[18]

Some military personnel feel that participating in peace operations dulls their warrior's edge. These soldiers and officers do not believe in their role as "global social workers." Peace operations are considered to be inappropriate for combat soldiers. As a Canadian soldier in Bosnia indicated, "This is not what we trained for, which was green." Similarly, Canadian politicians have been criticized for trying to make the military into NGOs in uniform. On the other hand, many soldiers and officers acknowledge that their presence in Bosnia makes a difference. As one non-commissioned officer (NCO) remarked, "In [the UN Protection Force] UNPROFOR, they were shooting at us and children were throwing rocks at us. In [the Implementation Force] IFOR, we were taking the guns away from the big guys. In [the Stabilization Force] SFOR, we see people coming back, children are waving at us."

Miller's work shows that in spite of the perceived benefits and a shift towards support of armed intervention in the regions where they work, relief workers remain essentially anti-military.

> An anti-military and anti-weapons bias persists in relief organizations because militarization and violence are still the primary causes of much of the suffering that these agencies are attempting to relieve. The crisis in Somalia, Rwanda, and Bosnia were all caused by clan or ethnic warfare. The human rights abuses in Haiti were the result of a military coup and a brutal dictatorship. NGOs accepted weapons as a necessary evil for reaching their goals when other methods no longer could provide a safe environment.[19]

Some differences concern motivation. Soldiers and officers participate in a peace operation because it is their job. They stay for their tour of duty and do what they are ordered to. In one Canadian study on ethics[20] the extra money earned was a strong motivation for participating in peace operations. "I have been on many tours, I do it for the money. I don't believe in peace, in helping people who don't want to help themselves."[21] The Ethics Report goes on to say that: "The often articulated motivator of extra dollars as the prime consideration for volunteering complicates the decision making process in high intensity ethical situations. The comment *dollars are the number one motivation, rather than duty* was not uncommon."[22]

In contrast, relief workers volunteer for hardship, often making many personal sacrifices in order to pursue altruistic goals.

> NGOs, who operate with much less individual security and often with fewer amenities than soldiers, are personally invested in the mission, and are committed for the long term to addressing whatever needs may arise. They are where they are by choice, and are devoted to their vocation. Many of them find it difficult to believe that soldiers could truly be committed to the same goals as they are.[23]

In Miller's study, relief workers expressed the view that soldiers were there simply because they were ordered to be there. This in turn led some relief workers to feel morally superior to soldiers. "In a number of interviews, distrust of the military was translated into comments suggesting that the US military or individual soldiers help out only because they are ordered to do so or have self-interested reasons for doing so."[24]

Differences in organizational structure can affect the way groups interact. What is the hierarchy in the organization? How are decisions taken? Organizations such as NGOs tend to have a more flattened hierarchy with decentralized decision making. When one American colonel in Bosnia referred to NGOs as "one general and many privates" the response of an NGO executive was "How about one general and many colonels?"[25] According to Colonel Bob Stewart, the commander of the first British deployment to Bosnia in 1992: "The military are hierarchical, authoritarian, centralized, large and robust, while the [United Nations High Commission for Refugees] UNHCR is flat, consensus-based with highly decentralized field offices."[26] Thus, the UNHCR's perceived lack of structure and tendency to delegate decision-making to people of a much younger age than the military can be a source of frustration from the point of view of the military.[27]

In addition, the gender and ethnic composition of the organizations in theatre may affect the way they interact with each other. Militaries in peace operations are predominantly male[28] while relief workers are often female in their late twenties to early forties.[29] Similarly, UN field staff are predominantly female. UN agencies such as the UNHCR recruit women on a positive-discrimination basis which means that half of the staff of UN agencies and NGOs operating in Bosnia are female.[30] Young male soldiers between 19 and 22 years old may have difficulty dealing with relief workers who are female and considerably older. Finally ethnic (including racial, cultural and religious) differences can impact on the way organizations behave with each other and with the local population. Miller and Moskos showed that military units that were mixed race and mixed gender had more humanitarian attitudes to the local population than all male uni-racial units which adopted a more aggressive stance towards locals.[31]

Tasks and Ways of Accomplishing Them

Ogata tells us the UNHCR's humanitarian activities have become closely entwined with the military, strengthening its humanitarian capacity but also complicating its efforts.[32] "If UN peacekeeping forces were to engage in offensive action, it would no longer be possible to maintain the non-political and impartial base of the UNHCR's humanitarian activities, however serious the needs of the victims might be."[33] Ogata expresses concern over the effect that military operations have on the neutral and impartial image of relief efforts. For example, while UNPROFOR convoy escorts provided protection and deterred attack, their presence in some cases heightened local hostility.[34] Similarly, in the Canadian Area of Responsibility in Bosnia, some NGOs in the town of Drvar refused to have any more contact with the military because they had been targeted during riots. They felt that they had been singled out for violence because of their association with the military. Therefore, tensions can arise between humanitarian and military actors because of their respective mandates and modes of operation. Humanitarian organizations are concerned with protecting people and ensuring basic human rights and the security of the victims on all sides of a conflict, whereas the military use of force might be directed just against one party in a conflict.

Of course the military is also concerned with maintaining objectivity and this can lead to distance from the local population. Because of security issues, military personnel find themselves in armed camps, behind fortified walls and barbed wire. They remain separate from the local population with little opportunity for extended social contact. Keeping distance from the local population can be perceived as demonstrating a lack of trust in the host population. This is not to say that the military does not help the community at all. In Bosnia, for instance, the Canadians rebuilt a hospital wing, set up a dental clinic, build a woodshed for a school, cut and delivered wood to the elderly, etc. However, militaries like to do things for people rather than with them. In contrast, relief workers often place themselves in the midst of the local population with few boundaries (be they physical or social) between. Because of the closeness, relief organizations often incorporate local cultural modes in the way they accomplish their tasks. This is reflected in work habits:

> [T]he military's standards and preferred way of completing its tasks (the most rapid, most efficient, highest quality way) do not mesh with the NGO approach, which employs, teaches, and gives control to members of the community, incorporates local cultural modes, and uses locally accessible resources when possible. In Bosnia the USAID director at that time observed, "[The US military] had a tendency to want to take over, so we had to stop that, I have to teach the military each time not to run things."[35]

The NGOs themselves can have mandates which differ from each other and this can lead to tensions with the military. In Bosnia in 1998 the inability of NGOs to collaborate with each other was often cited as a problem: "NGOs are a business, each with their own agenda and sometimes their own agendas don't coincide with other NGO activities. Sometimes NGOs don't want to talk to each other." One problem the Canadian military in Bosnia faced was that the UNHCR wanted to return refugees (Serbs), while another organization preferred to activate the (Croat) Council instead. "So they have different mandates and get into conflict with each other. Sometimes the NGOs here seem to be working at cross-purposes to each other." Another interviewee commenting on the SFOR mission said NGOs were not well coordinated, which created "duplication of effort, missed information, poorly completed projects and villages with rebuilt homes, but no electricity or water and a host of other problems."

Sometimes there is a gap between civilian and military understandings of the strategic goals of a mission. For example, Garofano notes that in Bosnia US military leaders did not believe that they had a mandate for nation-building (and may have wanted to avoid the burden of one).[36] On the other hand, humanitarian workers express frustration with the military's inability to act in certain situations:

> Our director witnessed a guy firing randomly in the air after leaving the scene of a crime. A UN peacekeeping truck was looking, trying not to get shot, but otherwise doing nothing. I'm sure they were careful because they didn't have a mandate to act. I imagine they were ordered not to do anything. That would be ok, but the military is here doing *what*?[37]

Relief workers commonly call upon military forces to become more actively and deeply involved. In Bosnia a relief worker complained:

> You cannot leave de-mining up to the [warring] parties. You have to take responsibility. You say you're not the police, fine; not de-mining, fine; not capturing war criminals, fine. What are you doing? You have to take responsibility for something.[38]

In contrast, in Haiti relief workers pushed for more military commitment:

> The UN [troops] should participate more in peacekeeping: patrols and police work. Foreign troops are not supposed to get involved in local actions, but people think they could have done more to disarm the local thugs.[39]

This is the same situation found during the Great Lake crisis. Many NGOs "seemed almost intentionally blind to the political and military implications of some of the suggestions and requests they made both privately and to the media".[40] This was reflected in different opinions as to what was an appropriate role for the military, i.e. some NGOs wanted the military to go into the refugee camps in Eastern Zaire and separate and/or disarm belligerents.[41] However, fulfilling the tasks the humanitarian agencies wanted would have involved serious risks and it would also have required important political decisions that many participating nations did not want to take.

Definitions of Success and Time Frames

According to Pope the long-term commitments of NGOs in a region may lead to substantial differences in how a mission accomplishment is defined.[42] NGOs may not declare a mission a success until all human suffering has been alleviated in the area.[43] Public opinion and the media, on the other hand, may simply want to put an end to fighting (send in troops in order to prevent the escalation of the conflict). The national politicians may have another definition of success (no casualties in the field, good publicity for their government, etc.).[44]

The military's definition of success is determined by the mission that has to be accomplished. In addition, according to European military commanders a mission may be considered a success if troops sustain no casualties and all are brought home safely – even if the actual mandate was not completely fulfilled. This can be interpreted by some as indifference to the local population or the humanitarian aspects of the mission. According to Miller the US military shares similar concerns about avoiding casualties among its own people and about "mission creep," i.e. extending and prolonging a mission because new objectives are constantly being added. "Many aid workers have detected these concerns, and look down on the military leaders as wanting to perform only the minimum required and then withdrawing as quickly as possible."[45]

The brevity of military tours (usually six months) can also cause tension with NGOs who are often the first to enter and the last to leave a troubled area.

> Once familiarized with local conditions, [military] officers have little time left to establish solid working relationships with their civilian counterparts, or acclimatize themselves to local values, culture and politics … . By contrast, it is unusual for civilians to serve for less than 12 months … . It was not unusual for civilians with UNPROFOR to be in their post for three years.[46]

In addition, different military units may have different forms of rotation, with some militaries rotating individuals while other rotate whole or parts of units at a single time. Moreover, humanitarian agencies sometimes demonstrate a misunderstanding of the speed with which the military can deploy. In the Great Lakes crisis, "there was a clear expectation that armies would be fully deployed in theatre almost instantly after a political decision was taken. It is not well understood that this operation involved the movement of tons of machinery and hundreds of people to Africa, and their establishment on the ground, all of which takes time."[47]

Last discusses immediate-term (two to six months), short-term (one to two years), medium-term (five to ten years) and long-term (more than ten years) intervention in the former Yugoslavia.[48] In each of these time frames the focus is different. For example, in the immediate- and short-term, military and civil security are the primary focus, while in the medium- and long-term the emphasis is on economic reconstruction, education and development. Each of these forms of intervention requires different resources (military and security forces vs. social and economic development projects) and different social actors (military and police vs. relief and development agents).

Thus, tension can occur when different social actors are operating with different time frames in the same theatre of operations.

Tensions can also arise when no end state has been adequately defined, or is controlled by one actor. As C. Dandekar and J. Gow have pointed out, one serious point of tension in a strategic peace operation is where the belligerents are in control of the end state and it is only when they decide that the conflict has been satisfactorily resolved will the peace operation end.[49] Thus, as long as the belligerents continue to fight, the operation in the former Yugoslavia could become a long Cyprus-type mission.

In peace operations where the goal of the mission is defined as humanitarian, it becomes more difficult to decide when the operation should come to an end. For example in the case of Zaire, when the refugees were freed from coercion and began to return to Rwanda, the international community then engaged in a debate over whether the military mission was still required. Those who defined the role of the military mission as humanitarian noted that there were still people in need and supported the extension of the mission. An opposing view, however, as Appathurai and Lysyshyn point out, notes that "there will always be people in need in eastern Zaire … ."[50]

Abilities to Exert Influence and Control Information

Different groups are able to exert influence at a number of levels. On the one hand, the decision to undertake a peace operation or send in troops may arise because of public pressure or public opinion informed by NGO and media reports.[51] On the other hand, the deployment of troops itself can attract media and political attention, which can then assist NGOs in publicizing their efforts and in raising funds.

Organizations such as NGOs and the media are able to exert influence not only at the national political level, but also in the international arena. This can frustrate military commanders who are not able to influence political and public opinion in the same way. During the Great Lakes crisis, the NGOs had political interests not unlike governments. According to Appathurai and Lysyshyn,

> These agencies have relationships with parties on the ground and with other national governments, and compete with each other for influence and financing. Some (not all) of these clearly tried to influence the Multinational Force during the crisis, providing suspiciously high numbers of refugees in need and using the media as a lever.[52]

The commander then finds him or herself trying to explain the disconnect between the information (s)he has about the local situation (numbers of refugees, etc.) and the portrait that is being painted back home.

Tied to the ability to exert influence is also the ability to control information. A military commander finds him/herself at the interface of many relationships where different organizations want access to the information (s)he possesses. For instance, according to Miller NGOs believe that the military can assist them in information gathering.[53] In this respect in Bosnia the Canadian military shares information with NGOs through population surveys and monitoring of returning refugees carried out by its civil-military cooperation people.

However, intelligence works in both directions and NGOs are expected to share information as well. Because NGOs often have a longer experience with the local population, their insights are frequently of value to the military. At the same time, the military is often unwilling to accept information that is not packaged appropriately for their use. According to one relief worker in Bosnia:

> There's no sense for the American military to reinvent the wheel. We had a lot of surveys and figures on refugees. The US military was starting to do it all over again. We saved them three to six months of work, and in return we have gotten a lot of support: they opened routes across the zone of separation, for example.
>
> Both of us come from very strong cultures and both of us think we're right and know how to do things best. Who's going to take the first step? We've gone through a process. In the beginning we were very reluctant, but we made the first step to help them learn how we think, how we work, to try to get them to understand the value of what we're doing. They started to realize how much we knew, that we had a sensitivity to what's going on in the country and that we could help them in situations in which they didn't know what to do.[54]

In addition, different organizations are often not aware of what others are doing. Thus, when NGOs criticize the military for "not doing enough," more often they simply are not aware of what the military is actually doing. In Bosnia the Canadian military tries to facilitate the sharing of information and promotes coordination between these NGOs. The CIMIC liaison section's role is to assist the international organizations in the military's Area of Responsibility, particularly the ICRC, the UNHCR, and their partners. Dealing with smaller NGOs in the Area of Responsibility can be problematic given their size which, while necessary to keep overhead down and be capable of direct action, undermines their ability to access current information and coordinate with other organizations.

Another gap in information-sharing relates to a lack of awareness or effort to become aware of the full scope of NGO activities. Globally Islamic-based NGOs are most affected in this way. For instance, the Canadian military contingent in Bosnia have little or no information of any development activities by Islamic groups which are quite active in the region. Not only is the military ignorant of Islamic group activities, but the media is similarly at fault. For example, Moskos reports that seven of the 33 NGOs with official standing in the United Nations operation in Somalia were Islamic. Yet, his computer search of US press reports revealed that, "Not one story was ever written on any of the Muslim NGOs – not one."[55]

To promote information-sharing, the Canadian military in Bosnia organizes regular meetings plus ad hoc information-sharing with NGOs. One of the mechanisms for this is called the Principals Group of NGOs which meets in the Canadian camp in Coralici.

The military facilitates the meeting and produces the agenda. "We decide the focus and explain why so we can have a common effort." The military tries to be sensitive to the NGOs. "We don't want to appear heavy-handed so we try to arrive at consensus." In this way, the military tries to develop and coordinate NGO strategy. As one officer said, "It is important to show consistency of effort."

Finally, one cannot discuss control of information without discussing the media. Both the military and NGOs are concerned about their relations with the media. According to Moskos, "NGO funding often depends of favourable press coverage."[56] And as a leading figure in the International Rescue Committee remarked, "You go where governments or UN agencies want you to go to get your share of contracts that otherwise would go to other agencies. And one way to get such contracts is by getting the press to publicize your work."[57] In this sense, the military presence in theatre can be a valuable resource since it often draws political and media attention to an area.

Moskos goes on to tell us that NGOs often have strained relations with the media, much the same way as the military does. As a senior officer in Sarajevo told him, "The media understand NGOs even less than we do."[58] The military and NGOs are often equally apprehensive about the media and particularly about negative coverage. For the military a bad news story may spell the end of an individual's career; for an NGO it may mean the end of funding.[59]

Control of Resources

In peace operations the different organizations often find themselves in competition for resources. The NGOs may be competing among themselves in order to secure funding and equipment at the same time that they may be competing over access to certain areas or regions which the military must safeguard.

From another perspective, resources among the different organizations sometimes are shared, especially by the military which deploys with valuable resources – food and medical supplies, money in the pockets of soldiers, communication equipment, construction equipment, transport and fuel, etc. Relief workers in Haiti described to Miller how early in the mission in 1994 thousands of soldiers assisted them:

> [A]fter Cyclone Gordon ... they volunteered. And they had an outpost next to our office. We knew each other, were friends, and they asked what support we needed. Engineers came out and set the course of the river back, which had just spread out all over. They made walls as barriers to prevent land degradation and protect the banks of the rivers. They also did an aerial survey with their helicopters for us. They worked well with the communities then.[60]

Similarly, the Canadian military contingent in Bosnia collaborates with IOs and NGOs. Once a month the head of the Canadian Medical Unit in Bosnia has a meeting with the World Health Organization in Bosnia, and (s)he also keeps in contact with other medical staff in the area (for example, Médecins Sans Frontières) about the main medical problems in the region. These are mainly TB, AIDS, communicable skin diseases, oral hygiene, and cancer. The Canadian military also co-operates with the UN Mine Action Centre: in response to the UN's request for someone to work in the mine action centre, a Canadian major was seconded to the Centre in Bihac as coordinator. In this capacity, he is responsible for safety, the techniques used to clear mines, and hirings. Canadians also work closely with UNHCR to anticipate resource needs in Bosnia and to provide them as appropriate. For instance, demands in 1998 were small compared to 1994-1995 when the UNHCR used Canadian military vehicles. As well, during the Kosovo crisis when NGOs on the ground were overwhelmed by the numbers of refugees, UNHCR asked NATO to coordinate all transportation of food, relief supplies, and medical care. NATO troops also helped to set up camps for the hundreds of thousands of refugees.[61]

As mentioned above, there are also misunderstandings as to the proper use of resources. Humanitarian agencies may want the military to disarm the local population or catch thieves and criminals.[62] At times, they also want the military to use its material resources more effectively. Different from the positive description above of NGO-military cooperation in the beginning of the mission in Haiti, by 1997 only a minimal US military force was present and appeared to be conserving its resources. A relief worker expressed the following frustrations:

> They have all that equipment here, money, people. Why not build roads, improve streets, build infrastructure? A lot of this is very capital-intensive and they have it. As it is, they're spending all this money to be locked up behind walls, and we don't know what they're doing.[63]

Similarly in Bosnia, some NGOs have been known to have requested the military to deliver goods and cattle for them which the military has refused to do. In this way, there is also competition over soldiers as resources. That is, there are a large number of competing demands placed upon a soldier's time and upon military resources to accomplish both humanitarian and military aims. According to one Canadian officer in the former Yugoslavia, they did not have the resources to meet the demands of the military and humanitarian tasks: "We are pushing the envelope and doing our damn best to keep all the balls in the air."

Conclusions

It is important to remember that NGOs and the military also share many things: a commitment to peace and stability; a hard working attitude; international experience; life with hardship and danger; personal risk of injury, illness and/or death; decision making under pressure; a "can do" attitude or a "make do with what you've got" attitude; an appreciation of competence; a willingness to work among the suffering, the dying and/or the dead; a frustration with conditions on the ground; a frustration with decisions they believe are political and make their work less effective, etc.[64] Moskos has advanced the hypothesis that in peace operations we can observe an embryonic convergence between the two institutions: "a 'softening' of the military, if you will, and a 'hardening' of the NGOs."[65] Thus, as the military and NGOs carry out overlapping missions in the same areas, they develop common ground for improved relations.

There appears to be a growing recognition by military forces of the value of working with NGOs. For example the US Joint Task Force Commander's Handbook has a whole chapter on civil-military relations which includes a discussion of NGOs, UN agencies and other international relief agencies.[66] Likewise, the relief community is developing an appreciation of the military's assistance in realizing humanitarian objectives. Efforts are underway to work more closely together. Flora MacDonald, former Secretary of State for External Affairs in Canada, went with NGOs to both Somalia and Rwanda. She noted at the time that there were about 200 NGOs operating and "the confusion was total." In contrast, in Kosovo MacDonald remarked that there was tremendous integration in the work being done by the Canadian military and the NGOs there – integration she had not seen elsewhere.[67]

Working together helps each community to view the other as equally professional and committed to common objectives. This is a very important point. In fact, Miller's central argument is that organizations that share common goals and depend on each other to reach that goal can develop a cooperative relationship and yet retain distinct organizational memberships and cultures.[68] Good working relations can be developed between culturally different groups. In this respect, such relationships should be encouraged outside of peace operations. For example, the Canadian Forces in 1996 began an exchange with CARE in which an officer is attached to the organization on a six-month basis. Some NGOs send personnel to the military for mine awareness training. These types of exchanges promote mutual understanding.

In the Bosnian theatre, the CIMIC coordination centres permit detailed cooperation between the many NGOs and local authorities. One such CIMIC centre consisted of 18 people and their role was to assist the international organizations in the Area of Responsibility, such as ICRC, UNHCR, and their partners. The CIMIC liaison section also assists in cooperation with the municipal and cantonment authorities in their efforts to successfully implement the civil aspects of the Dayton accords. For example, they coordinate with UNHCR assistance to returning displaced persons. CIMIC also conducts liaison efforts with international organizations such as UNHCR and the International Police Task Force, who are the Dayton Accord's implementing partners.

To be effective, CIMIC operations need to be finely tuned and staffed with competent people. Of course, for a military professional, a career in civil-military relations may not mean professional advancement the way combat does. Thus, there is a need for clear tracks of professional advancement in order to encourage participation in these functions. Another military option is to use reservists who have experience in dealing with civilians since they are civilians themselves.

Finally, the co-location of NGO and military headquarters in the same area would also promote better interface between the actors. Of course, being close to each other is not a guarantee of effective communication, but it could be facilitated. Dialogue can also be improved through pre-mission meetings between the military and NGOs, early agreement on responsibilities and objectives, central coordination, shared communications equipment, regular inter-agency meetings in-field, liaison exchange officers to name a few other methods. It is also critical that relief agencies be included earlier in the strategic planning stages of a military operation. In this respect, particular emphasis should be placed upon improving consultation at the policy level, information sharing and analysis. Thus, effective cooperation ensures the coordination of humanitarian, peace building, reconstruction, peace building, as well as other political and security aspects of the mission, thereby improving the strength and effectiveness of the mission itself.

Notes

1 This title was inspired by a comment by US General Shalikashvili at a 1995 conference on military efforts in humanitarian crises at which he referred to the military, humanitarian agencies and the media as "strange bedfellows [that] can be a very good combination." Cited in Charles Moskos, *The Media and the Military in Peace and Humanitarian Operations* (Chicago: Robert R. McCormick Tribune Foundation, 2000), p. 34.

In addition to documentary sources, particularly the work of US sociologists Laura Miller and Charles Moskos, research for this paper was carried out in the archives of the Canadian Department of National Defence Headquarters. During the 1996 crisis in the Great Lakes region of Central Africa, Canada attempted to lead the formation of a multinational coalition. The crisis resolved itself before the coalition could actually be deployed; however, there were a number of important lessons learned from this effort. See James Appathurai and Ralph Lysyshyn, *Lessons Learned from the Zaire Mission* (Ottawa: Canadian Department of Foreign Affairs and International Trade, 1997). Information also came from unstructured interviews and focus groups carried out with Canadian soldiers in Bosnia (October 1998) and in the Golan Heights (February 1999). In this respect I wish to thank the Canadian Department of National Defence and the soldiers and officers of the 3rd Battalion of the Royal Canadian Regiment Battle Group deployed in Bosnia and the Canadian Logistics group stationed on the Golan Heights for taking care of me. I am well aware that such trips require time and energy to organize and I am extremely appreciative of the support and information given to me during these trips. In addition to interviews with Canadian military personnel, I have also conducted interviews at NATO headquarters and with European battalion commanders who have been deployed to the former Yugoslavia. I have also consulted with members of large international relief agencies such as UNHCR, but have little interview data from the smaller NGOs who do not have contact with the military in an area of operations. This is an area for future research.

Funding for this research was received from the Defence and Civil Institute of Environmental Medicine [DCIEM], Canadian Department of National Defence. I wish to thank particularly Ross Pigeau for his support of this project. Research funds were also received from George C. Marshall Center in Germany. This research was also funded by US Army Research Institute Contract No. DASW01 -98- M-1868, 'Army Culture'. Finally, I wish to thank my research assistants Jason Dunn and Glenn Gilmour for their good humour and hard work on this project.

2 Please note that my use of the word "military" is very loose. Since the vast majority of my research experience is with the Army my knowledge of things "military" mostly refers to army knowledge and experiences in peace operations.

3 Michael Williams, *Civil Military Relations and Peacekeeping*, Adelphi Paper 321 (London: International Institute for Strategic Studies, 1998), p. 14.

4 Ibid.

5 David M. Last, "Defeating Fear and Hatred Through Peacebuilding: Multiplying the Impact of a Military Contribution," *Canadian Foreign Policy* 5:2 (Winter 1998): p. 162.

6 Maurice Baril, "Peacekeeping and Force," in *Peacekeeping with Muscle: The Use of Force in International Conflict Resolution*, eds. Alex Morrison, Douglas Fraser, and James Kiras (Cornwallis Park, NS: Canadian Peacekeeping Press, 1997), p. 119.

7 Judith Steihm, "The Challenge of Civil-Military Cooperation in Peacekeeping," *Airman-Scholar* (Winter 1998): p. 30; Mark Dearfield "The CJTF and NGOs: One Team, One Mission?" US Naval War College mimeo, 1998, p. 4; Major K. E. Bruno, "The Regional Civil-Military Operations Center: A Force Multiplier in Military Operations Other Than War," US Naval War College mimeo, 1999, p. 10.

8 Steihm, "The Challenge of Civil-Military Cooperation in Peacekeeping," p. 31; J. T. Dworken, "Military Relations with Humanitarian Relief Organizations: Observations from Restore Hope," US Center for Naval Analysis mimeo, 1993, p. 38.

9 I will use the term "peace operations" partly to avoid getting involved in a controversy over labels and to have one term to describe the wide range of activities which are often called peacekeeping. In fact, peacekeeping is NOT a term found in the UN Charter, but it has come to refer to a wide variety of actions and interventions, which renders the peacekeeping role itself both ambiguous and open to variable definition. F. Pinch, *Lessons From Canadian Peacekeeping Experience: a Human Resources Perspective* (Ottawa: FCP Human Resources Consulting, 1994), p. 17. In July 1992 an attempt was made by the then UN Secretary General Boutros Boutros-Ghali to identify various types of action in *An Agenda for Peace*. In Chapter II of this document peacemaking and peacekeeping are described. Peacemaking is the action to bring hostile parties to agreement, while peacekeeping is the deployment of a UN presence in the field. Other concepts found in this chapter are preventive diplomacy (action to prevent disputes from arising, to prevent existing disputes from escalating and to limit the spread of conflict); post-conflict peacebuilding (action to identify and support structures which will strengthen and solidify peace); and peace enforcement (restoring and maintaining cease-fire by force). Cited in M. Bertrand, "The Confusion Between Peacemaking and Peacekeeping," in *New Dimensions of Peacekeeping*, ed. D. Warner (Netherlands: Kluwer Academic Publishers, 1995), pp. 163-164. Bertrand tells us that although these terms seem clear, in fact the distinction between the different forms of actions is blurred, and that there is confusion among them. Bertrand, "The Confusion Between Peacemaking and Peacekeeping," p. 164.

10 P. J. Simmons, "Learning to Live with NGOs," *Foreign Policy* (Fall 1998): pp. 75-76.

11 Williams, *Civil Military Relations and Peacekeeping*, p. 39.

12 See Laura Miller, "From Adversaries to Allies: Relief Workers' Attitudes Towards the US Military," *Qualitative Sociology* 22:3 (1999): pp. 181-198.

13 P. Aall, "Nongovernmental Organizations and Peacemaking," in *Managing Global Chaos*, eds. C. A. Crocker and F. O. Hampson (Washington D.C.: United States Institute of Peace Press, 1996), p. 440.

14 Cited in Williams, *Civil Military Relations and Peacekeeping*, p. 41.

15 Andrew Natsios, "An NGO Perspective," in *Peacemaking in International Conflict*, eds. I. W. Zartman and J. L. Rasmussen (Washington D.C.: United States Institute of Peace Press, 1997), p. 354.

16 David Owen, *Balkan Odyssey* (London: Victor Gollancz, 1995), p. 208.

17 Cited in Jennifer Ross "Human Security in Peace Operations," paper presented to the workshop, *The Future of the Canadian Forces*, Centre for Security and Defence Studies and Canadian War Museum, Ottawa, Canada, 2 June 2000, p. 2.

18 Cited in Miller, "From Adversaries to Allies," p. 191.

19 Ibid.
20 Department of National Defence, Chief of Review Services, Defence Ethics Program, *Ethics and Operations Project Draft Report* (Ottawa: National Defence Headquarters, 1999) (hereinafter called *Ethics Report*).
21 *Ethics Report,* pp. 2-13.
22 Ibid., p. 13.
23 Miller, "From Adversaries to Allies," p. 194.
24 Ibid., p. 193.
25 Anecdote cited in Moskos, *The Media and the Military in Peace and Humanitarian Operations*, p. 33.
26 Cited in Williams, *Civil Military Relations and Peacekeeping*, p. 36.
27 Ibid., p. 37.
28 In traditional peacekeeping operations from 1957 to 1989 only 25 of the more than 26,000 troops were female. From 1989 to 1992 the number of females rose to 255 but that was still approximately one per cent of the total military members in peace operations. J. C. Beilstein, "The Role of Women in United States Peacekeeping," *Women 2000* Vol. 1 (1995): p. 1.
29 Miller, "From Adversaries to Allies," p. 193.
30 Williams, *Civil Military Relations and Peacekeeping*, p. 34.
31 L. Miller and C. Moskos, "Humanitarians or Warriors?: Race, Gender and Combat Status in Operation Restore Hope," *Armed Forces and Society* 21:4 (Summer 1995): pp. 615-637.
32 S. Ogata, "The Interface between Peacekeeping and Humanitarian Action," in *New Dimensions of Peacekeeping*, ed. D. Warner (Netherlands: Kluwer Academic Publishers, 1995), pp. 119-127.
33 Ibid.
34 Williams, *Civil Military Relations and Peacekeeping*, p. 40.
35 Miller, "From Adversaries to Allies," p. 192.
36 John Garofano, "The United States in Bosnia: Points of Tension and Learning for the US Military," US Army War College mimeo, 1999, p. 47.
37 Relief worker cited in Miller, "From Adversaries to Allies," p. 187.
38 Ibid., p. 189.
39 Ibid.
40 Appathurai and Lysyshyn, *Lessons Learned from the Zaire Mission*, p. 7.
41 Ibid., p. 9.
42 T. Pope, *Beans, Bullets, and Band-Aids: Attaining Unity of Effort in Humanitarian Intervention Operations,* Monograph of the School of Advanced Military Studies, US Army Command and General Staff College, Fort Leavenworth, Kansas, 1994.
43 Sweatt describes how differences in conceptual end-states negatively affects NGO and military relations. See S. Sweatt, *The Challenges of Civil-Military Relations at the Trailing Edge of War*, Monograph of the US Naval War College, Newport, Rhode Island, 1995.
44 National governments may also be responding to political imperatives, e.g. stopping the flow of refugees into the national country. See M. V. Metselaar, "Understanding Failures in Intelligence Estimates: UNPROFOR, the Dutch and the Bosnian-Serb Attack on Srebrenica," *Netherlands Annual Review of Military Studies, The Bosnian Experience* (1997): p. 27.
45 Miller, "From Adversaries to Allies," p. 191.
46 Williams, *Civil Military Relations and Peacekeeping*, p. 36.
47 Appathurai and Lysyshyn, *Lessons Learned from the Zaire Mission*, p. 12.
48 Last, "Defeating Fear and Hatred through Peacebuilding," p. 166.

49 D. Dandekar and J. Gow, "The Future of Peace Support Operations: Strategic Peacekeeping and Success," *Armed Forces and Society* 23:3 (Spring 1997): pp. 327-348.
50 Appathurai and Lysyshyn, *Lessons Learned from the Zaire Mission,* p. 11.
51 See J. S. van der Meulen, "Expectations of Peacekeeping: Dutch Public Opinion about Missions in the Former Yugoslavia," *Netherlands Annual Review of Military Studies, The Bosnian Experience* (1997): pp. 173-185.
52 Appathurai and Lysyshyn, *Lessons Learned from the Zaire Mission*, pp. 6-7.
53 L. Miller, "Relief Workers' Attitudes Toward the US Military in Peacekeeping Operations," paper presented to the Biennial International Conference of the Inter-University Seminar on Armed Forces and Society, Baltimore, Maryland, October 1997.
54 Relief worker quoted in Miller, "From Adversaries to Allies," p. 192.
55 Moskos, *The Media and the Military in Peace and Humanitarian Operations,* p. 46.
56 Ibid., p. 33.
57 Quoted in David Rieff, "Lost Kosovo," *The New Republic* (31 May 1999): p. 27.
58 Quoted in Moskos, *The Media and the Military in Peace and Humanitarian Operations,* p. 34.
59 Ibid., p. 46.
60 Relief worker quoted in Miller, "From Adversaries to Allies," p. 188.
61 Moskos, *The Media and the Military in Peace and Humanitarian Operations,* p. 50.
62 Miller, "Relief Workers' Attitudes Toward the US Military in Peacekeeping Operations."
63 Relief worker quoted in Miller, "From Adversaries to Allies" p. 188.
64 Steihm, "The Challenge of Civil-Military Cooperation in Peacekeeping," p. 30.
65 Moskos, *The Media and the Military in Peace and Humanitarian Operations,* p. 33.
66 See US Joint Warfighting Center, *Joint Task Force Commander's Handbook for Peace Operations*, Fort Monroe, Virginia: Joint Warfighting Center, 1997.
67 Cited in Ross, "Human Security in Peace Operations," p. 4.
68 Miller, "Relief Workers' Attitudes Toward the US Military in Peacekeeping Operations."

Chapter 8

Conclusion: Dilemmas of Peacekeeping at the Start of the Twenty-first Century

Timothy M. Shaw and Natalie Mychajlyszyn

"Peace is a development issue."

Darby and MacGinty[1]

"September 11 has begun a new chapter in the historic rivalry between states and non-state actors."

Booth and Dunne[2]

Over the last decade widespread expectations about a post-bipolar 'peace dividend' in the 1990s have been proven to be quite misplaced. Likewise, any anticipation that 'peace-keeping operations' (PKOs) would be either less frequent or less fraught after the end of the Cold War has also been shown to be rather optimistic. Rather, the dawn of the new millennium heralded profound challenges to the conceptualization and operationalization of humanitarian interventions and peace missions as this volume has indicated. By way of offering conclusions on the subject, this chapter draws from the others to offer some insight into possible answers to the questions posed in the introduction which frame our on-going concern and attention. It also points to emerging dilemmas in analysis and policy, approach and practice, at least until the end of the first decade of the new millennium.

The question of acceptable violations of sovereignty and non-intervention will likely remain highly controversial. The international community, regardless of its efforts to the contrary in the form of the International Commission on Intervention and State Sovereignty, has been unable to institute new mechanisms and doctrines that would provide clear and uniformly applicable guidelines as to which humanitarian crises warrant the violation of a state's sovereignty and that satisfy both sides in the debate. Indeed, as S. Neil MacFarlane argues in his chapter, the pre-11 September period showed itself to be more of a continuation from the Cold War era of politics as usual where interventions were concerned in that, at the end of the day, strategic consideration trumped collective norms as the motivation behind many intervention decisions. This becomes apparent in considering those crises where intervention did not take place despite ample reasons for proceeding with an intervention and the same international tools and mechanisms being available, save for the missing ingredient of strategic value. Thus, in this volume we see how intervention took place in Kosovo and Sri Lanka as Carment and Rowlands show due to NATO's growing concern with the regional consequences of Milosevic's treatment of the Kosovo Albanians and India's concern with regional instability and secessionist movements; and took place in a less aggressive form by France and the international community in Rwanda due to domestic political concerns about long-term involvement as Astroff and Meren note; or did not take place at all regarding Zaire due to a withdrawal of support in light of changed circumstances. Moreover, these cases show how international institutions and legal arguments are either disregarded or manipulated to suit the specific purposes of the primary actors, particularly where United Nations Chapter VII provisions are concerned. As much as 11 September 2001 is held up as a watershed in international politics, the actions of the international community in Iraq, Afghanistan and Haiti, or non-action in Africa, reinforces this point. Until the international community can move beyond state interests and the dissonance within it to either fashion new institutions and enforcement mechanisms that provide clear and uniformly applicable guidelines for acceptable violations of sovereignty, or respect those it has already created, interventions will continue to be a tool of international policy used by those who can, in effect, "twist arms and flex muscles".

It follows that the chapters in this book also shed light onto the nature of the humanitarian crises and conflicts themselves that precipitate interventions. Indeed, more and more the link between humanitarian crises and conflicts is appreciated and which goes beyond the violation of human rights as addressed by MacFarlane in his assessment of the legal justification for interventions. However, these linkages have a profoundly dynamic nature that not only renders them exceedingly overwhelming but also metastatic. Timothy M. Shaw profiles his rendering of this challenge in Africa as the "political economy of violence," appropriately highlighting the multi-faceted nature of the problem not only for the immediate area, but ultimately for the broader region. Shaw's chapter raises important reflections about how the international community responds (or doesn't, as the case may be) to such challenges. More specifically, for these challenges to be addressed effectively, the international community must consider equally multi-faceted and multi-disciplinary tools that are also regional in scope. The warning that emerges is that these crises and conflicts otherwise will proliferate and/or become more chronic with the result that more coercive and escalatory means of response, i.e. military interventions, might be taken but with no certainty of success. For some, 11 September itself and the response by the United States and its coalition of the willing exemplifies this syndrome.

That some cases of intervention are more successful than others can be better understood in light of the cases examined in the two chapters by Astroff and Meren and Carment and Rowlands. For their part, Astroff and Meren suggest a Conflict Intensity Abatement (CIA) Index to show what has become conventional wisdom in international politics that a successful de-escalation of a conflict is affected by the maturity of the conflict or crisis, the timing of the intervention, its nature (military or diplomatic or economic) and the extent of the commitment. Likewise, Carment and Rowlands take on an issue of great currency among conflict resolution analysts, that is the impact of bias on the success of an intervention. More specifically, they show how the consequences of action by an intervenor who favours one side in a dispute over another may just as easily escalate the conflict as de-escalate it, depending on the response to the biased intervention by the non-favoured combatant.

Lastly, we see that, as much as the international community attempts to overcome obstacles to building peace in post-conflict situations, other obstacles emerge. For instance, as evident in the chapters by Winslow and Last, close, purposeful collaboration between civilian and military agencies in the field has become in the post-Cold War era an unprecedented means by which societies can be protected and rehabilitated in order to prevent conflict from escalating or re-emerging. At the same time, however, as Winslow notes, the cultural differences between these two groups of actors can create tensions that complicate, if not undermine, the peacebuilding exercise. Likewise, as Last argues, the extension of the type of activities that military personnel are engaged in during peacebuilding operations beyond pure military tasks, i.e. security, governance, development and reconciliation, has emerged as an important feature influencing the success of peacebuilding operations and one that, arguably, should be institutionalized in order for 'peacekeepers to be put out of business.' However, military personnel face such limitations as knowledge of the local language, culture and conditions that prevent them from being more effective in carrying out 'civilian' activities, thereby threatening their credibility, that of the operation and the success of the mission itself. Thus, due to the nature of peacebuilding itself as an exceedingly complex and intense exercise demanding multiple actors, high levels of commitment and complementary skills and knowledge, it is likely that obstacles to peacebuilding can only be minimized rather than eliminated completely.

Taking these questions and answers into account, nine sets of inter-related issues concerning humanitarian intervention and informed by current conceptual and operational developments become apparent and serve to conclude this chapter and volume:

i) *Advancing from naïve, modest 'humanitarian interventions' to recognition of a major new security 'sector.'* As alluded to in the chapters by Carment and Rowlands and Astroff and Meren, the occasional, small-scale UN-orchestrated 'humanitarian interventions' characteristic of much of the Cold War period[3] now begin to look like picnics compared to the protracted, expansive, changeable character of, for instance, NATO missions of 'willing' coalition partners in Central Europe and Central Asia. Thus, the primary international arena and institution where crises are discussed and action initiated will shift away from the UN and toward ad hoc coalitions led by a dominant country such as the United States that has the necessary capabilities to do so, politically, economically and militarily. In this respect, for many countries joining such coalitions, their primary motivation may be less the fulfillment of alliance or other bilateral security obligations since these may not be present in the first place, but instead the political draw and economic benefit deriving from the extreme exhibition of such support. Indeed, as we have seen with the second Iraq war, this conceptualization suggests that the UN will be increasingly disregarded and the dominance of state-led responses will be reasserted. That a new security sector is under development is indicated by the number, scale and robustness of contemporary peace-enforcement duties as well as by the degree of their multilateralism in terms of both readiness and resources in response to the proliferation of such conflicts.

ii) *Recognizing the likelihood of a shift from short-term interventions towards a longer-term 'responsibility to protect.'* Most peacekeeping during the Cold War entailed the deployment of blue berets between two formal militaries and into situations featuring traditional sources of conflict. In the post-bipolar era, peacebuilding and military interventions are being deployed into situations characterized by irregular armed groups and humanitarian crises, i.e. conflicts of a non-traditional nature that derive from the character of many 'new' states as weak regimes and strong mafias, with both groups seeking to accumulate power through violent control over the economy,[4] as indicated in the next section, and in the absence of any established, transparent, and stable political, military and economic institutions that otherwise shoulder the responsibility to protect. In short, the 'al-Qaeda' 'fundamentalist' network was not unique, but rather the best-known or most notorious of such contemporary mafias. Thus, where institutional structures are present but are shirking from their responsibility to protect, or are absent altogether, the responsibility shifts to the international community instead, leading to the reconceptualising of the activity of intervening in terms of the 'responsibility to protect,' as recognized and legitimized by the ICISS.[5] In this respect, the nature of protection, of (re)establishing the institutions and mechanisms that secure the individual, the group, and society at large from threats from other individuals, groups and the state is recognized to require a long-term commitment, much more ambitious and ambiguous set of tasks such that previous Cold War-era responses in the form of quick 'in-out' interventions are no longer practical. In other words, interventions will be of a significantly longer duration and of a significantly deeper level of penetration in order to overcome the source of the humanitarian crises and to restore peace.

iii) *Appreciating the 'political economy of conflict' as the single primary cause of sustained conflict.* During the Cold War, conflicts and regimes were prolonged and endured in so far as they served the interests of the global rivalry between the United States and the Soviet Union. With the end of this rivalry, the regimes which had previously benefited from it turned to other means – such as 'blood diamonds' in West Africa – by which to sustain their power and ability to accumulate and in the process perpetrate and/or perpetuate conflict within and outside the state in question.[6] In this way, contemporary conflicts and humanitarian crises endure as a function of their political economy, as illustrated in Shaw's chapter. Thus, efficacious peacemaking now includes the additional, complicated and dangerous tasks of cutting-off illicit trade, such as drugs, forced migration, guns, money-laundering, etc.; otherwise, mafia-type networks will perpetuate violence which generates the resources by which they exist.[7] Such resource wars are likely to become more large-scale in the future as demand for gas, oil and fresh water, for instance, outstretch supply;[8] hence, Africa's growing indispensability for the West, especially the United States.[9]

iv) *Accepting the regionalization of many conflicts, especially in 'new' regions like Central Europe/Asia.* After the end of the Cold War and its global characterization, the world has witnessed a scaling-back of conflicts to a more regional scope. Indeed, many of the small and poor states in the middle of these conflicts, some newly independent, others already in existence, exert minimal control outside their capital cities and in the border areas. Thus, conflict nexuses are unfettered and easily spilled-over into neighbouring states, as occurred in Central and West Africa[10] as well as in the 'new' Central Asia and Central Europe. The presence of a regional power or the efforts of a state in the region to assert itself as a regional power by way of perpetuating or responding to a conflict or crisis reinforces the regionalization of contemporary conflicts and crises. As a result, the regionalization of conflict has witnessed regional-level responses, such as either ECOMOG in West Africa or NATO in Central Europe, which might lead towards at least some regional (in)security complexes or communities of both state and non-state groupings. At an extreme, it also may lead to a continuation of the process by which more global institutions such as the UN are increasingly disregarded and marginalized from the peacebuilding process.

v) *Encouraging 'new' divisions of labour among a variety of actors and interests.* With the end of bipolarity and reinforcing previous pronouncements regarding the UN and its marginalized role in post-Cold War peacebuilding, peace operations in the South are more likely to fall to the UN, where regional organizations are weak and where the most active of regional groupings, NATO, thus far has not shown itself. In contrast, peace operations in the North, including Central Asia and Central Europe, are monopolized by NATO in its effort to re-define its scope of interest and post-Cold War mandate to account for out-of-area conflicts and non-Article 5 activities. Furthermore, as contemporary peace operations necessitate some attention to causes and consequences, new actors have been incorporated in 'pre-packaged' responses, especially non-state actors.[11] In this respect, as Last alludes to in his chapter, non-governmental organizations (NGOs) have been assigned responsibility for education, habitat, health, etc. and multinational corporations (MNCs) for services such as communications, electricity, sewerage, transportation and water.[12] Such divisions of labour have also become apparent as national militaries are beginning to contract out some of their support services in part as cost-saving measures. The intention of dividing the labour is to assign tasks and responsibilities to actors, whether international or regional organizations, military or civilian groups, that are best suited and able to fulfill them without overtaxing and ultimately undermining any one actor. Indeed, the greater the complexity of peacebuilding and humanitarian interventions in a particular situation, the more evident and necessary a division of labour in order to better manage their scope and improve the likelihood of a positive outcome. Such divisions of labour become ever more inevitable given vii) below.[13] Nevertheless, these divisions should not be maintained in an absolute fashion and instead should retain some degree of flexibility in order to maximize opportunities and skills as needs arise.

vi) *Recognizing the range of 'new' issues generated by complex peace operations.* Complex peace operations[14] can no longer avoid a range of novel issues such as blood diamonds, child soldiers, diasporas, ecology, gender, HIV/AIDS,[15] land-mines, mafias and militias, individual security, etc. that have emerged as chronic dimensions – either as sources or consequences – of the humanitarian conflicts and crises to which they are deployed to address. Indeed, these issues in some respects have displaced and in others have been added to the more traditional preoccupations with conflicts such as disarmament. Which of these are recognized and prioritized depends on the operation and time period. Nevertheless, to enhance the chances of successful peacebuilding, humanitarian interventions and even multilateral negotiations like the Kimberley and Ottawa Processes that may result from them must take care to ensure that these issues are addressed in an integral and systemic way. The challenge, as this volume has demonstrated, is to do so.

vii) *Defining and incorporating the complexities entailed by the growing 'privatization of security.'* With the end of the Cold War, the means by which security is provided has been moving increasingly away from large-scale, full-service national armed forces towards private security groups. More specifically, security organizations and operations, including police and protection functions, are becoming increasingly privatized either formally and legally, as in contracting out, or informally and illegally, as in militias and mafias seizing aspects of the security sector.[16] The reasons for this movement range from the effort on the part of national governments to reduce costs – financial as well as political – associated with running a modern military and foreign deployments, the growing presence of MNCs as well as (although for different reasons) NGOs in areas of conflict who seek some measure of protection from encroaching (and armed) opposition groups or competitors, the inability of weak national governments to provide security in the first place, and the scope and complexity of the situations themselves. The complication of divisions of labor in peacemaking coalitions, i.e., public and private partnerships, even legal and illegal partners, is inevitable on many levels, including the placement of accountability, chain of command among others.[17]

viii) *Realizing the additional complication posed by the 9/11 syndrome of 'global terrorism.'* Terrorist attacks by 'fundamentalists' occurred before and after the horrors of 9/11, indicating a range of networks, allies and targets. While there can be no successful single 'war on terrorism', the threat posed by al-Qaeda complicates the future of peace operations as it will divert attentions and resources away from, say, another genocide like that in Rwanda a decade ago. At the same time, there is a risk that the terrorist lens will be inappropriately applied to all agenda-items, leading to inappropriate and ineffective responses. There is a need to identify and maintain conceptual and operational distinctions between anti-terrorist and pro-peace responses.[18] And finally,

ix) *Appreciating the centrality of such new forms of peacekeeping for an interrelated set of literatures/genres.* Several disciplines or fields are increasingly affected by conflict and peace-making reactions even if they do not always yet so appreciate.[19] This is so for established genres – e.g. economics, international relations,[20] political economy/science and security studies – as well as more recent ones – development and gender studies – and for policy debates as well as more academic theories. Such conceptual shifts are impacting NGOs and think tanks as well,[21] likely into the second decade of the new century.

Hence, the relevance of this collection: how to continually modify state and non-state analysis, policy and practice in response to changing patterns of conflict? In this way, the value of different perspectives on humanitarian intervention and peacebuilding appreciates and the task of identifying and understanding them will be never-ending, and the 'twisting of arms and flexing of muscles' will continue. As

Douglas Lemke recently asserted in a review article in *World Politics* on such parallel lessons from Africa for international relations:

> Because standard international relations research theorizes about and collects data only for official states, much of Africa's international relations are left out ... . But surely these lessons apply to the developing world more broadly. Without much effort one can create a list of de facto states in other parts of the developing world ... . Clearly, the existence of important de facto states carrying out traditional international relations activities with other de facto states as well as with official states, international nongovernmental organizations, and multinational corporations suggests the African lessons drawn here will apply globally too.[22]

Notes

1 John Darby and Roger MacGinty, "Conclusion," in *Contemporary Peacemaking: Conflict, Violence and Peace Processes*, eds. John Darby and Roger MacGinty (London: Palgrave, 2003), p. 271.

2 Ken Booth and Tim Dunne, "Preface," in *Worlds in Collision: Terror and the Future of Global Order,* eds. Ken Booth and Tim Dunne (London: Palgrave Macmillan, 2002), p. 13.

3 *The Responsibility to Protect*, Report of the International Commission on Intervention and State Sovereignty, International Development Research Centre, Ottawa, Canada, December 2001, Volume Two.

4 Patrick Chabal and Jean-Pascal Daloz, *Africa Works: Disorder as Political Instrument* (Oxford: James Currey for International African Institute, 1999); Mark Duffield, *Global Governance and the New Wars: The Merging of Development and Security* (London: Zed Books, 2001); William Reno, *Warlord Politics and African States* (Boulder: Lynne Rienner, 1998).

5 Ibid.

6 www.partnershipafricacanada.org; Reno, *Warlord Politics and African States.*

7 Graduate Institute for International Studies, *Small Arms Survey 2003: Development Denied* (Oxford: Oxford University Press, 2003); Graduate Institute for International Studies, *Small Arms Survey 2004: Rights at Risk* (Oxford: Oxford University Press, 2004).

8 Michael T. Klare, *Resource Wars: The New Landscape of Global Conflict* (New York: Owl, 2002).

9 Jonathan Stevenson, "Africa's Growing Strategic Resonance," *Survival* 45:4 (Winter 2003-04): pp. 153-171.

10 Timothy M. Shaw, "The Regional Dimensions of Conflict and Peacebuilding in Contemporary Africa," *Journal of International Development* 15:4 (May 2003): pp. 487-498.

11 Booth and Dunne, "Preface."

12 Tony Addison, ed., *From Conflict to Recovery in Africa* (Oxford: Oxford University Press for United Nations University/World Institute for Development Economics Research, 2003).

13 Darby and MacGinty, "Conclusion;" Rose M. Kadende-Kaiser and Paul J Kaiser, eds., "Phases of Conflict in Africa," *Journal of Asian and African Studies* 38:2-3 (August 2003): pp. 150-322.

14 Darby and MacGinty, "Conclusion;" Stephen John Steadman et al, eds., *Ending Civil Wars: The Implementation of Peace Agreements* (Boulder: Lynne Rienner, 2002).

15 www.businessfightsaids.org

16 Jorn Brommelhorster and Wolf-Christian Paes, eds., *Soldiers in Business: The Military as an Economic Actor* (London: Palgrave Macmillan, 2003).

17 For the first time, the International Institute for Strategic Studies included data on non-state armed groups in Part III of its annual review of military balances. International Institute for Strategic Studies, *The Military Balance 2003-2004* (Oxford: Oxford University Press, 2003).

18 Booth and Dunne, "Preface."

19 Marie Smyth and Gillian Robinson, eds., *Researching Violently Divided Societies: Ethical and Methodological Issues* (London: Pluto for United Nations University Press, 2001).

20 Kevin C. Dunn and Timothy M. Shaw, eds., *Africa's Challenge to International Relations Theory* (London: Palgrave, 2001).

21 Pamela Mbabazi et al, "Governance for Reconstruction in Africa: Challenges for Policy Communities and Coalitions," *Global Networks: A Journal of Transnational Affairs* 2:1 (January 2002).

22 Douglas Lemke, "Review Article: African Lessons for International Relations Research," *World Politics* 56:1 (October 2003): pp. 117 and 138. See also James D. Fearon and David D. Laitin, "Neotrusteeship and the Problem of Weak States," *International Security* 28:4 (Spring 2004): pp. 5-43.

Bibliography

"A Report of the Panel on United Nations Peace Operations." *The Brahimi Report.* United Nations (July 2000). www.un.org.

A Rough Trade: The Role of Companies and Governments in the Angolan Conflict. New York: Global Witness, 2000.

Aall, P. "Nongovernmental Organizations and Peacemaking." In *Managing Global Chaos: Sources of and Responses to International Conflict.* Edited by Chester Crocker and Fen Osler Hampson. Washington D.C.: United States Institute of Peace Press, 1996.

Abi-Saab, Georges. *The United Nations Operation in the Congo.* Oxford: Oxford University Press, 1978.

Addison, Tony, ed. *From Conflict to Recovery in Africa.* Oxford: Oxford University Press for United Nations University/World Institute for Development Economics Research, 2003.

Adler, E. and M. Barnett, eds. *Security Communities.* Cambridge: Cambridge University Press, 1998.

African Development Bank. *African Development Report 2000.* Oxford: Oxford University Press, 2000.

Amnesty International. *Political Killings by Governments.* London: Amnesty International, 1983.

Annan, Kofi. "Reflections on Intervention." 35th Ditchley Foundation Lecture, 26 June 1998. In *The Question of Intervention: Statements by the Secretary-General.* New York: United Nations, 1999.

———. *"We the Peoples:" The Role of the UN in the 21st Century.* New York: United Nations, 2000.

Appathurai, James and Ralph Lysyshyn. *Lessons Learned from the Zaire Mission.* Ottawa: Canadian Department of Foreign Affairs and International Trade, 1997.

Aron, Raymond. *Peace and War: A Theory of International Relations.* Malabar, FL: Robert E. Krieger, 1981.

Astroff, Robert E. *Scuttled Diplomacy: A Study of Intervention by the United Nations in Rwanda.* Master's Thesis, Carleton University, 1999.

Austin, Dennis. *Democracy and Violence in India and Sri Lanka.* London: Royal Institute of International Affairs, 1995.

Avant, Deborah. "The Privatization of Security and Change in the Control of Force." *International Studies Perspectives* 5:2 (May 2004).

Axworthy, Lloyd. "Human Security and Global Governance: Putting People First." *Global Governance* 7:1 (January-March 2001).

Ayoob, Mohammed. "Humanitarian Intervention and International Society." *Global Governance* 7:3 (July-September 2001).

Bard, M. and J. Zacker. *The Police and Interpersonal Conflict: Third Party Intervention Approaches.* Washington, D.C.: Police Foundation, 1976.

Baril, Maurice. "Peacekeeping and Force." In *Peacekeeping with Muscle: The Use of Force in International Conflict Resolution.* Edited by Alex Morrison, Douglas Fraser, and James Kiras. Cornwallis Park, N.S.: Canadian Peacekeeping Press, 1997.

Becker, Gary. "A Theory of Competition Among Pressure Groups for Political Influence." *Quarterly Journal of Economics* 98:3 (1983).

Beilstein, J. C. "The Role of Women in United States Peacekeeping." *Women 2000* 1 (1995).

Bercovitch, Jacob. *Social Conflicts and Third Parties: Strategies of Conflict Resolution*. Boulder, CO: Westview Press, 1984.

Bercovitch, Jacob, ed. *Resolving International Conflicts: Theory and Practice of Mediation*. Boulder: Lynne Rienner, 1996.

Berdal, M. and D. Malone, eds. *Greed and Grievance: Economic Agendas in Civil Wars*. Boulder: Lynne Rienner, 2000.

Berman, Eric and Katie Sams. *Peacekeeping in Africa: Capabilities and Culpabilities*. New York: United Nations, 2000.

Bertrand, M. "The Confusion Between Peacemaking and Peacekeeping." In *New Dimensions of Peacekeeping*. Edited by D. Warner. Netherlands: Kluwer Academic Publishers, 1995.

Bettati, Mario. *Le droit d'ingérence: Mutation de l'ordre international*. Paris: Odile Jacob, 1996.

Bettati, Mario and Bernard Kouchner. *Le devoir d'ingérence*. Paris: Denoël, 1987.

Betts, Richard K. "The Delusion of Impartial Intervention." In *Managing Global Chaos: Sources of and Responses to International Conflict*. Edited by Chester Crocker and Fen Osler Hampson. Washington, D.C.: United States Institute of Peace Press, 1996.

Biermann, Wolfgang and Martin Vadset, eds. *UN Peacekeeping in Trouble: Lessons Learned from the Former Yugoslavia*. Aldershot: Ashgate, 1998.

Bond, P., ed. *Fanon's Warning: A Civil Society Perspective on the New Partnership for Africa's Development*. Trenton, N.J.: Africa World Press, 2002.

Booth, Ken and Tim Dunne. "Preface." In *Worlds in Collision: Terror and the Future of Global Order*. Edited by Ken Booth and Tim Dunne. London: Palgrave Macmillan, 2002.

Boskey, James. "The Proper Role of the Mediator: Rational Assessment, Not Pressure." *Negotiation Journal* 10 (1994).

Boulden, Jane. *Peace Enforcement: The United Nations Experience in Congo, Somalia, and Bosnia*. Westport, CT: Praeger, 2001.

Boutros-Ghali, Boutros. *An Agenda for Peace: Preventive Diplomacy, Peacemaking and Peacekeeping*. New York: United Nations, 1992.

Boya, O. "Contentious Politics and Social Change in Congo." *Security Dialogue* 32:1 (March 2001).

Braathen, E. et al, eds. *Ethnicity Kills? The Politics of War, Peace and Ethnicity in Sub-Saharan Africa*. London: Macmillan, 2000.

Brommelhorster, Jorn and Wolf-Christian Paes, eds. *Soldiers in Business: The Military as an Economic Actor*. London: Palgrave Macmillan, 2003.

Bruno, Major K. E. "The Regional Civil-Military Operations Center: A Force Multiplier in Military Operations Other Than War." United States Naval War College mimeo, 1999.

Bryans, Michael, Bruce Jones and Janice Gross Stein. "Mean Times: Humanitarian Action in Complex Political Emergencies – Stark Choices, Cruel Dilemmas." *Coming to Terms* 1:3. Program on Conflict Management and Negotiation (January 1999).

Bull, Hedley. "Introduction." In *Intervention in World Politics*. Edited by Hedley Bull. Oxford: Oxford University Press, 1984.

Burton, J. W. *Conflict: Resolution and Provention*. London: Macmillan, 1990.

Byman, Daniel and Matthew Waxman. "Kosovo and the Great Air Power Debate." *International Security* 24:4 (2000).

Campbell, G. *Blood Diamonds: Tracing the Deadly Path of the World's Most Precious Stone*. Boulder: Perseus, 2002.

Carment, David and Patrick James. "Two-level Games and Third-Party Intervention: Evidence from Ethnic Conflict in the Balkans and South Asia." *Canadian Journal of Political Science* 29:3 (1996).

Carment, David and Frank Harvey. *Using Force to Prevent Ethnic Violence*. Westport, CT: Praeger Press, 2000.

Carment, David and Dane Rowlands. "Three's Company: Evaluating Third-Party Intervention in Intra-state Conflict." *Journal of Conflict Resolution* 42 (1998).

Carment, David and Dane Rowlands. "The Role of Bias in Third-Party Intervention: Theory and Evidence." Unpublished mimeo, Carleton University, 2000.

Carnevale, Peter J. and Sharon Arad. "Bias and Impartiality in International Mediation." In *Resolving International Conflicts: Theory and Practice of Mediation.* Edited by Jacob Bercovitch. Boulder: Lynne Rienner, 1996.

Chabal, Patrick and Jean-Pascal Daloz. *Africa Works: Disorder as Political Instrument.* Oxford: James Currey for International African Institute, 1999.

Chipman, John. *French Military Power and African Security.* London: International Institute for Strategic Studies, 1985.

_______. *French Power in Africa.* Oxford: Basil Blackwell, 1989.

Cilliers, J. and D. Christian, eds. *Angola's War Economy: The Role of Oil and Diamonds.* Pretoria: Institute for Security Studies, 2000.

Citizens and Governance: Civil Society in the New Millennium. London: Commonwealth Foundation, 1999.

Cliffe, L., ed. "Special Issue: Complex Political Emergencies." *Third World Quarterly* 20:1 (March 1999).

Coady, C. A. J. "The Ethics of Armed Humanitarian Intervention." *Peaceworks* No. 45. United States Institute of Peace (July 2002).

Cohen, Roberta and Francis Deng. *The Forsaken People: Case Studies of the Internally Displaced.* Washington, D.C.: Brookings Institution Press, 1998.

Collier, P. and A. Hoeffler. *Greed and Grievance in Civil War.* Washington, D.C.: World Bank, 2000. www.worldbank.org/research/conflict.

Conflict Diamonds: Possibilities for the Identification, Certification and Control of Diamonds. New York: Global Witness, 2000.

Dandekar, D. and J. Gow. "The Future of Peace Support Operations: Strategic Peacekeeping and Success." *Armed Forces and Society* 23:3 (Spring 1997).

Darby, John and Roger MacGinty. "Conclusion." In *Contemporary Peacemaking: Conflict, Violence and Peace Processes.* Edited by John Darby and Roger MacGinty. London: Palgrave, 2003.

De Waal, A. "What's New in the 'New Partnership for Africa's Development'?" *International Affairs* 78:3 (July 2002).

Dearfield, Mark. "The CJTF and NGOs: One Team, One Mission?" United States Naval War College mimeo, 1998.

Department of National Defence, Chief of Review Services, Defence Ethics Program. *Ethics and Operations Project Draft Report.* Ottawa: National Defence Headquarters, 1999.

Diehl, Paul F., J. Reifschneider and Paul R. Hensel. "United Nations Intervention and Recurring Conflict." *International Organization* 50 (1996).

Doyle, Michael and Nicholas Sambanis. "International Peacebuilding: A Theoretical and Quantitative Analysis (Statistical Data Included)." *American Political Science Review* (December 2000).

Doxey, Margaret P. *United Nations Sanctions: Current Policy Issues.* Halifax: Centre for Foreign Policy Studies of Dalhousie University, 1997.

Duffield, Mark. *Global Governance and the New Wars: The Merging of Development and Security.* London: Zed Books, 2001.

Dunn, Kevin C. and Timothy M. Shaw, eds. *Africa's Challenge to International Relations Theory.* London: Palgrave, 2001.

Dworken, J. T. "Military Relations with Humanitarian Relief Organizations: Observations from Restore Hope." United States Center for Naval Analysis mimeo, 1993.

Eckhardt, W. "Civilizations, Empires and Wars." *Journal of Peace Research* 27:1 (Winter 1990).

Evans, Gareth. *Cooperating for Peace: The Global Agenda for the 1990s and Beyond.* London: Allen and Unwin, 1993.

Farer, Tom J. and Felice Gaer. "The UN and Human Rights." In *United Nations, Divided World: The U.N.'s Roles in International Relations.* Edited by Adam Roberts and Benedict Kingsbury. Oxford: Oxford University Press, 1993.

Fenton, Neil. *Consent, Coercion and Sovereignty in United Nations Security Council Mandated Operations, 1991-1995*, D. Phil. Thesis, Oxford University, 2000.

Fetherston, A. B. "Peacekeeping, Conflict Resolution, and Peacebuilding: A Reconsideration of Theoretical Frameworks." In *Peacekeeping and Conflict Resolution.* Edited by Tom Woodhouse and Oliver Ramsbotham. London: Frank Cass, 2000.

Fortna, Virginia Page. "Inside and Out: Peacekeeping and Duration of Peace after Civil and Interstate Wars." *International Studies Review* 5:4 (2003).

Freedman, Lawrence. "Victims and Victors: Reflections on the Kosovo War." *Review of International Studies* 26:3 (2000).

Galtung, Johan. *The True Worlds: A Transnational Perspective.* New York: Free Press, 1980.

Garofano, John. "The United States in Bosnia: Points of Tension and Learning for the US Military." United States Army War College mimeo, 1999.

George, Alexander. "Case Studies and Theory Development: The Method of Structured Focused Comparison." In *Diplomacy: New Approaches in History, Theory and Policy.* Edited by Paul Gordon Lauren. New York, NY: Free Press, 1979.

Gibson, Kevin, Leigh Thompson and Max H. Bazerman. "Shortcomings of Neutrality in Mediation: Solutions Based on Rationality." *Negotiation Journal* 12 (1996).

Graduate Institute for International Studies. *Small Arms Survey, 2001.* Oxford: Oxford University Press, 2001.

______. *Small Arms Survey, 2002.* Oxford: Oxford University Press, 2002.

______. *Small Arms Survey, 2003: Development Denied.* Oxford: Oxford University Press, 2003.

Griffin, Michèle. "Where Angels Fear to Tread: Trends in International Intervention." *Security Dialogue* 31:4 (2000).

Haass, Richard N. *Intervention: The Use of American Military Force in the Post-Cold War World.* New York: Carnegie Endowment, 1994.

______. "Using Force: Lessons and Choices for U.S. Foreign Policy." In *Managing Global Chaos: Sources of and Responses to International Conflict.* Edited by Chester Crocker and Fen Osler Hampson. Washington, D.C.: United States Institute of Peace Press, 1996.

Harvey, Frank. "Deterrence Failure and Ethnic Conflict: The Case of Bosnia." In *Peace in the Midst of Wars: Preventing and Managing International Ethnic Conflicts.* Edited by David Carment and Patrick James. Columbus, S.C.: University of South Carolina Press, 1998.

Hassner, Pierre. *Violence and Peace: From the Atomic Bomb to Ethnic Cleansing.* London: Central European University Press, 1997.

Hauffler, Virginia. "International Diplomacy and the Privatization of Conflict Prevention." *International Studies Perspectives* 5:2 (May 2004).

Hay, John. *Conditions of Influence: An Exploration Study of the Canadian Government's Effect on United States Policy in the Case of Intervention in Eastern Zaire.* Master's Thesis, Carleton University, 1998.

Hazelton, R. *Diamonds: Forever or For Good? The Economic Impact of Diamonds in Southern Africa.* Partnership Africa Canada, Occasional Paper No. 3 (March 2002).

Hedges, Chris. "Kosovo's Next Masters?" *Foreign Affairs* 78:3 (1999).

Hennayake, Shatha. "The Peace Accord and the Tamils in Sri Lanka." *Asian Survey* 29:4 (1989).

Hillen, John. *Blue Helmets: The Strategy of UN Military Operations.* Washington, D.C.: Brassey's, 1998.

Hirshleifer, Jack. "The Analytics of Continuing Conflict." *Synthese* 76:2 (1988).
______. "Anarchy and its Breakdown." *Journal of Political Economy* 103:1 (1995).
Holsti, K. J. *International Politics*. 6th ed. Englewood Cliffs, N.J.: Prentice Hall, 1992.
Hope, K. R. "From Crisis to Renewal: Towards a Successful Implementation of the New Partnership for Africa's Development." *African Affairs* 101:404 (July 2002).
Hourani, Albert. *A History of the Arab Peoples*. New York: Warner, 1992.
Howe, H. M. *Ambiguous Order: Military Forces in African States*. Boulder: Lynne Rienner, 2001.
Human Development Report 1999. New York: United Nations Development Program, 1999.
Huntington, Samuel P. "The Clash of Civilizations?" *Foreign Affairs* 72:3 (Summer 1993).
International Crisis Group. "War Criminals in Bosnia's Republika Srpska: Who are the People in Your Neighbourhood?" *Report: Balkans* (2 November 2000). www.intl-crisis-group.org
International Institute for Strategic Studies. *The Military Balance 2003-2004*. Oxford: Oxford University Press, 2003.
James, Alan. "Peacekeeping and Ethnic Conflict: Theory and Evidence." In *Peace in the Midst of Wars*. Edited by David Carment and Patrick James. Columbus, S.C.: University of South Carolina Press, 1998.
Jentleson, Bruce. "Coercive Prevention: Normative, Political, and Policy Dilemmas." *Peaceworks* No. 35. United States Institute of Peace (October 2000).
Joulwan, George A. and Christopher C. Shoemaker. *Civilian-Military Cooperation in the Prevention of Deadly Conflict: Implementing Agreements in Bosnia and Beyond*. A Report to the Carnegie Commission on Preventing Deadly Conflict. New York: Carnegie Corporation, December 1998.
Kadende-Kaiser, Rose M. and Paul J Kaiser, eds. "Phases of Conflict in Africa." *Journal of Asian and African Studies* 38:2-3 (August 2003).
Kaldor, Mary. *New and Old Wars: Organised Violence in a Global Era*. Cambridge: Polity, 1999.
Kingma, K. ed. *The Impact of Demobilization in Sub-Saharan Africa*. London: Macmillan, 2000.
Klare, Michale T. *Resource Wars: The New Landscape of Global Conflict*. New York: Owl, 2002.
Kleiboer, Marieke. "Understanding Success and Failure in International Mediation." *Journal of Conflict Resolution* 40 (1996).
Klein, Naomi. *No Logo: Taking Aim at the Brand Bullies*. London: Flamingo, 2000.
Kreimer, Alcira, John Eriksson, Robert Muscat, Margaret Arnold and Colin Scott. *The World Bank's Experience with Post-Conflict Reconstruction*, Operations Evaluation Studies (Washington, DC: World Bank, 1998).
Kriesberg, Louis. *Constructive Conflicts: From Escalation to Resolution*. Lanham, MD: Rowman and Littlefield, 1998.
Kuper, Leo. *Genocide: Its Political Use in the Twentieth Century*. New Haven: Yale University Press, 1981.
Kuperman, Alan. "The Other Lesson of Rwanda: Mediators Sometimes Do More Damage Than Good." *SAIS Review* 16 (Winter-Spring 1996).
______. "Transnational Causes of Genocide: Or How the West Inadvertently Exacerbates Ethic Conflict in the Post Cold War Era." Paper resented at the Annual Meeting of the American Political Science Association, 2-5 September 1999, Atlanta, Georgia.
LaFeber, Walter. *The American Age: US Foreign Policy at Home and Abroad. Volume I, 1750 to 1920*. New York: Norton, 1994.
Laïdi, Zaki. *Les contraintes d'une rivalité: Les superpuissances et l'Afrique (1960-1985)*. Paris: La Découverte, 1986.

Lake, David A. and Donald Rothchild, eds. *The International Spread of Ethnic Conflict: Fear Diffusion, and Escalation*. Princeton, NJ: Princeton University Press, 1998.

Last, David. "Defeating Fear and Hatred Through Peacebuilding: Multiplying the Impact of a Military Contribution." *Canadian Foreign Policy* 5:2 (Winter 1998).

______. *From Peacekeeping to Peacebuilding: Theory, Cases, Experiments and Solutions*. Kingston, Ontario: Royal Military College 99/01.

______. "Organizing for Effective Peacebuilding," *International Peacekeeping* 7:1 (Spring 2000).

Last, David and Emma Kay. "The Spiritual Dimension of Peacekeeping: A Dual Role for the Chaplaincy?" *Peace Research: The Canadian Journal of Peace Studies* 31:1 (February 1999).

Lederach, John Paul. *Building Peace: Sustainable Reconciliation in Divided Societies*, Washington, D.C.: United States Institute for Peace, 1997.

Legault, Albert and Michel Fortmann, eds. *Les Conflits dans le Monde/Conflicts in the World 2000/2001*. Quebec: Institute Québecois des Hautes Etudes Internationales, Université Laval, 2002.

Luckham, R. et al. "Conflict and Poverty in Sub-Saharan Africa: An Assessment of the Issues and Evidence." *ID21 News* Issue No. 51. Sussex: Institute for Development Studies, 2001.

Lund, Michael. *Preventing Violent Conflicts: A Strategy for Preventive Diplomacy*. Washington, D.C.: United States Institute of Peace Press, 1996.

Luttwak, Edward N. "Give War a Chance." *Foreign Affairs* 78:4 (1999).

MacFarlane, S. Neil, Thielking, Carolin J. and Weiss, Thomas G. " The Responsibility to Protect: is anyone interested in humanitarian intervention?" *Third World Quarterly* 25:5 (July, 2004)

MacFarlane, S. Neil. *Intervention and Regional Security*. London: International Institute for Strategic Studies, 1985.

MacLean, S. J., F. Quadir and T. M. Shaw, eds. *Crises of Governance in Asia and Africa* Aldershot: Ashgate, 2001.

MacLean, S. J. and T. M. Shaw. "Canada and New 'Global' Strategic Alliances: Prospects for Human Security at Start of the Twenty-First Century." *Canadian Foreign Policy* 8:3 (Spring 2001).

Malone, David M. "The UN Security Council and Peace Operations." *Canadian Foreign Policy* 5:2 (Winter 1998).

______. *Decision-Making in the UN Security Council: The Case of Haiti, 1990-1997*. Oxford: Clarendon Press, 1998.

Matz, David E. "Mediator Pressure and Third-Party Autonomy: Are They Consistent with Each Other?" *Negotiation Journal* 10 (1994).

Mayall, James. *The New Interventionism, 1991-1994: United Nations Experience in Cambodia, former Yugoslavia and Somalia*. Cambridge: Cambridge University Press, 1996.

Mbabazi, Pamela et al. "Governance for Reconstruction in Africa: Challenges for Policy Communities and Coalitions." *Global Networks: A Journal of Transnational Affairs* 2:1 (January 2002).

McGowan, P. J. and P. Nel, eds. *Power, Wealth and Global Equity: An International Relations Textbook for Africa*. Second edition. Cape Town: University of Cape Town Press, 2002.

McLean, Denis. "Peace Operations and Common Sense." In *Managing Global Chaos: Sources of and Responses to International Conflict*. Edited by Chester Crocker and Fen Osler Hampson (Washington, D.C.: United States Institute of Peace Press, 1996.

Mekenkamp, M. et al., eds. *Searching for Peace in Africa: An Overview of Conflict Prevention and Management Activities*. Utrecht: European Platform for Conflict Prevention and Transformation, 1999.

Meren, David. *Destinies with Greatness or Delusions of Grandeur? Causes and Consequences of Prime Ministerial Interventions in Response to International Crises.* Master's Thesis, Carleton University, 1999.

Metselaar, M. V. "Understanding Failures in Intelligence Estimates: UNPROFOR, the Dutch and the Bosnian-Serb Attack on Srebrenica." *Netherlands Annual Review of Military Studies, The Bosnian Experience* (1997).

Miller, Laura. "From Adversaries to Allies: Relief Workers' Attitudes Towards the US Military." *Qualitative Sociology* 22:3 (1999).

Miller, L. and C. Moskos. "Humanitarians or Warriors?: Race, Gender and Combat Status in Operation Restore Hope." *Armed Forces and Society* 21:4 (Summer 1995).

Mills, G. and J. Stremlau, eds. *The Privatisation of Security in Africa.* Johannesburg: South African Institute for International Affairs, 2000.

Moïsi, Dominique and Pierre Lellouche. "French Policy in Africa: A Lonely Battle Against Destabilization." *International Security* (Spring 1979).

Moskos, Charles. *The Media and the Military in Peace and Humanitarian Operations.* Chicago: Robert R. McCormick Tribune Foundation, 2000.

Muni, S. D. *Pangs of Proximity: India and Sri Lanka's Ethnic Crisis.* New Delhi: Sage Publications and International Peace Research Institute, 1993.

Nafziger, Wayne E. and Juha Auvinen. "Economic Causes: The Political Economy of War, Hunger, and Flight." In *The Origins of Humanitarian Emergencies: War and Displacement in Developing Countries.* Edited by Wayne E. Nafziger, Frances Stewart, and Raimo Väyrynen. Oxford, Oxford University Press, 2000.

Natsios, Andrew. "An NGO Perspective." In *Peacemaking in International Conflict.* Edited by I. W. Zartman and J. L. Rasmussen. Washington D.C.: United States Institute of Peace Press, 1997.

Nederveen Pierterse, Jan. "Sociology of Humanitarian Intervention: Bosnia, Rwanda and Somalia Compared." *International Political Science Review* 18:1 (January 1997).

Oakley, Robert B., Michael J. Dziedzic, and Eliot M. Goldberg, eds. *Policing the New World Disorder: Peace Operations and Public Security.* Washington, D.C.: National Defense University Press, 1998.

O'Brien, Conor Cruise. *To Katanga and Back.* New York: Grosset and Dunlap, 1962.

Ogata, S. "The Interface Between Peacekeeping and Humanitarian Action." In *New Dimensions of Peacekeeping.* Edited by D. Warner. Netherlands: Kluwer Academic Publishers, 1995.

Pinch, F. *Lessons From Canadian Peacekeeping Experience: A Human Resources Perspective.* Ottawa: FCP Human Resources Consulting, 1994.

Pope, T. *Beans, Bullets, and Band-Aids: Attaining Unity of Effort in Humanitarian Intervention Operations.* Monograph of the School of Advanced Military Studies, US Army Command and General Staff College, Fort Leavenworth, Kansas, 1994.

Posen, Barry. "The War for Kosovo: Serbia's Political-Military Strategy." *International Security* 24:4 (2000).

Ratner, Steven R. *The New UN Peacekeeping: Building Peace in Lands of Conflict After the Cold War.* New York: St. Martin's, 1996.

Regan, Patrick. "Conditions for Successful Third-Party Intervention in Intra-state Conflicts." *Journal of Conflict Resolution* 40 (1996).

______. *Civil Wars and Foreign Powers: Outside Intervention in Intrastate Conflict.* Ann Arbour, MI: University of Michigan Press, 2000.

Regan, Patrick and Rodwan Abouharb. "Interventions and Civil Conflicts: Tools of Conflict Management or Simply Another Participant?" *World Affairs* (Summer 2002).

Reno, William. *Warlord Politics and African States.* Boulder: Lynne Rienner, 1998.

Report of the Sanctions Committee on the Violation of Security Council Sanctions against UNITA. New York: United Nations, 2000.

The Responsibility to Protect. Report of the International Commission on Intervention and State Sovereignty, International Development Research Centre, Ottawa, Canada, December 2001.

Roberts, Adam. *Humanitarian Action in War.* Adelphi Paper No. 305. Oxford: Oxford University Press for the International Institute for Strategic Studies, 1996.

______. "The Crisis in UN Peacekeeping." In *Managing Global Chaos: Sources of and Responses to International Conflict.* Edited by Chester Crocker and Fen Osler Hampson. Washington, D.C.: United States Institute of Peace Press, 1996.

______. "More Refugees, Less Asylum: A Regime in Transformation." *Journal of Refugee Studies* 11:4 (1998).

______. "NATO's 'Humanitarian War' Over Kosovo." *Survival* 41:3 (Autumn 1999).

Roberts, Adam and Richard Guelff. *Documents on the Laws of War.* Second edition. Oxford: Oxford University Press, 1989.

Roberts, David. "More Honoured in the Breech: Consent and Impartiality in the Cambodian Peacekeeping Operation." *International Peacekeeping* 4 (1997).

Rotberg, Robert and Ericka A. Albaugh. "Preventing Conflict in Africa: Possibilities of Peace Enforcement." *World Peace Foundation Reports*, No. 24 (1999).

Rowlands, Dane and David Carment. "Moral Hazard and Conflict Intervention." In *The Political Economy of War and Peace.* Edited by Murray Wolfson. London: Kluwer Academic Publishers, 1998.

Ruggie, John. "The New US Peacekeeping Doctrine." *The Washington Quarterly* 17:4 (1994).

Rwanda: The Preventable Genocide. Addis Ababa: International Panel of Eminent Persons, Organization of African Unity, 2000.

Rwanda: Death, Despair and Defiance. London: African Rights, 1995.

Saideman, Stephen. "Explaining the International Relations of Secessionist Conflicts: Vulnerability Versus Ethnic Ties." *International Organization* 51:4 (1997).

Schulz, Michael, Fredrik Soderbaum, and Joakim Ojendal, eds. *Regionalization in a Globalizing World: A Comparative Perspective On Forms, Actors and Processes.* London: Zed Books, 2001.

Securipax Forum. Paris: United Nations Educational, Scientific and Cultural Organization (UNESCO), 2000.

Seybolt, T. B. "The War in the Democratic Republic of Congo." *SIPRI Yearbook 2000.* Oxford: Oxford University Press, 2000.

Shaw, T. M. "New Regionalisms in Africa in the New Millennium: Comparative Perspectives on Renaissance, Realisms and/or Regressions." *New Political Economy* 5:3 (November 2000).

______. "African Foreign Policy in the New Millennium." In *Africa's Challenge to International Relations Theory.* Edited by K. C. Dunn and T. M. Shaw. London: Palgrave, 2001.

______. "Peace-building Partnerships and Human Security." In *Arnold Companion to Development Studies.* Edited by V. Desai and R. Potter. London: Arnold, 2002.

______. "The Regional Dimensions of Conflict and Peacebuilding in Contemporary Africa." *Journal of International Development* 15:4 (May 2003).

Shearer, David. *Private Armies and Military Intervention.* Adelphi Paper No. 316. Oxford: Oxford University Press for the International Institute for Strategic Studies, 1998.

Simmons, P. J. "Learning to Live with NGOs." *Foreign Policy* (Fall 1998).

SIPRI Yearbook of World Armaments and Disarmament. Stockholm: Stockholm International Peace Research Institute, 1999.

Slim, Hugo. "Violence and Humanitarianism: Moral Paradox and the Protection of Civilians." *Security Dialogue* 32:3 (2001).

Smillie, I., L. Gberie and R. Hazelton. *The Heart of the Matter: Sierra Leone, Diamonds and Human Security.* Ottawa: Partnership Africa Canada, 2000.

Smith, Chris. "South Asia's Enduring War." In *Creating Peace in Sri Lanka: Civil War and Reconciliation.* Edited by Robert Rotberg. Washington D.C.: Brookings Institution Press, 1999.

Smith, Dan. "Trends and Causes of Armed Conflict." In *Berghof Handbook for Conflict Transformation.* Edited by D. Smith. (2000). www.b.shuttle.de/berghof/BHandbook/articles/Core/Smith/CF.htm.

Smyth, Marie and Gillian Robinson, eds. *Researching Violently Divided Societies: Ethical and Methodological Issues.* London: Pluto for United Nations University Press, 2001.

Sollenberg, M. et al. "Major Armed Conflicts." *SIPRI Yearbook 1999.* Oxford: Oxford University Press, 1999.

Spearin, C. "A Private Security Panacea? A Specific Response to *Mean Times.*" *Canadian Foreign Policy* 7:3 (Spring 2000).

Steadman, Stephen John et al, eds. *Ending Civil Wars: The Implementation of Peace Agreements.* Boulder: Lynne Rienner, 2002.

Steihm, Judith. "The Challenge of Civil-Military Cooperation in Peacekeeping." *Airman-Scholar* (Winter 1998).

Stevenson, Jonathan. "Africa's Growing Strategic Resonance." *Survival* 45:4 (Winter 2003-04).

Strategic Survey 2000, International Institute for Strategic Studies, London.

Stremlau, J. "Ending Africa's Wars." *Foreign Affairs* 79:4 (July/August 2000).

Sweatt, S. *The Challenges of Civil-Military Relations at the Trailing Edge of War.* Monograph of the US Naval War College, Newport, Rhode Island, 1995.

Thomas, C. *Global Governance, Development and Human Security.* London: Pluto, 2000.

Thucydides. *History of the Peloponnesian War.* Harmondsworth, UK: Penguin, 1986.

Touval, Saadia and I. William Zartman. "Introduction: Mediation and Theory." In *International Mediation in Theory and Practice.* Edited by Saadia Touval and I. William Zartman. Boulder, CO: Westview Press, 1985.

The United Nations and Rwanda, 1993-1996. New York: United Nations,1996.

Vale, P., L. A. Swatuk, and B. Oden, eds. *Theory, Change and Southern Africa's Future.* London: Palgrave, 2001.

van der Meulen, J. S. "Expectations of Peacekeeping: Dutch Public Opinion about Missions in the Former Yugoslavia." *Netherlands Annual Review of Military Studies, The Bosnian Experience* (1997).

Wallensteen, Peter and Margareta Sollenberg. "Armed Conflict, Conflict Termination and Peace Agreements." *Journal of Peace Research* 34:4 (1997).

Walter, Barbara. "The Critical Barrier to Civil War Settlement." *International Organization* 51 (1997).

Watkins, Michael and Kim Winters. "Intervenors with Interests and Power." *Negotiation Journal* 13 (1997).

Weiss, Herbert. "Zaire: Collapsed Society, Surviving State, Future Policy." In *Collapsed States: The Disintegration and Restoration of Legitimate Authority.* Edited by I. William Zartman. Boulder: Lynne Rienner Publishers, 1995.

Weiss, T. G. "To Intervene or Not to Intervene? A Contemporary Snap-Shot." *Canadian Foreign Policy* 9:2 (Winter 2002).

Wheeler, Nicholas. *Saving Strangers: Humanitarian Intervention in International Society.* Oxford: Oxford University Press, 2000.

Williams, Michael. *Civil Military Relations and Peacekeeping.* Adelphi Paper No. 321. London: International Institute for Strategic Studies, 1998.

Wolfson, Murray. "A Three-Party Model of World Conflict." In *Essays on the Cold War.* Edited by Murray Wolfson. London: MacMillan, 1992.

Zartman, I. William and Saadia Touval. "International Mediation in the Post-Cold War Era." In *Managing Global Chaos: Sources of and Responses to International Conflict.* Edited by Chester Cocker and Fen Osler Hampson. Washington, D.C.: United States Institute of Peace Press, 1996.

Index